Subversive Expectations

Subversive
Expectations

Performance Art and Paratheater
in New York, 1976–85

Sally Banes

Ann Arbor / The University of Michigan Press

In memory of Michael Kirby

Copyright © by the University of Michigan 1998
All rights reserved
Published in the United States of America by
The University of Michigan Press
Manufactured in the United States of America
⊗ Printed on acid-free paper

2001   2000   1999   1998   4   3   2   1

A CIP catalog record for this book is available from the British Library.

Library of Congress Cataloging-in-Publication Data

Banes, Sally.
   Subversive expectations : performance art and paratheater in New
York, 1976–85 / Sally Banes.
      p.   cm.
   Includes bibliographical references and index.
   ISBN 0-472-09678-8 (cloth : alk. paper). — ISBN 0-472-06678-1
(paper : alk. paper)
    1. Performance art—New York (State)—New York.   2. Experimental
theater—New York (State)—New York.   3. Arts, Modern—20th century—
New York (State)—New York.   I. Title.
NX511.N4B28   1998
709'.747'1—dc21   98-6969
                                                  CIP

Acknowledgments

I owe a great deal to the editors who made the initial publication of these reviews and articles possible: Robb Baker, Wendy Perron, Denise Martin, Erika Munk, Ross Wetzsteon, Burt Supree, Thulani Davis, M Mark, Tobi Tobias, and Joan Acocella. Thanks go to Jeff Weinstein and Marshall Levin and the other copy editors who polished my prose. Special appreciation goes to Juliette Willis for her careful assistance in the preparation of the manuscript, Phil Auslander and Jon Erickson for constructive criticism, Fred Leise for creating the index, the anonymous readers of the manuscript for their helpful comments, Laurie Clark Klavins and Melissa Holcombe of the University of Michigan Press for their attentions, and my editor, LeAnn Fields, for her support. As always, I am grateful to my husband, Noël Carroll, for love, dialogue, and debate.

Contents

Introduction

This volume is a collection of my reviews of and articles about New York performance art and paratheater from 1976 to 1985. This was a decade when the mongrel, elusive, indefinable genre of performance art definitively emerged as *the* preeminent form of avant-garde art. Performance art historian RoseLee Goldberg has called the 1970s "the golden years" of performance art.[1] I count myself lucky to have moved to New York in 1976, at the height of this activity. An occasional performance art practitioner and a young critic with an interdisciplinary degree in the histories and theories of the arts from the University of Chicago, I felt I had finally found my proper milieu. As I compile this collection, I realize that in my reviews and articles (published primarily in the *Soho Weekly News* and the *Village Voice,* the two major alternative newspapers in New York at the time) I had the opportunity to chronicle a particularly rich, lively period—one that I had very little to do with creating but took a voracious pleasure in seeing, hearing, and thinking and writing about.

Unlike mainstream theater productions, which can flourish or die according to critical reaction, performance art—usually operating on a shoestring budget or with funding subsidies—did not depend on a critical mass of spectators for economic well-being. And alternative press critics like me certainly did not wield the make-or-break power of the mainstream press. In any case, most of the performances were one-night stands or short runs and had ended by the time my reviews were published. So I felt a certain freedom in knowing that my role as a critic was not that of judge, arbiter of taste, or consumer guide. Rather, my role was to join a longer-term conversation about performance art in a public yet immediate way.[2]

Performance art was officially christened in the critical literature only in the early 1970s.[3] But clearly the activity of that decade and after is the child of a century-old avant-garde performance tradition, stemming from experiments in theater, visual art, music, poetry, and dance, and from the various artistic movements in which those separate genres cross-fertilized, such as Futurism, Dada, and Surrealism. Its immediate forebears were the new performance genres that emerged in the 1960s, such as Happenings, Events, and Fluxus. Thus, performance art owes its patrimony to Richard Wagner, the Symbolists, and Serge Diaghilev (all champions of the *gesamtkunstwerk,* or total artwork) as much as to the provocative action/gestures of the Futurists and Dadaists; to the twentieth-century theater artists Antonin Artaud, Bertolt Brecht, John Cage, and Merce Cunningham as much as to the visual artists involved in Surrealism, the Bauhaus, and conceptual and minimalist art. Because, however, avant-garde movements of the late-nineteenth and twentieth centuries have had a complex relationship with both esoteric traditions and mass and folk culture—oscillating between becoming utterly hermetic, on the one hand, and expropriating the popular, the vernacular, and the exotic, on the other—performance art also has a genetic link to a variety of other performance modes besides the mainstreams of theater, dance, and visual art, not only in the West but also in Asia and Africa.

Against Definition

There are all sorts of popular, folk, and "high art" performances: opera, dance, drama, pageants, parades, pantomime, circus, monologues, stand-up comedy, magic shows, puppets, and so on. These are (or have been) done in a variety of venues, from churches, opera houses, and art theaters to burlesque and vaudeville houses to tents, cabarets, private residences, and city streets. There is also performance—historically, institutionally, and rhetorically situating itself as avant-garde—that borrows from any of these forms, sometimes attempts to dissolve boundaries among them, and often engages them in a dialectical critique. That is performance art.

Like expressionism and minimalism, performance art (also at times called art performance or artist's performance) seems to be a genre named by critics rather than artists. But, unlike expressionism and minimalism, it evades stylistic or generic description. It is a vague term, used indiscriminately to refer to a wide variety of events and incorporating a range of styles, intentions, methods, activities, and scales of production—from the matter-of-fact and banal to the baroque; from the solo to the crowd; from the autobiographical to the fantastical; from improvisation and chance procedures to the precisely set; from the political to the apolitical and antipolitical; from the serious to the comic; from the violent to the serene; from the technologically primitive to high-tech; from pure actor's theater to multimedia.

Performance art seems to defy definition, not so much because it comes in so many forms and styles but because it stakes out its territory, as performer and theater historian Michael Kirby has put it, "at the limits of performance."[4] In her 1979 history of performance art, Goldberg wrote that "performance defies precise or easy definition beyond the simple declaration that it is live art by artists."[5] This resistance to definition held a particular fascination for historians and theorists of performance art in the late 1970s, the cultural moment when I began writing about performance art in New York. During this period the theoretical difficulties surrounding definitions of performance art were crucial to the genre's attraction for artists, audiences, and critics alike; individual performances often were concerned with illustrating or probing precisely the problems of the identity, definition, and limits of art in general and of performance in particular, and this tendency was closely linked to movements in related art forms, like conceptual art and analytic postmodern dance.

Like critic Hugh Adams, who wrote that "performance [art] . . . is largely characterized by an abandonment of rules, shifting values, and an impermanent ground," Jerome Rothenberg suggested that one problem with trying to make a paradigm for performance is that one of its prime features is "an overt disdain for paradigms *per se*."[6] Still, this challenging feature itself emerged for a time as a persistent intellectual provocation.

So, especially in the 1970s, there were many attempts to define and classify the genre, and I want briefly to examine a few here. Rothenberg, despite his disclaimer, ventured several generalizations. First, performance itself is biological, a drive that is continuous over ethological and cultural grounds, thus linking traditional/oral performance with avant-garde performance and opposing the notion of "progress in art."[7] Second, in performance there is a breakdown between art and life, between discrete art forms, and between categories like "arts and nonarts" or "high and low art." Third, a process of dematerialization subverts artwork statuses like "masterpiece," or commodity, or even object, concomitant with the artist's change in status to a nonspecialist. Fourth, function is valued over form. Fifth, there is an emphasis on action and/or process, the presence of the artist in the artwork. Sixth, the spectators either become participants or, in some cases, disappear entirely (i.e., the role of the spectator and his or her relationship to the performer is altered). Seventh, time is used in nontheatrical ways—as real time, compressed time, or extended time.[8] In these remarks Rothenberg, a performance poet who also studies "ethnopoetics," collecting and comparing poetry from other cultures, asserts his own cross-cultural agenda.

Performance art critic and historian Moira Roth called performance art *either* that art "which thrusts itself into life" or the art of extending theater in an art setting.[9] According to film critic and historian Annette Kuhn, "a performance piece is a physical action which borrows from all the traditional performing media," in which the artist-performer is primarily a visual artist and conceives and realizes all aspects of the piece him- or herself. She characterized it as "a one-night stand," unlike "show biz." Moreover, she wrote that it posits a problem and then proceeds to resolve or complicate the situation; in a good performance the artist has revealed him- or herself to the audience, and the audience "wants to know more and more."[10] Both Roth and Kuhn show their commitments to locating performance art in the gallery art world.

Various performers and commentators called performance art amateurish and crude by nature: theater done by nontheater people. In 1977 the critic John Howell, editor of the short-lived *Performance Art Magazine* (later known as *Live,* then as *Alive*), described much of the activity in New York as " 'Almost Home Movies' . . . a homemade brand that presents the artist as the star of the show, acting out material from anecdotal (my life and its funny incidents) to esoteric (sexual extremes, specialized knowledge). . . . A certain nerve is all that's really needed."[11] Admittedly, there was a strong tendency toward the "primitive" and the infantile in much downtown New York performance art in the late 1970s and early 1980s. But Howell's own editorial choices gravitated as much to covering the sophisticated, precise techniques of Robert Wilson and Laurie Anderson at the Brooklyn Academy of Music Opera House and other high art venues as to documenting funkier events by the likes of Fluxus, Stuart Sherman, and the Kipper Kids at alternative spaces in Soho, Tribeca, and the East Village—such as the Kitchen, Franklin Furnace, Artist's Space, and P.S. 122.

The British performance artist and filmmaker Sally Potter saw performance art as having "evolved essentially as an anti-specialist area," creating an open-ended situation that was particularly attractive to women in the art world who would rather make new models than follow in male footsteps in painting and sculpture.[12] In fact, the notion of specialization was so unattractive during this period that many performance artists did not even want to be identified as such.[13] Eric Bogosian tendentiously insisted that performance art was simply nonliterary theater, and he advised "budding performance artists" to "(1) learn your history . . . ; (2) learn your medium (it's called theatre)."[14]

The concept of nonspecialization was closely linked to several other prominent features of both the "new theater" of the late 1960s and early 1970s and the performance art of the later 1970s and early 1980s. Historicizing Happenings, Events, Environments, and other types of new theater by tracing their roots to John Cage's influence and, farther back, to the Italian Futurists, Kirby identified one core feature as "nonmatrixed" performing, in which the performer works outside of the illusions of character and place, or "person-place matrices," created by the dramatic actor. Kirby also noted other aspects, including nonnarrative or nondramatic information structures and an emphasis on previously unaccentuated aspects of certain kinds of performance (for example, the musician's gestures, prized as much as or even above the sound he or she creates, as in the work of John Cage, Charlotte Moorman, and Philip Corner and other Fluxus artists).[15]

All these factors contributed to a hybrid, or "intermedia," situation, a provisional arena in which an artist in one medium could work in another or borrow structures from another or work in several at once. A musician might tell stories; a filmmaker might make a film composed of a scrim, lights, and moving human bodies; a sculptor might manipulate time; dancers might act, sing, or tell jokes. Glenn Lewis, a member of the Canadian performance group The Western Front, stated, "Performance does permit you access to everything, the whole gamut of what is available. . . . You can make direct reference to art, to history, to sociology, to anything. Performance is a way of presenting things in a contemporary context."[16] Laurie Anderson reworked the same theme when she wrote:

> Performance is freer [than theater] to be disjunctive and jagged and to focus on incidents, ideas, collisions. If you want to talk about earthquakes in a performance, you don't have to have a character who is a geologist or back from the tropics where an earthquake triggered a love affair or introduce someone who is otherwise suitably motivated to bring up the subject. . . . Personally I feel closer to the attitude of the stand-up comedian [than to the actor] . . . because the comedian works in real time.[17]

Dick Higgins called this working in the interstices between the arts the action of the "polyvalent" artist—an intermedia fusion of the arts, rather than "mixed media," in which a number of different arts can coexist but also can be separated out. He explained, "In my works I compose music with words, I make graphic images of gestures; and that is the world of intermedia. There can be a dance element to my sound poetry, a literary element to my lyrical pantomimes." For Higgins this aspect of performance art is, in fact, a way to evade identification with a single medium and thus to defy classification.[18] Of course, to identify performance art as intermedia is to create a definition. But Higgins here seems to be describing the evolution of his own work since the 1950s, rather than making global taxonomies.

Beyond these characterizations of performance art were numerous other statements about its nature or practices: that it uses real, not theatrical, space;[19] that it is the manipulation of physical materials, including the human body as object;[20] that it is establishing and living through a situation;[21] that it is an arena for the fusion of the social and creative lives of a community of artists;[22] that it is a ritual creation of a persona or mythical image with the audience as witness;[23] and that it might not even require an audience.[24]

Some of these statements were more in the manner of artists' manifestos than definitions. But the problem with trying to define performance art (like trying to define theater or art as a whole) is that almost any given definition can be challenged immediately with counterexamples. For instance, take Goldberg's statement that performance is "live art by artists." Either her meaning of the word *artist* is so wide that it includes all creative artists, or she means plastic artists specifically. In the first case her definition is too broad to be informative. In the second she provides her own counterexamples by including in her book performance works created by dancers, writers, musicians, and theater people. And, indeed, the performance art in the 1970s and 1980s that was regularly reviewed in publications such as *Flash Art, Performance Art Magazine* (and its successors), *High Performance, The Drama Review, Performing Arts Journal*, and *Avalanche* included work that bordered closely on various known performing arts (theater, music, dance) and that was made not only by art school graduates but also by trained theater people (such as the playwright Richard Foreman, actresses Amy Taubin and Rachel Rosenthal, and actors Spalding Gray and Eric Bogosian), musicians (such as Philip Corner, Phill Niblock, Robert Ashley, Pauline Oliveros, and David Van Tieghem), and dancers (Trisha Brown, Yvonne Rainer, Lucinda Childs, Meredith Monk, and Laura Dean).

Against the notion of the performance artist as the person who plans and realizes all aspects of the piece, there were the open formats of people like Jean Dupuy and Alison Knowles, who invited other artists of all kinds to contribute to their "anthologized" performance works (like Dupuy's *Grommets*), the later Full Moon Show variety evenings, and the ensemble work of groups like Mabou Mines.

The putative dispensing with plot and character was also a problematic characteristic to ascribe to performance art, challenged by Michael Smith's comic figure "Mike," the personae Dead Dog and Lone Horse (created by Bill Gordh and John Malpede), Robert Ashley's narrative epic *Private Parts,* Jill Kroesen's surrealistic ongoing narratives, and Eric Bogosian's cavalcade of male identities. The idea of performance art as autobiography may have been applicable to performance artists such as Linda Montano, Spalding Gray, and Tim Miller, but it did not apply to the imagistic manipulations of Robert Whitman and Sylvia Palacios, the fantasy personae of Eleanor Antin and Adrian Piper, the economic-analytic interventions of John Boone and Barbara Caveliere, or Robert Kushner's fashion activities.

Historical Narratives

Perhaps, as Noël Carroll recommends, rather than trying to pin down essential definitions of the mediumless genre of performance art, it is better to characterize it by telling narratives about its history and what one might call its genetic codes.[25] This is not the place to embark on an extended analysis of the various historical narratives about performance art that have appeared in the last 20 years. But I will briefly review several of them.

Carroll argues that there are two separate but often intertwining strands of activity that overlapped at various junctures in the 1970s and 1980s. One, which he calls "art performance," derives from concerns in the visual art world. The other, which he calls "performance art," is a descendant of the nonlinear, imagistic, presentational (rather than representational) theatrical avant-garde. Although Carroll's account is persuasive, it does have gaps. It limits the performance art "braid" to only two strands and thus fails fully to account for the participation in performance art of dancers, musicians, poets, and filmmakers, with *their* separate concerns and commitments. Moreover, although Carroll mentions the fascination with mass entertainment by the 1980s generation of performance artists, his account leaves out the historically continuous dialectical relationship between mass, popular, and folk culture (as well as non-Western performance forms), on the one hand, and the avant-garde, on the other.

Henry Sayre locates the history of performance art in an "other modernism"—a neglected, antiformalist branch of the historical avant-garde that he claims foreshadowed postmodernism by creating forms based on "contingency, multiplicity, and polyvocality."[26] Although he thus correctly argues that contemporary performance art is part of a historied continuum of avant-garde activity, his applications of postmodernist and poststructuralist theory from one period to performance artworks of an earlier one tend anachronistically to elide historical distinctions and to suggest improbable causal links.

Goldberg asserts not that there are two modernisms (one of which is Sayre's pre-postmodernism) but that performance art (a term she applies retroactively to earlier avant-garde "live art") characterizes a particularly fertile moment of *every* modernist movement in which ideas are tested and artistic problems resolved. Performance, according to Goldberg, thus functions as a laboratory for the avant-garde—"an avant avant garde."[27] Although Goldberg's account of modernism seems more accurate than Sayre's, her harnessing the term *performance art* to earlier manifestations of avant-garde performance also tends to be anachronistic and homogenizing.

More recently, taking issue with accounts like Goldberg's and Sayre's, Marvin Carlson has rejected narratives that locate performance art's origins solely in the avant-garde. He points out that there are similarities between contemporary performance art and various non-experimental performance precedents, from Renaissance royal entries to medieval popular entertainments to a quintessentially American form of one-person entertainment in Chautauqua entertainments and theater monologues.[28] While I completely agree that performance art has drawn from sources such as these, I contend that where performance art resembles elite, popular, folk, mass, or exotic spectacles, it does so not for genetic reasons (that is, because it is descended from them) but for strategic reasons (that is, because it alludes to them, either to criticize them or to explore aspects of them in a different context). For in terms of institutional formations and ideological commitments, even while being partially co-opted into the mainstream, performance art still locates itself as an oppositional, alternative culture.

In this I disagree with Philip Auslander, who posits in *Presence and Resistance: Postmodernism and Cultural Politics in Contemporary American Performance* that by the 1980s there was a "rapprochement between performance art and entertainment" and claims that in American culture in the 1990s "the distinction between 'high' or even 'vanguard' art and 'mass culture' is no longer at all clear, from either the producers' or the consumers' point of view" (although I agree with him that "the economy of mass communications has a decisive impact on artistic production"— as, I would point out, it has throughout the twentieth century). Since Auslander acknowledges that "anyone who has ever had to support herself as a performance artist will attest to the continued marginality of most performance art," it seems that a great many people must be able to tell the difference between mass art and performance art, at least on an economic basis.[29]

Certainly by the mid-1980s it was clear that performance art itself had changed, shifting venues from the elite art museum to the popular music club and often engaging dialectically with mass and popular entertainment—from television to rock and roll—rather than offering an intellectualized, avant-garde *alternative* to "kitsch," as it often had in the 1970s. Moreover, instead of delighting in the "primitive" aspects of nonspecialization, performance artists of the 1980s eagerly explored the realm of virtuoso specialists. They did not necessarily revert to matrixed performing. But neither were they simply themselves; they tried on the non-matrixed personae of the stand-up comic, the magician, the juggler, the puppeteer, the cabaret singer, the rock star, and the fashion model.

As I have argued elsewhere in regard to postmodern dance, it seems that performance art and its precursors—engaging with mass, popular, and folk culture in the 1960s and then again in the 1980s but eschewing them in the 1970s—shifted from an early, raw form of postmodernism to a high modernist concern with essences and abstractions to a later, highly sophisticated and technologically virtuosic form of postmodernism.[30] By 1988 a revised, expanded edition of Goldberg's book on the history of the genre had appeared, now titled *Performance Art: From Futurism to the Present*. In it she called the section on performance art in the 1980s "the Media Generation."[31] As Auslander has observed, rather than rejecting the entertainment industry, during this period a number of performance artists embraced it, and not always critically.[32] Yet neither Goldberg nor Auslander accounts for the fact that there has been a perennially high volume of two-way traffic between mass or popular culture and avant-garde performance—beginning at least with Filippo Marinetti's 1913 Futurist manifesto "The Variety Theater"—that long preceded the performance art of the 1980s.

As early as 1977, several commentators—both artists and critics—

had linked performance art to postmodernism, although the meaning of the term *postmodernism* was not then articulated nearly to the point it had reached by the late 1980s and early 1990s.[33] Auslander's intricate analysis of the nature and role of performance art in postmodern culture demonstrates the extent to which, by the end of the 1980s, performance art had become so widely known that it no longer needed to be defined; mass culture, especially television, had come to supply both structure and subject matter for much performance art; and several performance artists, including Laurie Anderson, Spalding Gray, Eric Bogosian, Willem Dafoe, and Ann Magnuson, had indeed become crossover artists in mainstream entertainment. (Besides Auslander's examples, in the other direction there is Martin Scorsese's *Life Lessons,* part of the film anthology *New York Stories* [1989], in which Steve Buscemi, who was then a downtown performance artist, plays the role of a downtown performance artist with whom Rosanna Arquette's character has an affair. In 1995 Janice Steinberg's mass-market murder mystery novel *Death of a Postmodernist* featured a performance artist as the victim.) *Presence and Resistance* shows that by the early 1990s the term *postmodern performance* had become a globally accepted synonym for *performance art* and also that "the postmodern" had been thoroughly theorized as a periodizing concept.

Auslander argues forcefully that, because it engages with aspects of both the style and content of mass culture, postmodern performance art can easily be absorbed into mainstream entertainment. Although he points out that there are performers, like Karen Finley, whose work is so extreme that one might not expect it could be shown on television, ultimately he still wonders whether, given the variety of extreme content on cable television—from pornographic imagery to fascist ideology— "there really is a content that exceeds television's institutional tolerance." For nearly everything, he asserts, can become "entertainment" in our increasingly mass-mediated culture: "if a particular mode of performance cannot be marketed on television as high culture or mass entertainment, it can still be recuperated as oddity or freak show." And he concludes that, given the heavy traffic between postmodern performance and commodified mass culture, "performance art . . . has become a discourse almost indistinguishable from other mass-cultural discourses."[34]

In my own articles "The Tradition of the Old" (1982) and "East Side Confidential" (1984), published in this volume, I took a similar position to Auslander's regarding the apparent congruence between performance art and mass entertainment. In retrospect, however, it seems to me that, if the boundaries between mass culture and performance art have become blurry and have been crossed in many places, they still have not entirely broken down or been erased, as Auslander suggests. Despite his useful point about the elasticity of mass culture, for every performance artist who crosses over into the mainstream, there are still myriad others who engage with popular and mass culture in ways that are either too critical, esoteric, or scandalous to be accepted by the mainstream or that by virtue of their structure or timing would not be easily tolerated there—even as an "oddity or freak show." And to present performance art as nothing more than a curiosity is not to absorb and accept it.

During the 1980s another strand of performance art began to flourish: the autobiographical confessional of identity politics. It was born partly of the widespread use of performance art by feminists (especially in California) in the 1970s, partly of the solo form that lends itself to autobiography, and partly of the changing demographics of the avant-garde art world as more persons of color entered it as well as of larger political discourses and the concrete realities of multiculturalism. In articles like "Consciousness Razing" (1980), "Men Together/Bloolips" (1981), "As, I, Like, It" (1982), and "Sentimental Journeys" (1983), I trace the rise of performance art about feminist, gay, and ethnic identity politics that took the form of personal storytelling.

Both of these tendencies—pop culturalization and identity confessionals—had already begun to emerge by the late 1970s and early 1980s, as my reviews and articles in this volume document. But at that time they were still only obscure currents; in the later 1980s and 1990s they became dominant modes of performance art—indeed, the way the entire genre began to be characterized by the culture at large.

Writing Performance Art Criticism

I was 25 when I began writing for the *Soho Weekly News,* having recently moved to New York from Chicago, where I danced, occasionally made performance art, and regularly wrote on dance and theater for the *Reader.* My performance commitments were antiessentialist, my academic training interdisciplinary, my politics actively socialist-feminist, and my critical method descriptive and formalist. I was also a dance critic, reviewing events, both paratheatrical and theatrical, that sometimes overlapped with performance art (although those dance reviews are not included here), and until 1982 my output as a dance critic far exceeded my yield as a performance art critic.

For the section of the *Soho Weekly News* entitled "Concepts in Performance," edited first by Robb Baker then by Wendy Perron and then by me, I wrote (along with other critics) not only about avant-garde performance art but also about various performances that did not fit neatly into the more traditional sections of the paper. Thus, religious ceremonies and political demonstrations, high art events from other cultures, popular entertainments, and folk performances of all kinds also fell under my purview, partly because I was interested in writing about them (as were my colleagues and peers) and partly because they were not easily parsed only as "music," "drama," "cinema," "dance," or "visual art." It was the critical act of framing some of these events as performance that drew them into the same world as the avant-garde. And this seemed to suit the temper of the times, for—given the reactionary national politics of the late 1970s and early 1980s—anything that did not fit into the bourgeois mainstream theater seemed part of an aesthetic equivalent to a Marcusian coalition of the disenfranchised. Translated into artistic terms, this coalition made strange, marginalized bedfellows of Soho and East Village denizens, rock star wannabes, circus clowns, and Hare Krishna devotees.

I wrote regularly about dance and performance for the *Soho Weekly News* from 1976 until 1980. I wrote occasionally for the *Village Voice* beginning in 1976, mostly on dance, but in 1980 was assigned a performance beat there. At first it was published in the Art section, but by 1982 it became a regular page, titled "Performance," with its own discrete heading and its own listing in the table of contents. These two weeklies, identified with the two most visible artists' neighborhoods in New York, were the newspapers in New York committed to covering alternative culture in depth, devoting space to the avant-garde, the politically marginal, the out-of-the-way, and that which for any other reason was overlooked by the mainstream press. The *Soho Weekly News,* originally founded as an alternative to the older, more established (and more widely circulated) alternative *Voice* (which we at the old SWN criticized for its mainstream co-optation), sometimes ran two or three articles in the "Concepts" section. Under new management in 1980, the *Soho Weekly News* became both more ambitious and more culturally conservative, and suddenly the *Voice* once again seemed like an oasis for covering the avant-garde.

As a writer, I often deliberately adopted as my critical strategy the Russian Formalist technique of *ostraniene,* or "enstrangement," attempting to write about events without preconceptions, as if I were visiting from another planet.[35] My stance of "knowing innocence" and curiosity was consciously calculated. I went to each performance with subversive expectations. This was one method I used for resolving the challenge that performance art, flouting known rules and conventions, posed to the spectator and critic. Writing about paratheater—that is, nontheater events reframed as theater—in this way meant changing frames to "make it strange" from a theatrical point of view. (Tolstoy, in his description of a visit to the opera in *War and Peace,* had changed frames in reverse by *removing* the theatrical frame.)[36] Intentionally constructing an event as "exotic," and thus requiring description and explanation as if it had just happened for the first time (which, often, it had), gave me a sense of critical freedom that seemed to parallel the artistic freedom performance art offered as a practice. In this way I approached even traditional performances—the Japanese tea ceremony, the circus, the rodeo, the cat show—and nontheatrical events with the same sense of wonder I brought to performance art events: partly irreverent and partly probing. While in one sense this approach may have decontextualized the events, opening my reviews to charges of homogenization, deracination, or even disrespect, I still believe that it served a salutary purpose in bringing previously unnoticed aspects of those events to light.

Over the course of my ten-year career as a performance art critic in New York, I matured as a writer, a process that I think is evident in the reviews and articles and that is especially marked by the difference between my days at the *Soho* (1976–80) and my days at the *Voice* (1980–85). During that decade I entered (and finished) graduate school and became a full-time academic. As a student in the Department of Graduate Drama at New York University (NYU), my own predilections were strengthened by the focus of the program and the faculty. We studied the histories and theories of every kind of performance *but* mainstream theater, from the avant-garde to popular entertainment to folk festival to ritual. The ethnographic approach I learned from Richard Schechner dovetailed neatly with the descriptive documentation of the avant-garde I learned from Michael Kirby, buttressed by Brooks McNamara's historical perspective on popular and folk performance. (I was not yet Kirby's student when I reviewed him, in "Up against the Perceptual Wall," in 1976; he was a polymath who was a practitioner as well as a scholar of performance art and its precursors.) Every kind of nontheatrical event became, as we learned to call it, "paratheater"—worthy of study. It was *how* one analyzed and framed the event, rather than *what* the event was, that turned it into performance. The NYU program, now known as the Department of Performance Studies, drawing on ethnographic as well as aesthetic methods, has been instrumental in forming a new intellectual approach to theater and its relatives that in the 1990s is becoming academically institutionalized in various universities. At the same time, the performance paradigm has entered other academic fields, previously far removed from theater, from literature to anthropology.[37]

By the mid-1980s, I was in my mid-30s, a full-time university professor, and I had gotten used to writing in academese. I still lived in a seedy loft in lower Soho, but I no longer had the time or stamina to hang out in East Village clubs until three in the morning, and I was frustrated by the brief, superficial newspaper format. I took a leave of absence from the *Voice,* in order to write (in my book *Greenwich Village 1963: Avant-Garde Performance and the Effervescent Body*) in greater depth about more historically distant performance events. But the leave became permanent, as I moved away from New York City and became more enmeshed in academic discourse. C. Carr took over my column at the *Voice,* and the performances documented in her book, *On Edge,* reveal a vastly different scene from the one I had quit in 1985.[38]

Today I am struck by the ingenuousness of some of my reviews as well as by my youthful political dogmatism, my equally youthful aesthetic contentiousness, and my general preference then for description over interpretation. If I could time-travel to the 1970s now, I would not write most of these reviews the same way again (nor could I). Certainly, they should not be mistaken for theoretical analyses of performance art and paratheater. They are simply journalistic criticism.

Nevertheless, I render them here as a collection of materials documenting both a particular cultural moment and a style of criticism that was its product. The very emphasis on description, I think, is useful. The reviews and articles chronicle the mid-career work of people like Meredith Monk, Robert Wilson, Eleanor Antin, Joan Jonas, Ping Chong, and Laurie Anderson as well as events by well-established avant-gardists like the Bread and Puppet Theater, Robert Whitman, Nam June Paik, Charlotte Moorman, Robert Ashley, Jack Smith, Richard Foreman, Tony Conrad, and Chris Burden. They record revivals of earlier avant-garde performances, from the Russian Futurist opera *Victory over the Sun* (1913) to Happenings and Fluxus performances in the 1960s to an early feminist performance by Yvonne Rainer. They register appearances by emerging performance artists such as Anne Bogart, Tim Miller, Karen Finley, Whoopi Goldberg, Spalding Gray, Eric Bogosian, Robert Longo, Komar and Melamid, Steve Buscemi, and Annie Sprinkle—all of whom later gained fame, if not notoriety, in mainstream culture. (In fact, I believe I was the first to review the early New York performances by Bogart, Miller, Finley, Goldberg, Buscemi, and Sprinkle.) They also describe the works of lesser-known or forgotten performance artists, whose work nevertheless constituted part of the incredible flurry of performance activity at the time. And these reviews document the economic transformation of Soho from a marginal artists' neighborhood to a flourishing upscale center of art-commerce, fashion, dining, and entertainment as well as the migration of the performance art scene to new, not-yet-gentrified artists' neighborhoods—Tribeca and the East Village. Although beginning in 1981 I wrote about the emergence of New York hip-hop culture in several of my *Voice* columns, I have not included most of those articles here, since they are easily available in another collection.[39]

To be selected for inclusion in this volume, each article had to meet at least one of three specific criteria: (1) Was the artist important historically? (2) Was the work exemplary? (3) Was the performance part of an important movement within avant-garde performance art or in the performance scene generally? Some artists appear several times in this collection, an indicator of how prolific they were. Since I tried to vary the format of my columns from time to time and to provide context for understanding the work of certain artists—and because, practically speaking, not every week provided something to review—this collection includes interviews and feature stories as well as reviews. Sometimes, as in the case of articles like "Reading the Circus" (1980) and "Dario Fo's Theater of Blasphemy" (1983), I tried to create hybrid forms of critical writing by combining interview, review, and background material. Because I conceive of this volume as a historical chronicle, I have arranged all the articles chronologically, with footnotes indicating the provenance of each piece.

In one sense these articles are "just documents," as Jonas Mekas once described his documentary films of 1960s theater and dance performances to me.[40] But, of course, neither filmmaking nor criticism can be totally transparent. They are interpretations, and they are products of their time. The reviews and articles collected here convey the texture of a vital moment in history. I offer them to the reader as a view of a recently bygone world.

Notes

1. RoseLee Goldberg, "Performance: The Golden Years," in *The Art of Performance: A Critical Anthology,* ed. Gregory Battcock and Robert Nickas (New York: Dutton, 1984), 71–94.

2. Of course, I acknowledge that, while performance art critics do not (or at least did not, in my day) necessarily serve as consumer guides for their readers, as part of artists' press packets, reviews can certainly influence curators and funding agencies.

3. Bruce Barber found that the term *performance art* first appeared under a separate heading in *Art Index* in 1972–73 ("Indexing: Conditionalism and Its Heretical Equivalents," in *Performance by Artists,* ed. AA Bronson and Peggy Gale [Toronto: Art Metropole, 1979], 187).

4. Michael Kirby, "Performance at the Limits of Performance," *The Drama Review* 16 (March 1972): 70–71.

5. RoseLee Goldberg, *Performance: Live Art 1909 to the Present* (New York: Harry N. Abrams, 1979), 6.

6. Hugh Adams, "Against a Definitive Statement on British Performance Art," *Studio International* 192 (July–August 1976): 3; Jerome Rothenberg, "New Models, New Visions: Some Notes toward a Poetics of Performance," in *Performance in Postmodern Culture,* ed. Michel Benamou and Charles Caramello (Milwaukee: Center for Twentieth Century Studies; Madison, WI: Coda Press, 1977), 12.

7. Cf. Richard Schechner, "Postmodern Performance: The End of Humanism," *Performing Arts Journal* 4, nos. 1–2 (1979): 9–22.

8. Rothenberg, 12–17.

9. Moira Roth, "A Star Is Born: Performance Art in California," *Performing Arts Journal* 4, no. 3 (1980): 86.

10. Annette Kuhn, "Why Is Performance Art Different from All Other Art?" *Village Voice,* February 23, 1976.

11. John Howell, "Art Performance: New York," *Performing Arts Journal* 1 (winter 1977): 35.

12. Sally Potter, with Marc Chaimowicz, "Women and Performance in the UK," *Studio International* 192 (July–August 1976): 33.

13. See Linda Frye Burnham, "Performance Art in California: An Overview," *High Performance* 2 (September 1979): 2.

14. Eric Bogosian, in "What Is Performance Art?" *Performance Art Magazine* 1 (1979): 23.

15. Michael Kirby, "The New Theatre," *The Art of Time: Essays on the Avant-Garde* (New York: E. P. Dutton, 1969), 75–102; "On Acting and Non-Acting," *The Drama Review* 16 (March 1972): 3–15.

16. Glenn Lewis, comp., "Performance Notes from the Western Front," in Bronson and Gale, *Performance by Artists,* 274.

17. Laurie Anderson, in "What Is Performance Art?" 22.

18. Dick Higgins, in "What Is Performance Art?" 22.

19. RoseLee Goldberg, "Space as Praxis," *Studio International* 190 (September–October 1975): 130–35.

20. Higgins, in "What Is Performance Art?" 22; Scott Burton, "An Article on Scott Burton in the Form of a Resumé," *Art Rite* 8 (1975): 8–10.

21. Chantal Pontbriand, "Introduction: Notions of Performance," in Bronson and Gale, *Performance by Artists,* 19–20.

22. Eric Bogosian, "Art World Underground," *The Drama Review* 23 (December 1979): 32.

23. Joan Jonas, in "What Is Performance Art?" 23.

24. Kirby, "Performance at the Limits of Performance"; James T. Hindman, "Self-Performance: Allan Kaprow's Activities," *The Drama Review* 23 (March 1979): 95–102.

25. Noël Carroll, "Performance," *Formations* 3 (Spring 1986): 63–79.

26. Henry M. Sayre, *The Object of Performance: The American Avant-Garde since 1970* (Chicago: University of Chicago Press, 1989), xii.

27. Goldberg, "Performance," 6.

28. Marvin Carlson, "Performance in Its Historical Context," in *Performance: A Critical Introduction* (London: Routledge, 1996), 79–99.

29. Philip Auslander, *Presence and Resistance: Postmodernism and Cultural Politics in Contemporary American Performance* (Ann Arbor: University of Michigan Press, 1992), 59, 65, 64.

30. "Is It All Postmodern?" *The Drama Review* 36 (Spring 1992): 59–62.

31. RoseLee Goldberg, *Performance Art: From Futurism to the Present* (New York: Harry N. Abrams, 1988), 190.

32. Auslander, "Performance Art and Television Culture," *Presence and Resistance,* 57–81.

33. See the articles in Benamou and Caramello, *Performance;* as well as Higgins, in "What Is Performance Art?"; and Schechner, "Postmodern Performance." Rothenberg, however, disagrees with the use of the term *postmodernism,* arguing that it sets up false historical binaries, and calls for "a viable American modernism," at least in poetry, that simply includes twentieth-century work participating in "*a poetry of changes, experiment, destruction and creation, questioning old structures and inventing new ones, blurring fixed distinctions, opening the domain, and so on*" (17).

34. Auslander, *Presence and Resistance,* 64–65, 78–79.

35. In "Art as Device" the Russian Formalist critic Viktor Shklovsky discusses his use of *ostraniene,* which has been variously translated as "making things strange," "defamiliarization," and "enstrangement." (In his translator's introduction to Shklovsky's writings, Benjamin Sher argues convincingly that his neologism *enstrangement* is a better translation than *defamiliarization,* which Lemon and Reis had used in their 1965 anthology and which therefore is more familiar to English-speaking readers of Shklovsky [xviii–xix].) A technique that Shklovsky saw as operative in literature for the purpose of enlivening perception and routing automatic responses to life, enstrangement was adapted from Russian literary theories to the theater by Bertolt Brecht, who in turn influenced the American and European avant-garde of the 1960s and 1970s. (Viktor Shklovsky, "Art as Device," *Theory of Prose,* intro. Gerald L. Bruns, trans. Benjamin Sher [Elmwood Park, IL: Dalkey Archive Press, 1990], 1–14.)

36. Tolstoy partly describes the opera scene in *War and Peace* thus: "There was a certain devil on the stage who sang, with arms outspread, until someone pulled the board from under him and he fell through" (qtd. in Shklovsky, "Art as Device," 9).

37. See Jill Dolan, "Geographies of Learning: Theatre Studies, Performance and the 'Performative,'" *Theatre Journal* 45 (December 1993): 417–41.

38. C. Carr, *On Edge: Performance at the End of the Twentieth Century* (Hanover, NH: Wesleyan University Press/University Press of New England, 1993).

39. Sally Banes, *Writing Dancing in the Age of Postmodernism* (Hanover, NH: Wesleyan University Press/University Press of New England, 1994).

40. See Sally Banes, "Just Documents," *Village Voice,* October 18, 1983.

Subversive
Expectations

Up against the Perceptual Wall
(Michael Kirby)

In *Revolutionary Dance,* last week's presentation by the Structuralist Workshop, we are first of all confronted with Michael Kirby's "Structuralist Manifesto" as we enter the theater. Kirby states that everything has a structure, whether consciously acknowledged or not; that what the Structuralist Workshop tries to do is to isolate that structure and make it the focus of performance, rather than simply an armature on which to hang the action and the characters; that performance structures have to do with an experience of time: expectation and then memory comprising the two directions of a continuum stretching out from the central instant of performance itself; that this kind of structuralism, however, is not related to theories of the unconscious developed by Freud, Jung, or Lévi-Strauss. And, finally, he states, someday structuralism will fade away, but that day is far in the future.

The audience is seated on chairs lining the sides of a long, narrow playing area. Various light sources are lined up along this strip: a fancy floor lamp, a little pile of plastic logs with an orange light bulb underneath, a floodlight, a bulb rigged up to a table, a lantern hanging from a log tripod. At each end of the playing area are tables piled with props, nothing mysterious: forks, a knapsack, simple surgical equipment, a camera, coffeepot, tape recorder, lots of little packages neatly wrapped up.

The performance begins. The room is darkened, and people enter and exit with different lighting devices. Their actions are sometimes repeated, appear to be purposeless—although at times they have a definite but not articulated effect (e.g., someone rushes backward with a flashlight as if searching, though that particular meaning isn't resolved or played out). The actions are accompanied by a series of entrances and exits with tapping sounds created (tapping a wrench against a pie plate taped to the floor; tapping a foot; clicking the button on a telephone up and down; tapping fingers against a matchbox).

There are abortive lightings of cigarettes, observations of objects, unwrappings of tiny packages, falling things.

Husks of the Scenes

And now another stage of the performance begins. In a series of scenes, all using the same dialogue, the previous actions are fleshed out with linear content. In one scene people in formal dress are dancing then interrupted by a messenger, and finally one of the tuxedoed men attacks the other; in another a stretcher is rushed in, a body dumped on it, an operation takes place; in another a bound body on the floor is outlined in tape while a photographer snaps away; a man and a woman look for a plane to rescue them while another man lies silently by a pile of logs; men sit and play cards while a woman discovers a deadened phone line.

The scenes go on and on. The same three or four lines of dialogue serve for each, inflected differently each time. "Wait!" . . . "Hear?" . . . "It's one of theirs." . . . "What is it?" . . . "Here."

Then the action returns to the first stage: husks of the scenes—their movements—are enacted again, this time made recognizable as parts of the second section shorn of meaning.

So Kirby has forced the structure to emerge from a grouping of scenes with similar themes. He has shown us, by relentless variation (within strict limits) on dialogue and action, how meaningless content finally is. Ultimately, the meaning is random and incomplete, while the structure is familiar and concrete. And he reveals another structure besides that patterning the movements: that of memory and recognition. What seem random acts in the first section become integrated and reveal themselves as parts of a structure in the second section. In the third section, then, while the events return to their abstract and unconnected state, they have a new correspondence based on their prior cementing by content.

How are we to understand the name of this performance, its claim to be *Revolutionary Dance?* If we look at the surface, at the content, the scenes seem to be about revolution, or at any rate about some kind of critical military situation. We attach the title to the scenes and interpret them as bits and pieces of a revolution. Thus, if we were to value content and draw lessons from it, we might conclude that a lot of parts don't necessarily add up to a whole: forks dropping, impromptu hospital beds, dead phone wires, people waving down planes, bound-up bodies, and a revolutionary label may be present in certain situations but don't form a revolution unless some gigantic underlying thing orders them thusly. Or, extending the meaning of meaninglessness, we might conclude that, if you take all the revolutionary scenes you can imagine, repeat them ad infinitum, and realize that at some (structural) level they are interchangeable, then revolutions are meaningless.

Up against the Walls

First, we have to assume that this is more than a gimmick, that the pedantic posturing in the Structuralist Manifesto is not simply self-parody. This assumption we make because it's practically inconceivable that anyone would spend their time at this unless they meant it seriously. Yet the very seriousness of the endeavor manages to suffocate any breaths of creative or subversive life in the thing.

Yes, we are forced up against a perceptual wall; yes, our habits are undermined; yes, we are shaken and subverted. But, finally, no structures are disrupted, only displayed. The furniture is moved around, but the walls are still there. Revolution is about gaining competence and seizing power. Making a strategy for action, using subversion and disruption—whether the barricades are in the mind or on the street—to make something new, different, and better. *Revolutionary Dance* provides us with neither material nor tools for changing; it is, finally, an interesting but exceedingly dry academic exercise.

Soho Weekly News, July 22, 1976

Einstein on the Beach

(Robert Wilson)

First, it was *The Life and Times of Sigmund Freud.* Then, the 12-hour-long *Life and Times of Joseph Stalin.* And, last year on Broadway, *A Letter to Queen Victoria.*

Einstein on the Beach is the latest in Robert Wilson's series of spectacles revolving around historic figures in recent history. Four and a half hours long, performed without intermissions, *Einstein* is a collaboration among Wilson, a grand architect of time and space; composer Philip Glass; and choreographers Lucinda Childs and Andy de Groat.

Wilson's not-quite-biographical works—his oeuvre has included other themes as well—are not strict or even approximate histories of his subjects but, rather, evocations of an era or worldview through associative symbols and images.

Wilson's scene sketches for this opera (on view in December at Paula Cooper Gallery) disclose an austere vision of light and mass. Huge geometrical shapes interact, human figures diminish. Compared to *Stalin,* for instance, with its profusion of characters, animals, special effects, and tracks of activity onstage, the production of *Einstein* is spare, lucid, and linear.

The work of both Glass and Childs is characterized by repetition and accretion of simple sounds or movements. Wilson could have found no better style to affirm the most elemental of subject matters—Einstein, in other words, time and space.

Wilson's pieces have always played around with time, slowing down motions, repeating actions at long intervals, or performing extremely lengthy activities. *Einstein,* though, seems to distort time in a strategic manner, verifying, by its very structure, tenets of the relativity theory. For example, the second act, which took one hour, seemed twice as long as the first act, which took two hours. Is a Wilson opera a separate system in which clocks change their rhythms?

Space, too, becomes both subject and form, as Wilson, Childs, and de Groat demand our special attention to scale and spatial patterns. One scene consists solely of the manipulation from horizontal to vertical, and ascension, of a huge bar of light. Childs's hypnotic dance on the diagonal in the first scene cuts through the different layers of stage space, as do the two all-over field dances by de Groat. But other scenes mark the division of space, rather than divide it: the five connective knee plays happen in a small downstage corner; the gigantic space machine looms up at the very back of the stage; a train is seen in profile and full view both down and upstage. And marking off the orchestra from the stage sits a violinist made up to look like Einstein.

The train is one of the important visual symbols used throughout the opera. Not only does it represent nineteenth-century technology, later transformed into the more modern spaceship, but it is in fact a much more specific Einsteinian symbol: it is an example he often used in proofs. The velocity of light remains the same whether observed from a moving train or from a static point.

Clocks, transparent elevators, all the rich, elegant imagery of the scientific proofs are here, grandly set into motion.

But, just as relativity explains the world rather than mystifying it, this is a theater of disclosure. Each magical occurrence is prepared for by stagehands in full view. Despite the massiveness of the scenery and the lights, despite the contentlessness of the songs (the syllables are either numbers or do-re-mi), it is the voices and motions of the human beings that fill the space and time of the performance. Another aspect of the demystification process in the opera is the conception of genius it proposes: for everyone is Einstein—those on trial, those who calculate, those who watch, those who sing, those who dance, those who judge, those who drink coffee and eat doughnuts, the one who throws paper airplanes, and the one who listens to the vast, infinite sound within a conch shell.

The most dazzling moment in the performance is the atomic explosion. And "on the beach" alludes not only to infinity but to the novel about nuclear holocaust. But, though the explosion itself is dazzling, the contradictions it provokes have already been indicated: Einstein has been on trial throughout much of the play.

Einstein is not always easy or intelligible. At times it makes the audience work; at times it makes us hallucinate. Ultimately, it provides us with extraordinary frameworks and systems with which we can re-discover basic realities.

Unpublished, November 1976

Roots and Rituals

(Geoff Hendricks / Grommets)

Geoff Hendricks makes performance pieces and exhibits that are about roots and rituals. A simple event—the shaving of a beard—becomes an occasion for meditations on transformations, ritual preparations, witnessing and celebration.

Unfinished Business was a 12-hour piece in two sections. On Friday, December 3, at noon, 3 Mercer Store, a tiny storefront near Canal Street, had become a Vermont woodshed cum sauna. On a windowsill, neatly folded white towels and ivory soap. A stack of prayerbooks and missals. Branches and twigs laid out on the floor, along with burlap bags, scissors, string, tape, labels, sandpaper, saws, small axes. An old desk stood by the door, with a bronze plaque on it: *Write a Dream*. A sawhorse stood in the center of the room, with another plaque: *Saw Wood*. Lines of stones marked the shadows of pillars.

Hendricks, assisted by his small son, Bracken, and two young men, starts sawing small rounds from a branch and scatters them about. A man arrives, writes a dream about fir trees, and teaches Bracken a Quaker song.

I come back at intervals throughout the day. The room is strewn with bits and slices of wood. Two white strings dangle from the ceiling, studded with white feathers. A twig broom rests against a corner. People are fashioning bows out of branches, sanding a chair, taking photographs, talking quietly about beards, blind seers, past performance pieces. A notice of the performance, taped to the door, notes that the piece is subtitled "Education of the Boychild" and dedicated to Bracken, Dick Higgins, Meredith Monk, Ray Johnson, and Teiresias.

I wonder whether the ritual keeps going when no one's there to watch it. They persist in the same relaxed way whether I peer over their shoulders, wander around, or, later, bicycle by surreptitiously. What kind of education is this for a boychild, I think. Who needs to learn how to be a Vermont peasant in New York City in 1976? Let him learn about power, and the fiscal crisis; let him learn to cook and clean. Teiresias was both man and woman.

Saturday noon. A huge bronzecasting apparatus is firing up outside the store. Inside, Bracken asks me to sign a petition, which says: "We the undersigned, do herewith petition the removal of Geoffrey Hendricks's beard: understanding that each of our signatures effects the removal of a lock of said beard, and that we in turn do each freely give a lock of our hair in exchange."

A label with my name on it is affixed to my hair, which is tied to a chair, and another label to the corresponding lock of beard, which Bracken solemnly removes and hangs in a reliquary.

The room is now totally adorned with relics. Bundles of twigs hang in rows from the ceiling. A branch is wrapped in burlap and rope; a hammer is buried in a bundle of twigs and hung from a ladder. A pair of work shoes stands in the corner, half-buried in a pile of loose corn kernels.

Outside, sand-encrusted molds are being plunged into the upper part of the kiln and filled with wax, while metal scraps are thrust into the glowing orange bottom.

3:45. The razor is applied to a closely trimmed beard. The chair is festooned with tagged locks of hair in several colors. Outside, a mold is packed into a mound of sand, and a pale river of glowing metal poured into it. But the mold cracks, and the bowl turns out to be only fragments.

5:30. The beard is gone; the sideburns are disappearing quickly. Three people are taking photos. The sculptors are packing away their equipment. Kids are riding on the sawhorse and kicking the wood bits around. The moustache goes. George Maciunas gives Geoff a haircut. Even in the midst of depressions and election years, the world is wonderful enough to contain mythic actions and transformations. The gentle, Nordic fairy-tale quality of the second day's activity muted the maleness of the previous day, not only by actually removing Hendricks's beard but by crystallizing real and ordinary activities into symbols and metaphors.

• • •

Meanwhile, a few blocks up from Canal, in Jean Dupuy's loft, another performance turning private into public action was going on all week-end. But while Geoff Hendricks's activity was a 12-hour-long process available for continuous viewing, *Grommets* presented around 20 different events simultaneously for an hour. Each event, taking place in its own discrete area of a two-story structure, was masked by muslin and visible only through a grommet.

A grommet is a metal eyelet that reinforces a hole in fabric. This is the second of Dupuy's grommet pieces; the first, at P.S. 1 earlier this fall, presented simultaneous activity in one room that could be viewed through grommets in the canvas door hanging.

Because the structure generated an aura of voyeurism, it's not surprising that many of the pieces were about private activities, or private parts. Elaine Hartnett, surrounded by stuffed animals, flowered curtains and pillows, chatted to Charlemagne Palestine, visible only on a video monitor, about being watched. Larry Miller hypnotized each willing viewer via rotating fans, an unblinking eye at the end of a spiral tunnel, and a seductive voice over earphones. Suzanne Harris sat among arcane objects muttering about dance and revolution, while two dancers moved in and out of vision so close to the grommet that you could only see flashes of the edge of an eye, the crease of an elbow, an expanse of back.

Olga Adorno's two grommets were focused on her face and bare crotch. As she whispered obscene messages, one looked from one disembodied part to the other, both distorted by lenses corresponding exactly to the grommets. Maureen Connor's silhouette, hanging upside down in gynecologists' stirrups, was backed by a field of huge flies. Jana Haimisohn, in boots and workclothes, did a sober dance punctuated by the bored, vagina-framing gestures of a 42d Street stripper.

But some of the cubicles created other universes entirely, universes made huge by the telescope-like perspective of the grommet. Julia Heyward sang old songs into your ear as you looked back through a seemingly infinite room containing courtyards and windows; Carmen Beuchat seemed to exist on several planes, as, dancing among mirrors, her body could be seen in the distance and then her face, suddenly, right in front of you.

Thursday night I heard Pooh Kaye was throwing dirt around with some kind of fantastic machine, and I saw Laurie Anderson's tiny 3-D projection of *Mary Hartman*. Saturday night, Anderson was playing one violin note, obsessively, and the *Mary Hartman* grommet was taped over. Kaye was throwing punches, moving her body around abruptly, moving close to the grommet, punching at it, moving away.

The place was getting crowded. There wasn't enough time to see everything, since everything only lasted an hour, and only one or two could look at a time; standing on lines sometimes for ten minutes at a time required blind judgment and haphazard strategizing, especially since those exhibits with the shortest lines were static, but the changing exhibits one *wanted* to review yet in the limited time had the least chance to. *Grommets* tantalized but couldn't fully gratify.

Soho Weekly News, December 9, 1976

About Quarry, about Meredith Monk

Ladies and Gentlemen, Meredith Monk will attempt the death-defying feat of presenting history as both a circle and a line in the opera *Quarry*, a four-ring circus of the Holocaust, at Brooklyn Academy of Music, beginning December 15.

It's terrifying. It's hilarious. It's gigantic, and it's tiny. It's a person: it's the world. It's a grotesque reflection and a prayer.

Like most Monk works, *Quarry* looks like a narrative but refuses to act like one. Events occur, but their meanings shift and are wiped away. Time and space become shattered and rearranged; in newly constructed frameworks, individual lives and objects become metaphors for larger systems, and theatrical relationships symbolize real situations.

Quarry begins with a child's complaint: "I don't feel well. I don't feel well. I don't feel well. It's my eyes. It's my eyes. It's my eyes. It's my hand, it's my hand, it's my hand. It's my skin, it's my skin, it's my skin." Little Meredith? A child's memory of World War II, hopelessly en-tangled with biblical mythology and Freudian fears of parents? In the four corners of the performing area four households function simulta-neously: ordinary people eat dinner, rehearse their lines, discuss their research. But among these twentieth-century people, whose world is permeated with radio broadcasts, lives an Old Testament couple. Later, people from all the different households will become dictators. Later still, they will become victims. And will the child survive?

Juxtaposed against the possibilities of individuals are the actions of the chorus of 30. They appear three times: once neutrally to wash away the past, once to rally in support of the mesmerizing dictator, once to sing a requiem. The changing scale is reiterated in a film. Among what at first looks like a pile of tiny pebbles, even tinier people emerge, and we realize that the stones are enormous. History can change its scope as well as its shape. Will the child survive, will the nation survive, will the world survive?

• • •

QUARRY. 1. (from the Latin quadrus, *a square) A flat, square or diamond-shaped piece of glass or tile.*
2. (from the Medieval Latin quarreia, *place where stones are squared) A place where stone is excavated for building purposes. To excavate.*
3. (from the Middle English querre, *parts of a slain animal placed on the hide and given to dogs) An animal, or anything, that is being hunted down.*

• • •

Is it autobiographical, I ask Meredith. Her mother was a radio singer, as is one of the dictators; Meredith was born during the war; her great-grandfather was a cantor in Russia. Is she excavating the history of a people by digging into her own past?

Of course, the answer is yes and no. She says it's not, though there are a few details from her own life. In the Monk lexicon, anyway, personal references are only a jumping-off place. She hadn't even wanted to cast herself as the child, Monk explains. She had auditioned children for the part, but they didn't have the necessary vocal stamina; she'd auditioned other people but finally decided she'd have to do it herself. She'd originally wanted to play the dictator. Or the radio singer.

But, actually, her role as a child in *Quarry* is a fitting inversion of her real-life role as director (dictator, mother). Everyone has it in them to become a dictator, she says. It's something she's struggled with for a long time as a director, and that's why it was much more interesting to see the material unearthed when six different people played dictators in the piece.

And now, writing this, I remember that, during the performance at LaMama Annex last spring, I had wanted to be shown more clearly how a dictator comes to exercise power. What's the relationship between the comic, banal, and evil dictators and the chorus, with its beautiful rituals? Are they dances of complicity? The leader and the led don't simply exist side by side; there is a political relationship which the dictator manipulates to his or her advantage.

It was frustrating to have so much going on at once in the four corners scenes, I complain. I never knew where to look. I was afraid I'd miss something.

Oh no, Meredith protests. All of that activity was timed and manipulated perfectly so that your eye would be drawn first to one place and then to another.

How often are we really choosing freely at circuses, sideshows, theaters, supermarkets, in elections and wars? For Monk spectacle is a metaphor for freedom, its possibilities and its frustrations. Monk's use of sound, for instance, shows us how subtly we can be controlled. The radio is the central image in the opera: a means to power, a source of information, both true and distorted. So many people can be reached via radio, yet we see the radio announcer in the sound booth, lonely and insulated. Listening to songs and speeches without words, we realize that content is only part of meaning. We don't understand the dictator's words, but we understand his tone, and we are terrified. We hear a weather report that has all the wrong words, but we know it must be a weather report because formally it resembles one.

Meredith Monk, benignly dictating our theatrical visions and aural imagery, warns us gently and mourns our pliancy. Look and listen to what we can become: victimizers or victims. Monk's vision, usually utopian, in *Quarry* turns dark.

Soho Weekly News, December 16, 1976

Concrete in the Flesh
(Jared Bark)

The veil of Maya is probably made out of Krishna concrete.

Jared Bark's performance—incorporating slides, video, live actions by stage workpeople and objects, disembodied voices and music, darkness, flames and statues—is called *Krishna Concrete* after one of the contradictions (to the Western mind) of Hindu culture: the most mundane objects are named after the gods, and in their visual representations the gods look like nearly ordinary creatures (snakes, elephants, blue children, etc.). Cows are holy and so on. The title comes specifically from an anecdote Bark tells in the performance about seeing a calendar in India advertising this particular brand of concrete.

The joke, of course, is that Krishna is the concrete form of the Hindu god Vishnu, the Sun and the Preserver. Krishna actually means dark, or black.

Krishna Concrete explores with a wry, gentle humor the polarities and double meanings emerging in our culture as that curious hybrid, American Hinduism, gains popularity. Here Christ and Krishna are inextricably amalgamated.

Real human actors never appear except to manipulate objects (or to serve as objects). Instead, a video monitor atop a column shows us various faces that recite mythic legends about Christ and Krishna. Their bodies change as different slides—of Egyptian statues, knight's armor, people in modern dress—are projected onto the column. As the bodies, faces, and voices switch around with no regard to gender, an otherworldly effect is generated.

Two plastic pumpkins light up erratically, carrying on a proleptic argument on why it's okay to make a performance about religion and another argument on the recent religious fad and its relation to political activity.

A monumental pumpkin face, constructed out of umbrellas, a long light-tube fixture, and a plastic traffic cone, all carried by stage hands, advances menacingly and retreats.

Bark, on videotape, tells stories about his trip to India and about his childhood: how he thought he was entering sainthood when beams of light began to appear at his bedside; how he would burn bridges of bark in his fireplace; and how he became obsessed with setting things on fire. He interrupts himself to chant in Sanskrit about holy flames banishing darkness forever.

The piece is structured as a mosaic of separate elements: the repeated appearance of light, in different forms; anecdotes from Bark's personal history and religious legends; slides and videotapes of religious icons (both Indian and Western, popular and "high" art); and music—Indian and Gregorian chants, a blues hymn, and "The Road to Mandalay" sung by Frank Sinatra. It's a rich, colorful mosaic, playing on incongruities and ambiguities, as when a white-cloaked disciple steps in front of a slide projection and becomes an Indian deity.

But, though *Krishna Concrete* has a didactic format (mimicking religious structures) and uses an iconic vocabulary, Bark isn't really making categorical statements about anything. The two most spectacular effects in the piece are two of the light sections (I think of them as little theatrical miracles)—involving a tiny house and bridge built of matchsticks that burn up and a series of slides (beams of light and entire engravings) that leave pale after-images. The piece is fundamentally a playful celebration of light and the ways we come to express our experiences with it.

Soho Weekly News, February 24, 1977

Pumping Air
(Charlemagne Palestine)

Charlemagne Palestine's piano performances (which I've never seen) impress people, as far as I can tell, partly because of the audacity of his sheer physicality, the stress on endurance and breaking past material limits (of piano, vocal chords, etc.).

When he shifts media—from sounds to movements, from musical instruments to the body itself—this aspect in Palestine's work leaves me cold. He's no dancer; he's no Arnold Schwarzenegger. Instead, he chooses to present himself as a typically shleppy guy, his undershirt revealing plump and slightly hunched shoulders and a rigid back. I'm not arguing that only beautiful or muscular bodies are acceptable on-stage. But you can immediately see that virtuosity will not be an issue here, since Palestine makes clear that his body is neither trained nor strong enough to reach extremes, let alone transcend them.

An ordinary body can also do plenty of useful and wonderful things. But these body works are not about the ordinary actions of the pedestrian body. The shlep persona precludes this option. From the moment he enters (nearly an hour after curtain time), slugs some brandy, takes off his jeans, and off-handedly introduces the pieces, Palestine reveals his presence in the world as not altogether comfortable. The works prove to be about vulnerability, about battling with different kinds of forces. But Palestine approaches this generic human predicament with a special handicap, a sort of willed (or willful) infantilism.

In the first two pieces of *Battling the Invisible* he resists "the invisible": first he holds his hands parallel in front of his body, as if compressing something, then holds them out at arm's length facing away from his body, as if pushing something away. He grunts, pushes, displays extreme effort, and makes no progress; neither does he lose his ground. In the next work he walks around in a circle, making ghoulish sounds and throwing his arms out in front of himself repeatedly. All these pieces are transparently reminiscent (remember, he's dressed in a red undershirt with a bare bottom) of a baby's actions: in the first two pieces, attempts to defecate; in the third, a game of make-believe horror.

The sensibility, rather than the literal action, of the fourth piece reminded me of a child's: Palestine got under a large wooden box, kicked around inside it until it came crashing apart, then dragged off the fragments. (He had put his pants and shoes back on for this work.) It had the form of a destructive tantrum, but most disturbing to me was the insensitivity—both of the performer and the onlookers—to the safety of the spectators directly in the path of the ruptured box. Though he'd obliquely warned people that the piece might be dangerous, he didn't spell out how. When huge pieces of wood came dangerously close to hitting him and then nearly slid onto the legs of two women in the audience, Palestine continued casually, and many people in the audience laughed—as though we were watching cartoon characters being flattened by a truck.

Palestine asked for a woman to volunteer from the audience. All she would have to do is to take off her top and relax, he said, as the spectators snickered. One did, and he proceeded to "penetrate the whatever," as he put it. Not any part of her body but an invisible shield that now seemed to surround her. He rushed at her, circled her slowly, his arms outstretched, making loud buzzing noises. In his expressed frustration at not being able to clasp the imperturbable breasts, I again was reminded of a baby looking irritably for the nipple, his anger paralyzing him and further foiling his efforts.

In another piece Palestine lowered the lights and handled a dagger, growling fiercely but ambiguously. In the final piece he turned out all the lights and dared an unseen adversary to show himself, cursing, cajoling, and finally falling to the floor and struggling. The intimation of violence in both of these pieces was somewhat frightening; we had already seen Palestine's disregard for people's safety. In the dagger piece there was little reason to suspect that he would attack anyone in the audience but no reason to think he might not hurt himself. And in the last piece, though an illusion of two people fighting was created aurally, in fact the sounds resulted from Palestine's throwing himself on the floor.

The risks Palestine takes in his body works just aren't worth taking. The sounds are often affecting, but each piece is only provocative, disgusting, amusing, scary, or meaningful up to a point—a point that is close to boredom. In fact, Palestine's isometric battles remained confined in the narcissistic, circumscribed world of the unsensing infant, which believes its body to be the only reality.

Soho Weekly News, April 28, 1977

New Mysteries

(Theodora Skipitares)

The confessional substance and autobiographical format of so many recent performances make theatrical experience for the viewer these days somewhat akin to voyeurism; one is asked to witness on the stage or in the gallery private acts, personal idiosyncracies, expressions of narcissism, of self-loathing. Not all personal narratives create this kind of situation, of course. The best of the overtly autobiographical works can powerfully convey general truths and perceptions through one person's special vision of the world.

Theodora Skipitares's *Venus Cafe* is a short, haunting piece that evokes Greek theater, myths, and mysteries but does so through a juxtaposition of old forms, original imagery, stories from her own life, and references to Greek culture both on the islands and transplanted in America.

Even before the performance begins there is a flat landscape on the surface of the arid yellow wall. Three ascending shelves hold three masks: one next to a clutter of dusty wineglasses, one next to a mirror and a hammered metal icon, one beside a candle burning in a cage. A tiny paper effigy hangs on the wall; near it a two-foot-high androgynous nude mannequin stands on a pile of books. An object that looks like a lampshade, made of a straw hat and a fringe of chopsticks, hangs on the wall near a huge bundle of white clothing, which hangs near a cascade of colorful china plates hanging from ribbons.

Into this landscape comes Skipitares. At first we don't see her face. She stands pressed against the wall like an ancient sentinel, immobile, her bare back to us, her hands above her head, which is covered by the lampshade/hat. As she intones Greek words, titles projected over her tell a story in English about a shoulder that remains obstinately numb because it hasn't been loved enough.

The author goes to each shelf in turn, eerily poking her head up through an opening and donning the mask, emitting strange primordial sounds—ranging from an untongued ululation to a hoarse braying—which she sustains for several minutes.

In between the shelf rituals the paper effigy is set afire, and there are more stories told. One is of the transformation of the heroine's appearance from that of whore to virgin, as her 65-year-old aunt in Athens gives her dowdy clothes to fend off the constant catcalls. "Sort of like a Byzantine fairy tale," the woman narrating the story on tape explains. Like the Empress Theodora, who went from dancing girl to Holy Empress. A slide of a Byzantine painting appears, and Theodora Skipitares, who's been covering herself with layers and layers of white shirts and pants, stands against the wall in the slide's projection path and suddenly becomes the empress, as a man's voice on tape repeats the story. A film tells the tale of the Venus Cafe, the luncheonette Skipitares's father opened when he moved to the United States. "His name was Demosthenes Skipitares, a hand writes on a blackboard. They called him Jimmy." A Greek menu soon appears below the epigraph as the performer puts on her next costume, the veil of plates, and clatters slowly across the room.

Finally, the small mannequin's arm wags as slides of Athenian ruins flash on and off. Skipitares, sitting atop a ladder, shouts through a megaphone, recounting the village gossip about the Skipitares clan— the failures, the successes, the runaway wives.

Playing off the ambiguities inherent in both material and format— the contradictions arising from the clash of two cultures; the use of Greek theatrical techniques (the mask, the megaphone) in a chamber situation; the several ways that the information is detached from the author's personal presence; the one story repeated with two separate meanings—Skipitares transcends the cult of personality to create a mythic geography filled with a panoply of objects and signals that range from the familiar to the bizarre.

Soho Weekly News, June 2, 1977

Within You/Without You

(Robert Ashley)

For Robert Ashley our most private parts are our minds. The three songs he performed at the Kitchen are existential dramas, mapping structures of consciousness in words and music. Each song is also a portrait, a nude, gathering images, culling fantasies and habits into a specific shape: the contours of the subject's unclothed thoughts.

The heroes and heroines of Ashley's story-portraits in *Private Parts* are nameless; one doesn't call oneself anything, in particular, to oneself. They have their concerns, their ways of understanding the world, their ways of making categories and organizing experience. For some it is necessary to project an external vision. For others it is better to follow the thoughts deeply into the imagination. Ashley draws these processes of thinking for us, his spoken words disappearing the way thoughts do, invisible but leaving imprints on our minds.

He stands in the middle of a very wide and shallow space, very still and tall, with a lean face and shades on. He watches a video monitor, which shows the same image to the pianist—"Blue" Gene Tyranny— and the PolyMoog player, Peter Gordon. All three watch this image of a score that has the words and chord changes written on sheets of paper that turn every few sentences. We can see the score too.

Ashley stands in the middle of this space, facing us, and Gordon sits all the way to the right, and Tyranny sits all the way to the left. In the spaces in between are speakers and plants and four video monitors that show another image: a live image of the piano keyboard and Tyranny's hands playing on it, a big red ring on one pinky. Jill Kroesen, who did the video work, walks around checking things out and, in the second song, sings the chorus with Tyranny. Recorded sounds of tablas and drums emanate from somewhere unseen.

But back to the songs. The first one is "The Park." A man is in a motel room, opening his suitcase, pouring himself a drink. And inside these moments are stuffed other moments, actions, space, directions, his way of talking, his lines of preference.

> He had arrived and there were rooms, and all rooms were not the
> same, some better than others, he thought, better view, a better

layout, better shower, softer bed, not so far from noise, more like home, etcetera, etcetera.
Very abstract.

The pianist spins out jazzy patterns knotting chords intricately and unraveling them, underscoring with dramatic crescendos the crises in the narrative. It's ironic that these minute changes are accompanied by almost cocktail lounge music, yet the changes *are* dramatic and gigantic from a certain perspective. The piano music sets up certain expectations for the text: a pressing problem with a lover or an ongoing problem like loneliness. Ashley's cool deportment, his tuneless incantation, the drone of the synthesizer and the gurgling tablas mix with the hot jazz setup to make a strange solution; the words tell of a different order of issues:

> He was unhappy with the world.
> He worked with the forwardness and the backwardness.
> He worked with what things are ahead of us and with what things are behind us.
> I guess the other kind would be to work with things that are alongside, the attachments.

or

> (The numbers on the telephone, the parts of the book, the notes of the scale, they are the same, are they not?
> They come from the sameness of the idea of the outsideness, not the alongside the outsideness, the differentness.)

or

> How can we pass from one state to another?

Sitting inside his motel room, he sees an image, a frozen shot of two men (perhaps they are both him) sitting on a park bench, dividing everything into two categories: the permanent and the impermanent. He thinks about the town, the way its inhabitants use directionality in their language, and all this while writing down tomorrow's breakfast for room service.

"The Supermarket" is more like a rock song, with its short, loud chords and its repeating choruses. The narrative in this song unfolds differently: we don't know right away who or where. We edge toward the character, which turns out to be two characters—two old people who would like to get married but whose tax situation makes it impossible. Besides, they met in an old people's home, which doesn't allow married inmates. So every so often they check out of the old people's home for the weekend and check into adjoining rooms in a hotel, and now they're in the supermarket, thinking about all this and other things as they shop. As she reaches the end of her row, he reaches into the depths. That's the difference between them. They contemplate style, remembering, getting old.

Our work with our bodies is to move rocks.
Our work with our minds is to dignify eating.
Museums are a good example.

And the chorus chants, "Pro-per fold / Ex-tra teeth / In a bowl," and later, "Ne-ver know / Tu-na fish / Ca-sserole." This song is not about city space and rhythms but about horizons, the low shelves of certain supermarkets, the vastness of places where supermarkets resemble "a small Versailles."

You wonder, when Ashley sings about space, whether it all bounces back to the metaphysical: does he ever refer to the space of the body, or is it all the space of the mind? He sings of style; you think he means the style of his own songs, and then he says, "For instance, they are more dissimilar now than when they met." There is a certain unity of referents being explored. There are different levels of meaning in concrete language. Maybe looking out of one's body in time with the mind's eye is exactly the same as looking out a window and apprehending objects with the senses. In the song, finally, everything exists in virtual space, packed together, the 2 minutes or so of physical action and the 20 minutes or so of sung thoughts.

The third song, "The Backyard," begins with the throbbing of tablas, like a heartbeat, or like the Beatles' song about life going on within you and without you. For me it is the most mysterious and delicate of the songs, a meditation about the occult powers of numbers and systems. It is about a woman or girl who stands in the doorway of her mother's house at sunset, while guests gossip in the backyard. She thinks mostly about two things: elevation and proportions. She is systematic but experiences wonder. She meditates on her breath; the music echoes the structure of her mental process. First, the tablas repeat a simple pattern that becomes a pulse, as Ashley chants:

My mind turns to my breath, one
My mind watches my breath, two
My mind turns and watches my breath, three
My mind turns and faces my breath, four

My mind faces my breath, five
My mind studies my breath, six
My mind sees every aspect of the beauty of my breath, seven
My mind watches my breath soothing itself, eight
My mind sees every part of my breath, nine
My breath is not indifferent to itself, ten

As she sinks deeper into meditation, the synthesizer creeps in with stretched tones. She approaches numbers in her mind, dwelling on the number 42, facing it, studying it. She circles the number that is her father's age, calculating it by coming at it from different perspectives, in relation to different numbers. She thinks about Giordano Bruno.

The song suddenly becomes an imaginary film, as the image expands into a planetary system, superimposed over a point-of-view shot, where we see her in the doorway, and we hear the chatter of the guests, the piano entering with soft background music. But then we move inward again, and the piano fades away. The sustained tones of the synthesizer predominate, ascending, approaching a still point.

This is the hour of the mystery of the barnswallows
One: where do they go in daytime?
Two: do they never rest?
Three: when you buy them in the store, made in China, on the end
    of strings, they do exactly what they do alive.
Four: how is that possible?

When Ashley says this is sentimental, does he mean to comment on his image of a beautiful woman hypnotized by the elegance and mystery of proportions or on his song, or is it another thought passing through her mind?

We sense that the time for the light to change is almost near, as the music drowns out Ashley's quiet voice, and still we hear, filtering through, words about waves of colors and soft textures, descriptions of the sun's angles.

Dear George
What's going on?
I'm not the same person that I used to be.

Soho Weekly News, January 19, 1978

Words from *Private Parts* © 1977 Robert Ashley. "The Park" and "The Backyard" are recorded on *Private Parts*. Lovely Music Ltd., distributed by Performing Artservices.

Historical Immaterialism
(Ann Wilson)

Ann Wilson's romantic idealization and canonization of generations of artists in her recent "art environment and collaborative theatrical performance" offers a view of the artist as martyred genius—the "exemplary sufferer," as Susan Sontag so neatly put it. In our day such a view seems antiquated and reactionary, if not downright sentimental.

Unfortunately, Wilson invites comparison to Robert Wilson, both because she and many of her collaborators are longtime associates of the author of *Einstein on the Beach, The Life and Times of Joseph Stalin,* etc., and because her venture is as monumental as, if not more so than, those of the other Wilson. Unlike the lavish aesthetic visions of R. Wilson—in which strange creatures, inhabiting fabulous original landscapes, speak recognizable words to make abstract, musical patterns that move in and out of meaning—*Butler's Lives of the Saints* is sparse, ascetic in a way that seems stingy and narrowly focused, rather than spiritual. Where R. Wilson's spectacles are rich and resonant, A. Wilson's seems poverty stricken, despite the large funds obviously spent on the production. The resemblance between the two Wilsons is clearly only name deep.

Wilson (Ann)'s view of art is antimaterialist. In the glossy 25¢ brochure and the $2 libretto, she registers the requisite complaints about the artist's economic situation in American society. Yet accompanying these criticisms—and expressed throughout the performance—is the contradictory notion of art as a mysterious, selfless activity; the artist as a person with only one foot in the real world.

For example, Wilson writes: "Like an orchestra, this work involves the talents and energies of many people. It is hours of time in an exchange, a mind made up of all our minds. There is no way to thank all of those who so generously gave hundreds of hours, often with no pay, to make *Butler's Lives of the Saints*. My deepest gratitude goes to so many for the selfless understanding of the true communal nature of this endeavor. I hope that some day there will be a culture which values its artists enough to pay them for their work."

I should think that one way to start improving this condition would be for Wilson to pay the artists, making that a priority over elaborate, nostalgic sets and glossy brochures. But then the condition of artists wouldn't be tragic and selfless, and Wilson would have to revise her conception of art.

The performance everywhere supports this quasireligious notion that art is spiritual rather than material; that the souls of artists commune in some virtual realm beyond time and space and dwell in a stream of genius-martyrdom that spirals up toward heaven. The chorus seems liturgical. Then Ishmael, played by a child, walks across the stage in a misty haze. Wilson trots out a parade of "saints," most of whom are connected in their exaltation of the spirit at the cost of physical, often sexual, denial. Van Gogh, Dickinson, Weil, Saint Theresa of Avila . . . the list goes on and on. The climax, in dead center, is selections from *The Song of Songs*. The aspiration of the elements in this parade is toward a holy, bodiless state, whether the means is art or religion.

Wilson's method of connecting all the characters is to have them refer sketchily to their philosophical positions by reading a few lines of text, as each appears briefly in the small space surrounded by the monumental Gordon Craig setting. The similarities between the characters are magnified by montage juxtaposition. This pageant is sometimes punctuated, sometimes accompanied by the songs of the chorus and brief dance sequences. All this is further elaborated with plastiques that refer lightly to famous paintings and sculptures. For those who did not invest in a libretto or who didn't have a clear sightline to the diagrammatic representation of the action (which was posted on a side wall, dimly lit), the performance became a game of "Botticelli"—that irritating, elitist game of one-upmanship in which one flaunts one's arcane knowledge of the trivia of art history. At *Butler's Lives* the way to stay awake and afloat in the dizzying vortex where everyone became everyone else—each saint seemed to be a reincarnation of a single spiritual force—where art became religion, and everything was everything, was to quiz oneself and one's neighbors. Who could be the first to guess the painting, sculpture, character, or author?

A friend told me that she criticized the production to someone standing nearby when it was over, and he happened to have worked on it. "You'll be glad some day you saw it," he told her. "This was a historic occasion." But I can think of lots of historic occasions that have been neither good performances nor pleasant events. And, given the view of history *Butler's Lives* projects—without shape or concrete meaning—who would want to participate in it?

Kenneth King's tribute to Simone Weil was a gem burning in the abyss. Without literal or literary reference to his subject, he saluted her with electrifying chains of motion, his arms rapidly slashing and pointing through space, or spiraling against his torso.

In these unstable times, when much of society is turning to religion as an escape hatch, I expect art to propose positive alternatives. Rather than making art an agent of increasing mystification, we need radical, creative methods for thinking about and coping with the real problems of life. The spiritualism and hieratic otherworldliness of *Butler's Lives,* at this historical juncture, is a dodge and an opiate that denies the responsibility of art to liberate in the concrete here and now.

Soho Weekly News, January 26, 1978

Double Vision

(Yvonne Rainer)

Yvonne Rainer first showed *Inner Appearances* at a program called "Dancing Ladies" organized by James Waring in 1972. People saw it then as a militant feminist statement, especially since in the space on the program for her biography Rainer attacked the sexism of the program's title. Later, the piece was incorporated into her *Performance* and *This Is the Story of a Woman Who. . . .* In her book *Work 1961–73* Rainer says that she felt ingenuous for not foreseeing that the work would be taken as a political statement; she then deliberately rewrote it for a male performer to make it more political, changing the text slightly to suit certain cultural images of male behavior and thoughts.

At the Whitney performance on January 27, the female (played by Margot Norton) and male (John Erdman) versions of *Inner Appearances* were performed back to back, a repetitive structure that intensifies the formal oppositions in the piece and underscores its political content.

A woman plugs in a vacuum cleaner and proceeds to vacuum the stage, humming a simple tune now and then, and stopping at times to lie on a mattress downstage or to sit on one of two chairs placed upstage. Projected on the wall behind her is a series of slides, which might be her thoughts, feelings, motivations. The character wears an eyeshade. The vacuum cleaner, sometimes on and sometimes off, creates a soundtrack that alternates between a soft roar and silence. After the entire space has been cleaned, she unplugs the machine and winds up the cord. Then the man does the same task, also humming now and then, also sitting or lying, also turning the vacuum cleaner on and off. Both use the same spatial pattern for vacuuming. His slides provide a narrative that is almost, but not quite, identical to hers.

The physical activity in *Inner Appearances* is a neutral task. Performed in an abstract setting in dim light, the behavior is cool and somewhat melancholy. But rubbing against this almost clinical outer appearance is the other visual track: those slides, verbal descriptions of anger, contempt, love, erotic fantasies, irritation, shame, jealousy, grief, and joy. The narrative is ambiguous in terms of time and referents: one slide tells about a conversation the character had on the way to the performance; another, of the traumatized state of the character's spine when she or he vacuums. Memories of childhood mingle with the present thoughts of making love and performing. A passage from a novel recalled only partially and a Sappho poem mix freely with anecdotes about friends and clichés about female intuition. Despite its emotional weight, its heat, its potentially melodramatic intensity, the narrative is distanced, because it is typed on file cards, and disembodied from the performer.

When the text is repeated with variations for the man, you see the action from another angle, partly because the words have changed, partly because the image of a man vacuuming is not as familiar. And because he has a different style of vacuuming, sitting, and humming (more assertive? more deliberate? more self-assured?) you see the text from another angle, too. You see the dissolution of what had seemed a fixed situation. Yet you also see a complex thought process becoming codified into cliché.

Rainer disassembles the various channels of a drama to present them matter-of-factly, dry in their discreteness, clotted with passion if you choose to piece them together to make stereotypes. But the final title warns us against falling into the trap of easy habits. Cliché, it states, seduces us by offering clear and rigid structures with which to order our lives and thoughts.

The unsettling disjunction between the flow of inner life, with its emotional extremes, and the opaque, neutral outer behavior keeps us from reassembling the components into a melodrama, a formula. And the repetition flattens the emotional impact, further preventing a histrionic reading. Yet, by presenting performance as a means for both heightening and crystallizing psychological content, *Inner Appearances* generates a complex tension between the expressive power of drama and the numbing effects of its formulas. The political question the work poses is never as simple-minded as "What is the nature of this woman's oppression by a vacuum cleaner?" but a more profound and difficult problem: What kind of culture do we live in, that invites us to freeze our lives wholesale into clichés and stereotypes?

Soho Weekly News, February 16, 1978

Engineering Images
(Sylvia Whitman)

Sylvia Whitman's performance vignettes are like tiny machines of consciousness—phantasmagoria manufactured out of ordinary things. Their titles are commonsensical, almost mundane: "With five cups," "Soft frame for a small black telephone," "Going in," and so on. The deadpan presentation, too, makes you think of someone unpacking a carton of dishes or pushing a hand truck. Small-scale chores.

Often the raw materials Whitman transforms with these performance engines are quite ordinary: a middle-aged woman dressed in black, a man in a business suit; a set of teacups, a telephone, a bed. She favors brown wrapping paper, which turns up covering a huge package or as stuffing for the enormous sausagelike edges of the frame that's hoisted to fill the stage, leaving a space in the center for the telephone.

But mixed in with these ordinary things and people are quite extraordinary items and activities. As in a dream, a man opens his briefcase, takes out a can of Maxwell House coffee, opens it with a can opener, and pulls out of it a piece of blue fabric that is just large enough to tack up over his shadow. The shadow, painted on a piece of brown cardboard, has been acting as a cumbersome traveling companion. His actions are matter-of-fact but uncanny.

Or, in "Yellow tube," Whitman appears at one side of the stage, places on her head a yellow tube suspended from the ceiling, and slowly walks to the other side. The tube, taller than the performer, moves along a simple string track. The image is startling: our entire visual field is taken up by this unusual, extremely vertical object and by the way Whitman's body strains slightly forward to pull the tube along. Yet at the same time the familiar picture of a woman wearing a hat is never completely undermined.

In "Bed," a white bed stands on end facing us, and on it lies/stands a man in white clothing whose body is outlined in blue neon. The entire construction moves inexorably across the space. Again, fantastic details transfigure a commonplace sight. In "With five cups," there are five crossings by two women, each involving the transportation of a teacup and saucer—one time the cup and saucer are pulled by a string like a small dog on a leash, another time stuck to the back of a jacket, another time encased in a transparent sphere, with a small blue bird fluttering around the cup and perching on its edge to drink.

There is a satisfying sense of closure in each small piece, an economy of timing, color, shape, and movement that forms a compact, vivid composition. There are the blue and brown tones, the rough surfaces of the paper, the smoothness of the drapes, the diagonal edges of things. Whitman generally treats the space as flat, rather than dealing with it sculpturally. It's as if each small performance produces a painting—but one that is rendered enigmatic because it moves and is moved by silent human agents.

Each vignette in *Around the Edge* uses simple but curious stage machinery—the neon frame for the body, the rigging that hoists the soft frame, a plastic casing that attaches a tiny house behind the woman ("The house that follows"), a draped hole in the wall through which Whitman is pulled by three pairs of red hands ("Going in"). A fanciful delicacy underlies the straightforward efficiency with which each concept is carried out. At the performance I saw, there were lags before some of the more technically complicated acts, which detracted slightly from the rhythm of the entire stream of phantasm machines. It was so satisfying to watch the pieces in which the riggings and tracks were visible that the long preparations backstage seemed to mask and puncture the easy flow of marvelous visions.

Soho Weekly News, March 16, 1978

Flu as Fashion and
Art as Business

(Richard Foreman)

The Byrd Hoffman Theater at 147 Spring has been replaced by Victoria Falls, the antique clothing store that used to be on the other side of West Broadway. It's strange to see racks of expensive gauzy lace dresses and silk camisoles arranged on the floor that has been the scene of Robert Wilson's smaller spectacles, performances by Kenneth King and others, as well as open house dancing and spinning sessions.

Maybe it's not so strange, though, that in a neighborhood where culture *is* commerce—even the paper I write for, after all, is deeply enmeshed in the network that packages art for sale—a clothing store would use art to merchandise goods. Well, Martha Graham's posed for mink ads, and last year Rudi Gernreich collaborated on a dance with Bella Lewitsky. But Richard Foreman doing a Soho fashion show called *Fever*? Next thing you know, Dean and Deluca will ask Robert Morris to build cheese displays. Grand Union will retaliate by trying to get Joseph Kosuth to design their sale signs. And Miso, the dress shop, will up the ante by planning a fashion show for next season, to be choreographed by Merce Cunningham. The possibilities opened by marrying art and commerce are endless—and rather offensive.

At Victoria Falls the crowd mills around for a while but soon runs out of clothes to look at. When a stage light goes on, we all turn expectantly toward the illuminated wall, pushing our way to the front. Music comes on—a faded recording of "Der Fuhrerschein" ("The Driver's License") by Paul Graetz, a Weimar cabaret composer. A line of seven fading beauties, dressed in pale lace and silk chemises, teddies, petticoats, gowns and bloomers, pink ballet slippers and high-heeled sandals, and clutching turquoise kleenex, swoons against the wall. They look feverish. Some delicately wipe their foreheads; some press their stomachs.

Rena Gill, the owner of the store and a sometime Foreman actress, announces, "Ladies and Gentlemen, there will be a fashion show against the East Wall!" A column of seven militaristic women marches in to stand in front of the feverish ones. Their clothes are dark and masculine—vests, pants, boots, mandarin jackets, a dark red rose, a purple belt. They look like they could become a punk rock militia. They hold thermometers over their heads ominously. Gill counts out orders. "Very slowly now, ONE!" They shake down the thermometers. "TWO!" They march over to the wall, brandishing their weapons. In a continuing series of exaggerated, arrested poses, the thermometers are plunged into pale mouths, the punk doctors stand back to watch their patients, hands on hips. They scratch their own backs then step forward again to read the temperatures. The feverish ones cower. But then, after the hussars slap them, they leave, and their places against the wall (and their disease) are assumed by their healer/conquerors.

In a matter of minutes some of Foreman's favorite themes and structures materialize: women's mysteries are embodied, polarized into dominant/passive, dark/light, healthy/sick, strong/frail; references are made to decadent European culture; metaphoric allusions to violence and sexual violation are deftly subverted at the last minute (one expects the thermometers to plunge forcefully into anuses, rather than mouths, for instance). But the fashion show is not a play. Ultimately, it is simply advertising, and its ideas and associations are always subservient to the subtext, which reads, "BUY CLOTHES."

Soho Weekly News, May 18, 1978

A Family Affair

(Festival of Saint Anthony)

Since 1951 the parish of St. Anthony of Padua Church has celebrated the festival of its patron every June. For about ten days Sullivan St. is transformed; instead of cars, the curbs are lined with booths selling sausages, pizza, zeppole, nuts, calzone, sweet pastries, clams on the half shell, Italian ices, candy, and in recent years Filipino and Chinese food. There are game booths, a raffle, clothing and souvenir sales, religious items and St. Anthony's Church T-shirts. The street is crowned with glittering decorations that blaze with light at night. Children's rides appear suddenly in the parking lot across from the church.

According to the flier the church puts out, "St. Anthony's is more than equal to the task of living on the edge of bohemia. The Italian love of pageantry, the flair for the picturesque, combine to usurp the Village's neon brilliance . . . Unlike some of the commercialized Italian street festivals in the city, the one at St. Anthony's is run by the priests and the parishioners. Everyone who works at the feast must be recommended by the priests."

Saint Anthony of Padua was born in Lisbon in 1195 and at 15 was a canon regular of Saint Augustine. My childhood book of saints describes his calling: "Five friends of his were missionaries in Africa. One evening while he was reading in his study, he was told that his five friends had been killed by savages. Then and there Saint Anthony closed the heavy book he was reading and said: 'Is it right for me to sit here and read while my friends sacrifice their lives for Christ?' " He set out for Africa but, falling ill, ended up in Italy, where he met Saint Francis, became a wandering preacher like his mentor and, as a Franciscan friar, worked miracles and saved souls. Sometimes he worked so hard that he forgot to eat or sleep; he wore himself out and died at 36, on June 13, 1231. A year later he was canonized.

On the first Saturday of the Sullivan St. festival in the saint's honor, a day dedicated to children, there is a general blessing of young people. The next day there's a special service and blessing for the sick. Then there are the masses, novenas, confessions, devotions, and bingo games, which happen every week. At least six extra friars are assigned to the parish during the festival.

But the most spectacular and solemn event during the celebration happens on the last day, June 13, the saint's day. A statue of Saint Anthony holding the child Jesus (a replica, in colored plaster, of the statue at the apex of the church's façade) is carried by four men through the streets, embedded in the center of a parade of hundreds of people. First come three boys bearing a crucifix; then about 30 small boys, ascending in size, dressed in white robes, then a group of scouts in uniform, then 15 pairs of girls and boys dressed like miniature brides and bridegrooms and closely surrounded by mothers. Several friars carrying baskets of medals and receiving contributions precede the statue. Then, after a hiatus, comes a monsignor carrying a monstrance, the hem of his white robe held up from the street by two assistants. Next, a band of young and old men plays liturgical tunes on trombones, trumpets, and drums. Behind them are more ranks of parishioners: little girls dressed in Italian country costume—shawls and aprons worn over long, full skirts, kerchiefs and hoop earrings—and then a crowd of students from St. Anthony's school, in their school uniforms, and, finally, marching behind a banner that reads, "St. Ann's Married Association," lots and lots of women of all ages and a few men.

The games close as the procession, which has gone from the church up to W. Fourth St., down Thompson, and across Broome, comes back up Sullivan St. for the final leg of the route. That is, they close on the street side but most keep the sidewalk side open. Most of the festival goers ignore the gaming anyway, as the parade marches slowly by them. A few run to kiss the statue (the security cop flinches—the statue is draped in dollar bills) or to get a medal from the priests.

This year, while strolling down the block eating and drinking and drifting willy-nilly wherever the crowds swept me, I was struck by the subtle ways the feast, like so many religious celebrations in different faiths, promotes domesticity. One signal wasn't so subtle. Among the food and game booths was a table where a young woman handed out anti–abortion rights literature. "Four Ways to Kill an Unborn Child," one flier proclaimed in red, under a photograph of a bloody fetus. It went on to describe luridly four methods of abortion, analogizing all four methods to the most brutal, messy murders. "The bits and pieces of the baby are then disposed of," concluded the outline of the D & C procedure. Another flier, distributed by the Knights of Columbus, told the "thoughts" of an unborn child, ending with "Today my mother killed me." It stated that abortion in the case of a deformed child is no different than killing the child after it is born or after it has grown up; that in the case of rape or incest the crime is "rarely capable of being legally proven" and that true justice wouldn't "kill an innocent child for the crime of its father." To the pregnant woman terrorized by these crude, alarming broadsides, the only comfort is the suggestion that she go into seclusion, put the child up for adoption, and put herself up for "rehabilitation." And all this from a group that doesn't identify itself on its literature.

The attack on the rights of women to choose abortion is knit into a more lowkey promotion and embodiment of domestic values generally. There are the acceptable thrills—the rides, the liquor roulette, the gambling neatly enveloped off the main track (the poker, etc., in the basement of the church and the pinball and video games in a parking lot off the street). But these are easily countered by the pervading themes of home, church, and family. There are the tiny bridal couples in the parade. The street itself seems to have become a private domain, its roof the golden archways that form a cathedral ceiling between the buildings, just high enough to create a perfectly scaled frame around St. Anthony's statue as it is borne toward the church. In this street that has temporarily become a sanctuary for the feasters, the eating takes on a special symbolic function: sharing food, the crowds are united into a metaphorical family. St. Anthony watches over the crowd like a father. Bread, not only the staff of life but the basis of *family* life, is an important, holy symbol here: small loaves, blessed by the parish priest, are available for a small donation.

The first and second prizes in the church raffle are family cars. The third prizes are color TV sets. And at the various other church booths you can buy a tiny statue of the saint to turn your car into a chapel, a little plastic broom with the motto "God Bless Our Home," and a one-inch square plastic TV with a permanent image of Jesus and Mary. Or you can win, also at official church booths, Corning Ware blenders, mixmasters, pressure cookers, and toasters.

Considered as a bunch of disparate activities, the festival at most amounts to a pleasurable, sensual celebration in remembrance of a saint. Considered as a unified performance, it projects and promotes a stern, repressive vision of private life, bound equally by obligations to family and faith.

Soho Weekly News, June 29, 1978

All the World's a Sideshow
(Roy Faudree and the No Theater Company)

John Merrick, a nineteenth-century freak whom Leslie Fiedler has called "the Ugliest Man who ever lived," is the point around which Victorian society orbits in Roy Faudree and the No Theater Company's *Elephant Man*. Merrick was born deformed with a series of skeletal and skin disorders that made his flesh appear like hide and hang in great swells from his bones. Given the temper of the century, its fascination with Missing Links, evolution, and the moral as well as physical absence of a sharp boundary between man and beast, the misshapen Merrick was billed as a pachyderm much in the manner that Stephen Bibrowsky was renamed Lionel the Lion-faced Man.

Faudree's play doesn't dwell on Merrick's carnival years but on the last period of the Elephant Man's short life, when a doctor named Treves installed him in a hospital room where he could live, reading and building tiny houses, far from the derision, repulsion, and yet unquenchable curiosity of a rough public. High society briefly turned Merrick into a cause, launching charity balls to insure him a quiet lifetime tenure of privacy, in contrast to his earlier years when to live he had to parade naked before cruel sideshow audiences. Unfortunately, Merrick did not live long enough to take much advantage of his reprieve. After only three and a half years he died, his neck broken by the weight of his own outsized head, when he attempted to "sleep like other people," in contrast to the sitting posture his anatomy dictated.

Merrick remains masked and cloaked throughout the play so that we never actually see his much discussed deformity. The dramatic justification is not simply suspense, though a sense of horrible anticipation does pervade much of the performance. Instead, the main reason is that Merrick is used as a point of entry into the society that surrounds him. His story is interwoven with disjointed vignettes about the lives of the doctors, nurses, famous people, and servants that tangentially touch him. He is the center of a Gordian Knot, the nexus of a web of social relations that Faudree illuminates by displaying Merrick's position in the system as a metaphor or symbol for the preoccupations and prejudices of the whole culture.

Like Fiedler, Faudree is interested in freaks iconographically, rather than biologically. He wants to exemplify how physical deformity can function almost like a figure of speech—specifically, like a term in a metaphor. Early in the play a scene shows a medical examination of the actress Madge Kendal; she is corseted in a manner the doctor finds unhealthy. Juxtaposed to Merrick's tale, the point seems to be that the fashion is really deformity, a theme underscored later when we briefly see Treves's wife awkwardly strung up in an antique beauty contraption that looks disconcertingly like a gallows. Merrick's plight is also used to comment on the position of women in English society. His tale is interlaced with an argument for feminism, the correlation impelling a metaphoric comparison: Victorian women are also freaks, disenfranchised and oppressed because of biological differences.

Often in this production characters appear at the primmest of parties only half-dressed. The effect is quite jarring, given the overdressed, overly formal, and repressive atmosphere. Here the juxtaposition to Merrick's deformity serves as a generic image for the period's attitude to the body as something animal or half-human or even unnatural, to be covered or hidden. Male actors playing female roles cavort in tight dresses, their muscles obscenely bulging in badly proportional garments, literalizing a Victorian attitude toward all flesh as gross. The difficulty and ill ease Merrick has inhabiting his body metaphorically stands for a whole society's discomfiture "with the baser part of man." The basis of the Victorian disdain for the physical in sexual repression is quite explicit. As the doctor loosens Kendal's corset, on the pretext that the natural look is the healthiest, he is actually involved in a furtive seduction.

The narration is easily understood but quite elliptical. There are flashbacks and scenes begun in media res. Most often, the action from one vignette to the next is not overlapping—the play jumps from one event to another that is temporally parallel but not causally connected to what precedes. This style bids the audience to link the scenes associatively, since the causal bonds are so loose. The strongest element in the story line is Merrick, the freak, a central image that can be constantly mined for associations that metaphorically reflect on the rest of the action.

Faudree strives to show that deformity is a rich symbol, dense with multiple connotations, each of which can be mobilized separately when incorporated into different settings. Like a word, it is polysemic, shifting its emphasis and significance as it shifts contexts. For instance, one aspect of a freak is that it is on display. Faudree juxtaposes Merrick to a production of Gilbert's *Pygmalion and Galatea*. Not only is Merrick trapped in flesh as Galatea was initially trapped in stone; his freakishness also stands for the suspect social position of actors, as exhibitionists of sorts, in society. The freak is also used to elucidate Nora's crisis in Ibsen's *Doll House*. Here the Elephant Man serves both as an analogue to woman's oppression and an emblem of alienation. As Nora complains of her husband's lack of communication and her sense of isolation and powerlessness, excluded from the world of men, you realize that the general idea of the freak is the perfect expression for the feeling of being a misunderstood, misjudged outsider. (The excerpt from Ibsen is recited simultaneously by Kendal, putting on her makeup backstage, and Lady Treves, reading the lines from a book.) And, in this case, Merrick literally cannot be understood, because a flap of skin obstructs his mouth and distorts his speech.

As the play ends, a group of cloaked Merricks limp onto the stage for a moment. The freak is transformed in a metaphor for human life. The pathos we feel for Merrick, like the pathos felt for a freak like Karloff's Frankenstein monster, is symbolically transferred to the imperfect condition into which everyone is born.

The Elephant Man is basically a play of ideas, a meditation on the multiple layers of meaning sedimented in a symbol. It requires an abstract mode of presentation, in order to distance the audience by subverting empathy and encouraging the spectator's associative imagination. The brisk scene changes, the fluidity and stylization of the staging, are appropriate. The five major zones in the long, narrow corridor the troupe has constructed in the Envelope at the Performing Garage shift between different social arenas: the circus, society, the stage, the hospital, Merrick's room. Finally, the street outside the theater is also used as Lady Treves, becoming Ibsen's Nora, walks out of the playing space with a suitcase. As the actors go from one zone to another, sometimes in the middle of a line, they shed clothing or add clothing to become different characters. Men play women, and women play men at times, complicating the text poetically, since in it women express the desire to be treated like men in order to achieve equality.

The play also comments on its own position in theater history, its situation as a modern experimental work contrasting with traditional genres like circuses, melodramas, extravaganzas, and serious dramas.

Madge Kendal was, in fact, a well-respected actress and manager who, with her husband and partner, William Kendal, did much to raise the status of actors. In the play Kendal speaks of her brother, T. W. Robertson, who inaugurated naturalistic domestic dramas in England. Ibsen, the great naturalist, is also invoked. And W. S. Gilbert's work appears not only because it is thematically important but also because T. W. Robertson first encouraged Gilbert to write plays. Merrick is taken to Drury Lane to see the pantomime—which, anachronistically, is portrayed by a mime (i.e., dumbshow) that turns into a quasi-Noh drama. (The Christmas pantomimes at Drury Lane—a theater also renowned in the 1880s for its realistic melodramas—were extravagant spectacles featuring double transvestitism, acrobatics, ballet and precision dancing, slapstick, and songs, centering around a few familiar folktales.)

The major failing of the production is the acting. The rapid changes in mood, often leaping from comedy to melodrama, and the diversity of historical material demand that the troupe command a wide range of acting styles. But the No Theater seems to have a no-style, except perhaps for a tendency to forced declamation, that it uses to allude to historical genres in its own vernacular, rather than, like the text, carefully quoting its sources. The result is a loss of the sense of fragmentation and distance that this sort of post-Brechtian exercise requires.

Soho Weekly News, August 3, 1978. Cowritten with Noël Carroll.

Hats and Hierophanies
(Robert Kushner/International Society for
Krishna Consciousness)

Robert Kushner's *New York Hat Line* presented 25 hats in a mock fashion show of four different lines: the New York Line, the Bedroom Line, the Puerto Vallarta Line, and the Cheese Line.

It seems like haute couture is deemphasizing hats these days—maybe because hair itself is beginning to be treated as an objet d'art. But Robert Kushner's performance reminds us what strange objects hats have always been. When you consider the vagaries of headgear, Kushner's concoctions of foam rubber, chopsticks, pot lids, frisbees, unstretched oil paintings, and airline bags really look only slightly outlandish. They are exaggerations of *la mode* but not violations.

Hats have always come in so many bizarre shapes that the basis of Kushner's transformations lies primarily in the combinations of materials, rather than the size or shape of the objects. Some, like the *Persian Salt Bag,* a tapestry rectangle that stands straight up from the head, and several biomorphic foam rubber numbers, are reminiscent of medieval chaperons and jester's hats. Others, with turbans, silk veils, chinoiserie, or liripipes, seem more like between-the-world-wars versions of antique and foreign styles. But I guess there are no precedents for things like the *Dynel Pipeline,* a wig of silver curls with a plexiglass tube, charred and bent, protruding a foot or so, and the *Homage to the Bay of Flags,* with banners attached to wire hoops ending in front of the face.

The performance is an almost perfectly straight rendition of a regular fashion show. The models smile somewhat vacantly, push their hips forward, turn around to show every angle to the audience, and point out details with languorous gestures. But the cleverest part of the satire is the text, by Ed Friedman, which Kushner and Barbara Barg read as commentary during the modeling. Friedman burlesques the ad copy jargon that makes everything sound strange and chic:

Half-inch double-stitch petite pleats wiggle their way around your scheming consciousness hoisting themselves into a bulbous brim that climaxes in a penultimate pinnacle with an antique, Bakelite, badminton birdie of Middle Eastern art deco origin.

After the first set of hats, the idea behind the whole thing wears thin fast. Kushner stops to have his models change clothes between sets, perhaps to demystify fashion show glamor, or perhaps only because he has six models. *New York Hat Line* would be funnier if it were even more like a real fashion show, whipping its way past our eyes.

• • •

On Saturday the Hare Krishna people came down to Washington Square to hold their annual Festival of Chariots in the park. The celebration included Vedic weddings, a fire sacrifice, and dancing. Being around blissed-out people makes me nervous. Usually I just make my escape when they gather. But after I innocently wandered into the thing, the dancing kept me riveted. It was infectious, though ultimately insidious in ways that confirm every one of my premonitions.

The chanting, cymbals, and drums were highly amplified so that the whole park was soaked with the repetitive rhythm. It was hard, even for a cynic like me, not to get swept into jumping and stepping along with the devotees. They were sure-footed, in their earth shoes, sneakers, or sandals: bouncing madmen in transcendental motion, throwing arms up toward the sky, snaking bare torsos, landing softly on the stage as if it were a trampoline, every movement light and resilient. A couple of tiny boys, probably not even old enough to talk yet, had already indoctrinated their feet to spring from side to side just like their elders. (The women were down on the street, bowing with their faces pressed against the pavement or, at certain climactic points, acting like shills to incite the audience to jump and dance.)

Those religious people sure know how to organize a performance. And they're pretty sneaky about using music and dancing to bolster their propaganda. The head guy explained after the dancing men sat down that their ecstasy was an incarnation of godhead and so on, which everyone feels to some degree even if they aren't lucky enough to realize a direct connection to Krishna . . . after all, he asked cannily, hadn't each one of us felt some strange exhilaration during the chanting of the sacred names?

Soho Weekly News, August 17, 1978

Subway Stops

(Lawrence Kucharz)

Canal St. is a series of views, stories, and sounds connected both by content and by simultaneous projection. The correspondences are never literal, but all three are about subways.

The views are 24 slides of the Canal Street subway station (BMT, I think), arranged and projected in modules simulating perspective shifts. We seem to move toward or away from a vanishing point, and then the view changes radically so that an entirely new vanishing point is established. The camera is a free agent that changes positions and sides of the track. The rapid projection of the slides, which lasts for about 20 minutes, gives the impression of a film rhythmically zooming up to various objects—a tiled wall, a clock, the opening of the tunnel illuminated by the headlights of an oncoming train. The same goals of vision are repeatedly set forth, only to be dropped for new goals. Thus, the spectator never achieves a single point of view. The presentation of the slides establishes a visual structure the human eye could not duplicate. Yet the fragmented image is strangely familiar. It reminds me of the feeling of standing on the platform, staring at the walls, noticing different details, checking the time, looking again and again for the sign of an approaching train.

The words that accompany the visual track are an aural serial projection, on tape, of a poem called "City Street Scenes 1." Kucharz applies Schoenbergian, 12-tone music compositional techniques to 12 words: *lights, subway, passing, waiting, man, quiet, train, riding, woman, station, dim, deserted.* Kucharz explains in an article in *Ear* that in his serial poetry he must take into account the differential between tones and words—e.g., words have syntactical meaning, there are more than 12 words in the English language, and, to find correspondences between words parallel to those which flow structurally from the relationships between tones on a given scale, one must invent them arbitrarily.

In "City Street Scenes 1" Kucharz's operations yield 48 arrangements of these 12 words. They function like 48 tiny stories, changing meaning with each arrangement.

dim station
woman, . . . quiet, deserted, waiting
riding train
passing subway, lights man

An image is overlaid on the pulsating actual image of the empty Canal St. Station. It seems like a scenario for a story. Subway sounds—the crescendos and decrescendos of passing trains, the bell ringing a warning of closing doors—supply a dramatic, atmospheric framework, a sense of climaxes never quite reached, a mysterious quality of foreboding. At first the stories sound muffled and unintelligible, like the announcements you hear in subway stations. Gradually, as they are repeated, you decipher the meanings in the sounds. But, as with the visual track, the object changes, undercutting any possible resolution.

quiet woman
man
train passing, . . . lights waiting dim subway
deserted, . . . riding quiet
station dim train
man
subway waiting, lights woman, . . . passing
deserted riding, . . . quiet

The stories shift from inside to outside, from train to platform, from man to woman.

And we are confronted with a resonant total text, unified in its fragmentation, static because it is constantly transforming.

Soho Weekly News, August 24, 1978

Words from "City Street Scenes I" © 1978 Lawrence Kucharz.

Performance Art in California . . .

(Women's Performance Art)

This is a report on a report. Three feminist artists from California—Barbara Margolies, Mary-Linn Hughes, and Micki McGee—have been traveling around the United States this summer, bringing with them information to share on feminist performance in southern California, in the form of a slide talk. They trace the beginnings of the genre to the establishment of the Feminist Art Program at Fresno State College by Judy Chicago (painter and author of *Through the Flower*) in 1970. The following year the program moved to California Institute of the Arts (Cal Arts) in Los Angeles, a school that was to become a center for performance art, feminist and otherwise, throughout the 1970s.

Judy Chicago advocated performance as a suitable feminist form from the beginning, since she felt that performance was available to unskilled students and that it could be fueled by pent-up rage in a way that painting and sculpture couldn't. Her students' performances were powerful, she reports, because they sprang from authentic feelings.

The first group of slides shown at Franklin Furnace skipped the early Fresno performances and began with 1972 pieces at Womanhouse, a fantasy environment built by the women in the Feminist Program. These performances questioned not only women's roles in everyday life but also the use of commonplace actions in art performance. That is, an act like sweeping the floor, treated as "cool" material by New York avant-gardists, became a hot, charged symbol in a feminist context. In *Scrubbing* the audience watched while Christine Rush literally and simply scrubbed the floor. In *Waiting* Faith Wilding sat in a chair and rocked, reciting a litany of situations that add up to a lifetime of waiting.

Ablutions, a collaboration among Chicago, Suzanne Lacy, Sandra Orgel, and Aviva Rahmani, was a series of scenes suggesting mysterious feminine rituals, one involving immersions by two women in three bathtubs. One tub was filled with eggs, the second with animal blood, the third with clay. The floor was strewn with broken eggs shells, ropes, chains, and animal kidneys. After their ablutions the women were wrapped in sheets and tied up, while on tape women's voices told of rape experiences.

Margolies, Hughes, and McGee see feminist performance as a process that has developed over time from expressing weakness and anger to asserting strength. They cite Chicago's interpretation of *Ablutions*—that women are bound by self-victimization—and performances like Barbara Smith's *Feed Me* (1973), in which the artist, alone and naked all night in a room filled with food, wine, flowers, oils, incense, and pillows, received the audience one at a time. The rumors circulating about what did or could happen sexually conflicted with the actual experience of engaging in conversation and mutually agreeable acts of feeding, making the myth of feminine vulnerability and sexual passivity the subject of the piece, in the form (as in many of Smith's performances on other subjects) of a ritual meal.

In contrast, many recent performances are tough political statements, often embodying strategies for change. *Three Weeks in May,* a protest against the high incidence of rape in Los Angeles organized by Suzanne Lacy in 1977, involved artists, feminist groups, and city officials and included a documentation on a city map of each day's rapes, a speakout and healing ritual for women who had been victims of sexual violence, performances by men showing how American culture trains men to be potential rapists, self-defense demonstrations, and public meetings. *Record Companies Drag Their Feet* (1978), done by Leslie Labowitz with Women Against Violence Against Women (WAVAW), was an agitprop event criticizing record album covers with a skit about record company executives, which concluded with a successful press conference by WAVAW.

Cheri Gaulke's *Red Shoes/The Big Feet of the Empress Tu Chin/Mud* (1978) is a more personalized statement affirming, through storytelling and the symbolism of feet and shoes, the earth and nature as the source of women's identity and vigor. Gaulke is one of three members of the Feminist Art Workers collective: the many collaborations and collective performances, of the 20-odd pieces documented, attests to the success of the feminist art community in southern California at putting principles into practice in art, work, and daily life.

Soho Weekly News, September 7, 1978

Kroesen's American Dream

(Jill Kroesen)

A few days after I saw *The Original Lou and Walter Story* I saw *Oklahoma* on TV. I was amazed at how much they reminded me of each other. In both, not too much goes on except that people fall in love, have strange dreams, and the world is divided into farmers, women, and others. In each, the plot is basically an excuse for a lot of singing and dancing. Of course, there are also certain differences. If *Lou and Walter* is an American musical, it is one that has been radically transformed in style and content.

As in Kroesen's various versions of *Stanley Oil* (an economic analysis of the entire history of the Western world), in *Lou and Walter* a complicated story is set up primarily by asides, introductions, and notes. The actions done by the performers advance the plot only slightly; for the most part they function to illustrate salient moments repeatedly. One gets a vague idea of the plot first by reading the program notes, and then Kroesen sits in front of the audience at a microphone, explaining everything again like an earnest child, bouncing a ball, grinning, embroidering on the details. One finds out about the long-standing battles between the Share If and the farmers, including the time the Share If stole the farmers' sheep. One learns about the social structure of the town, including an important division of the sexes. "Women who are in the town have to go to the outskirts of town where they dance when they become 14. It isn't against the Share If's law like many other things are, but it is unthinkable in this town for things to be any other way. There is one exception: the Share If can have a wife in town, but it is against the law for her to do anything except cook roast beef, and she has to do that very well."

Not surprisingly, people are rarely born in the town. Also, all the farmers belong to the Sodom Union, where they have meetings often to make decisions about all the problems daily life creates, they plant potatoes, they sleep, and they play. The farmers have to give away most of their potatoes so the sun won't fall down.

Once all that information is out of the way, the performance can begin, with the next installment of the plot. Lou (Kroesen) has gone away to Disappeared because of his "abnormal love" for one of the other farmers. Abnormal love is what we know as a consuming, unrequited crush. But in this town abnormal love has a debilitating physical effect—you literally fall apart, your arms fall off and come back on, and you might even disappear. The farmers have a seance, and Lou emerges from a box, but he has lost his "thing" (and suddenly Walter finds he has two "things"). Now Lou is a she.

But this new development has to be kept from the Share If, who would send Lou to join The Women if he found out. The Women are symbolized by two dancers dressed in typical ballet outfits, doing pointe work that continuously traces out the borders of the performance space. Also, Lou confides to the audience that now she has to join a new club (instructions received in Disappeared) and choose someone else to join with her, but if she makes a mistake the other person might die. The Share If's wife cooks roast beef by sitting at a piano upstage drawing cows and coloring them in red. Toward the end of the play, she gets to come downstage and show the audience her artwork. But mostly she gets yelled at by the Share If because she keeps breaking into spells of piano playing, which cause Lou either to sing a countrified lullaby to the farmers ("Raaahk-a bah ba-ay-bee-ee . . . ") or to slide up to the Spot to have a dream and sing. It is in the dreams, which punctuate the repetitive routine of meetings, planting, Share If's yells and threats, and lullabies, that things happen. A tap dancing stranger, Lee You, arrives, and Lou falls in love abnormally again.

Here is the crux of the problem. Lee You seems like the proper candidate to ask to join the new club. But, on the other hand, abnormal love might be clouding Lou's reason. Lee You shows up in real life and teaches the farmers how to enter the mysterious Spot by tap dancing. But then he's arrested by the Share If, who mistakes him for Lou. He is let out of jail, but Lou is gone, once again to Disappeared.

For me the best things about Kroesen's performances are their repetitiveness and inconclusiveness. There is something haunting about the way everything happens over and over, songs begin again and again, and the piece doesn't really end. And there is something deeply satisfying about the constant return to the plaintive songs that lead nowhere, the inevitable farmers' banter, silly and comic, that frames every turn of the plot. It is an infantile, obsessive structure that suits the mythopoeic manipulation of symbols and the illogical interweaving of real circumstance and fanciful causation (as when Kroesen, who really has a slipped disc, which made her hobble slightly throughout the performance, explained that Lou has pelvic inflammatory disease [PID] and that's why she'll have to walk funny). A childlike confusion of sexual identity, literalized in Lou's transformation, is also suggested by the range of feminine types— from the big woman who plays the Share If, that is, a big scary man (Marsha Carlson), to the ethereal ballerinas floating around the edges (Judith Hanfield and Debra Weiss) to the subversive, spaced-out Share If's wife (Regina Beck).

This infantile projection of a world, supported by Jared Bark's wonderful sets, which include a Plexiglas potato patch illuminated in green and house frames that sway gently as people come and go, is dominated at its center by Kroesen's extremely engaging performance presence. As Lou she is the child/God, the animating force whose anxieties and desires populate the fantasy. The fact that in group scenes Kroesen often speaks into a microphone exemplifies and underscores this role.

The Original Lou and Walter Story is in many respects charming, brilliant, beautiful, touching, and mysterious. But it left me with one nagging question. Underneath its sexual confusion and attacks on authority, it hints at a message similar to *Oklahoma*'s. That is, *Lou and Walter* could be interpreted as preaching a typically conservative, even anti-gay morality. In some ways, the story hints that to grow up, one must leave childish (i.e., homosexual) relations behind and find "normal love" (heterosexual). I hope that future installments will prove my interpretation wrong.

Soho Weekly News, January 11, 1979

Monk's Chant

(Meredith Monk)

Meredith Monk's music often sounds simple in terms of instrumentation: her basic strategy is to spin out a single melodic phrase, to repeat and vary it (usually on piano or organ) with a gentle obstinacy. The melodies, in their simplicity and circularity, are reminiscent of lullabies or folktunes. Yet over this clear, secure base Monk builds a complex superstructure of vocal adventures—including warbles, ululations, murmurs, wails, drones, tattoos, chirps, hums, sighs, breathy flutters, twangs, falsettos, and bell-like clarity—that derives from years of experimentation, refining images and emotions into musical forms. Her songs are wordless, but, because the sound clusters and intonations she uses seem to strikingly resemble human conversation, there is both an emotional content and, often, a charmingly humorous quality in the songs.

For 12 years Monk, who has had classical voice training and as a teenager did a lot of folksinging, has been working with the solo voice—her own. During the past two years she has taught others her vocal techniques and at the same time composed pieces utilizing the special qualities of their voices. Monk's concert at The Kitchen, including the solo "Procession" from *Quarry* (1976), a trio version of three songs from *Vessel* (1971), as well as the more recent *Tablet* (1977), written for three voices, piano, and recorder, and her newest piece, *Dolmen Music* (1979), was a chance to hear nine years' worth of Monk's music.

Dolmen Music, for six voices and cello, seems to mark both an increase in complexity and an inclination toward more conventional composition. The typical Monk dissonances and distortions are woven into the piece, but so subtly and delicately one barely realizes it. The overall impression of the piece is one rich with variety in harmony, melody, texture, and range of pitch. Using three female and three male voices (the singers are Meredith Monk, Andrea Goodman, Monica Solem, Julius Eastman, Robert Een, Paul Langland, and Een also plays cello), Monk alternately separates and unites them, compares and contrasts them, both in terms of formal design and in terms of implicit social meaning.

A dolmen, the program notes explain, is "a prehistoric monument found especially in Britain and France, consisting of two or more stones supporting a horizontal stone slab." Dolmens are thought to be ancient tombs, my dictionary tells me. A Monk music concert always has theatrical impact, and the way the singers enter to sit in a circle, men on one side and women on the other, the dim, bluish lighting, the way the singers seem to follow a certain protocol in joining or stopping the song, all lend a slightly melancholy, ceremonial, archaic quality to the exquisite performance of *Dolmen Music*.

The piece begins with a faint note played on the cello, sounding as if it comes from very far away, a distant call or a memory. Then one female voice begins a series of sustained tones, with tiny ridges—almost like melodic hiccups—creating slight punctuations. She is joined by another woman, and then the three men sing a deep chant, alternating its sureness with scrambled sounds, semblances of grumbling. Now all six sing in rich counterpoint. Now the women's voices sneak in ornamental variations, and Solem's voice emerges from the group to make *n-n-n-naw* sounds, and then Goodman enters with open, higher *ah-ah ah-aah* sounds. The piece ends with a loud finale that satisfyingly resolves the contrasts, repeating and weaving together each motif. In the constant alternation and mixing of male-female, low-high, fading-returning, clear-muted-twangy, solo-group, a cappella–to cello, the pieces take on many meanings, sometimes sounding like early church music, sometimes like a Jewish temple service, sometimes like a homespun community gathered around a campfire, sometimes like a lonely shepherd's call, and sometimes like a celestial choir.

Soho Weekly News, February 1, 1979

The Squirming Point

(Eleanor Antin)

I'm not sure how to write about Eleanor Antin's recent performance without making it sound better than it was. To describe the plot makes the "narrative" more intriguing—and more important as a component of the performance—than it is in reality. But with that caveat, let me begin.

Eleanora Antinova (played by Eleanor Antin, who is white) is a black woman, a ballerina who has been trained by Luba Tchernicheva and who dances with Sergei Diaghilev's Ballets Russes. Frustrated by Diaghilev's refusal to let her play classic roles in the "white" ballets—*Swan Lake, Giselle, Les Sylphides*—Antinova decides to create her own ballet, about Marie Antoinette on the eve of the French Revolution. The rest of the "action" in *Before the Revolution* is that ballet, in which the starring role is played by Antinova and the supporting roles by Diaghilev, Tamara Karsavina, Igor Stravinsky, Vaslav Nijinsky, and Tchernicheva. Of course, they're not really played by all these dead people; they (and those people as themselves) are played by life-sized, painted cardboard cutouts on wheels, rolled about by a lackey in eighteenth-century dress (Tere Foley). Their lines are spoken by Antin, whose voice changes pitch and accent rather easily. These characters change roles by having clothing and wig cutouts clipped to them with clothespins, in the manner of paper dolls (Marie Antoinette even has two children clipped to her voluminous skirt).

The performance and the ballet within it surprised me with their conventional theatricality, even though I know that Antin has for years been interested in the creation of personae, which include, besides the Black Ballerina, the King of Solana Beach, the Nurse, and the Black Movie Star. The entire performance—with its arcane references to the actual world of Diaghilev (of course, there were no blacks in his company, though there were Moors and slaves in his ballets played by whites in blackface), its studiously constructed allusions to the court life of Louis XVI and Marie Antoinette, its arch artworld jokes—seems like an over-researched, double Stanislavsky étude, in which the actor builds the role by improvising myriad details of the character's life. Except for the lack of other actors, the situation is so traditional that its amateurish realization seems like a flaw rather than the endearing virtue one would hope for; its dullness—and the performance *was* boring—flows more from pretension than from postmodern aspirations. Antin's Russian accents were usually so good that it grated when her Nijinsky had an accent that sounded more Jewish than Polish. Her wobbly arabesques and attitudes were not quite adequate by real ballet standards (which, of course, they never claimed to emulate), but neither were they bad enough, or distanced enough, to serve as commentary on ballet. At one point Antin speaks as Antin, explaining that the performance is an attempt to "fill in the space between me and my name with credit." The tactic remains just so much rhetoric, never providing a frame for the disparate images and messages in the rest of the performance.

Antin's working drawings for *Before the Revolution,* on display (with the cutouts) this month at Ronald Feldman's Fine Arts (74 Street and Madison Avenue), show not only her amazing ability to copy other styles but also, in the character studies, suggest a great deal of movement and vitality. I wonder why Antin chooses to leave these obvious aspects of dance offstage.

Not only does the role of the Black Ballerina, as Antin plays it, seem like a bad racist joke, and not only were many lines in the dialogue offensive in other ways (a Polish joke about Nijinsky, for example), but the very basis of Antin's theater is lifeless, snide, and (literally) manipulative. With Antin at the center, speaking all the roles, and getting all the attention, the structure of the performance denies anything or anyone outside Antin. It is a vehicle for absolute narcissism.

Soho Weekly News, March 8, 1979

Multiple Exposure
(Jill Kroesen)

Jill Kroesen has been burnishing two basic plots in various performances for as long as I've known about her work. Now she has a new narrative, which I assume she will continue to revamp. To summarize briefly: USSR (Kroesen) is trying to take a lot from the US (Marisa Lyon), including her boyfriend, the undeveloped country (Steve Piccolo). In the meantime the weather (Joel Bergman) is tapdancing his grand design, often sending a storm that carries a virus (Sharon Mattlin) to infect the superpowers.

Condensing political events with soap opera plots and infantile rationalizations about the way the world works, Kroesen draws parallels between them. She equates the stupidity of the SALT talks with two little girls trading toys and sticking their tongues out at each other. US sits and reads *Glamour* magazine with a transistor radio plastered to her ear; USSR lies down on her little blanket hugging a big illustration board that says *Das Kapital*. Whenever USSR sees the underdeveloped country (his T-shirt reads "Raw Material"), via satellite, at US's house, she calls him on a red plastic telephone and asks him over to make a deal: "Hi honey. If you promise not to give the US any more coffee so they can't wake up in the morning, I'll untie one of the knots around your hands, if you promise not to shake your head back and forth, except when I tell you to, OK?"

The virus is a kind of chorus. After she invades the countries (giving them stomach virus, VD, and rabies) she can tell us what they're like inside and out. They're both inferior. Like the superpowers, the virus feels like multiplying. The need to multiply, Kroesen explains in her prologue, comes from the need to be secure, and it's much easier to get security by multiplying than by being creative. That's why people have kids, and that's why big countries need lots of little countries. Also, Kroesen confides disarmingly at this point, though this performance deals with current events, "It's not supposed to be completely factual."

As in the rest of her work, Kroesen uses a basic da capo structure in *Excuse Me I Feel Like Multiplying*. There are certain actions that repeat over and over again—the storm, getting into makeshift shelters, which signals the beginning of a round of SALT talks, the invasion of the virus, getting sick and going home to bed, making a deal. Although the plot is complicated, Kroesen tells it all in the prologue, leaving only the variable but repetitious details to be embroidered in the action of the relatively simple performance. Sometimes more exposition comes later in a song. There are five new songs, mainly clustered together at the end of the piece, and they are wonderful, especially the "I Think I'm Good if Someone Wants to Fuck Me Blues"—which explains how to become a *prima desirable assoluta* (sung by USSR, of course, who desperately wants to be No. 1 and knock US off her complacent, blue-jeaned ass). Lyon, a soprano, gets to sing as well ("Don't Steal My Boyfriend"). The songs have the same da capo form, basic repeating chord changes on electric organ or guitar creating a strong base for the obsessive returns of Kroesen's deep, rich, pleasingly nasal voice. Peter Gordon, who as the telephone company delivers peace to the two nations, also provides a very nice jagged ornamentation to the songs with a saxophone.

The casualness of *Excuse Me . . .* , with its makeshift shelters and beds, the way the performers are free to behave as if "offstage" when not singing or speaking, the way Kroesen explains and comments on the action, creates a diffuseness that is generally an agreeable aspect of Kroesen's work. In the Customs House the hugeness of the space sometimes exaggerated the scattered feeling, and, though generally people used microphones, their voices were instantly lost when they did not. I'm looking forward to the next installation of Kroesen's satire, structured to replicate a fixation, on world politics/women's roles/public health/meteorology, etc.

Soho Weekly News, May 31, 1979

Take Tea and See
(Masters of the Tea Ceremony Society of Urasenke)

The tension between artifice and nature (key to the Tea Event, or *Chanoyu*, literally, "hot water for tea"; the young American masters who are demonstrating this ritual prefer not to call it a ceremony—too formal, they say) is redoubled in the downstairs lobby at Japan House twice daily this month. Here the highly stylized act of making tea, to the Western eye (mine at least) so intricately stiffened by conventions and thus ceremonial in appearance, is distanced and formalized an extra time, because one doesn't participate as a guest in the actual rite but watches from outside the tea hut (two walls have been left open—like the "fourth wall" of a proscenium stage in naturalistic theater). Two guests and a host, all trained in performing the ritual, enact only the *temae*, or climax of the form. The witnessing by the guests of the perfectly realized performance by the host is mirrored here by the watching of this witnessing by the interested public.

The Way of Tea, *Chado*, has its roots in Zen Buddhism and Taoism (like *Kendo*, the Way of the Sword, and *Shodo*, the Way of the Brush, or calligraphy) and in the aristocratic practice of holding tea parties when tea was a luxury item imported from China. The rising merchant classes borrowed the samurai and noble practice, codifying it during the fifteenth and sixteenth centuries and refining it with the Zen sensibility of finding spiritual serenity in meditating on the simple details of everyday life. The Way of Tea provides time to study art and think on nature. It is a paring down of gesture, word, and artifacts that urges one to find beauty in simplicity. Life itself becomes aestheticized. It is interesting to me that the word *suki*, "liking of tea," also means artistic taste. Also that, as Seno Tanaka writes in *The Tea Ceremony*, the custom of drinking tea in such an elaborately conscious manner might never have been created if tea had been a native crop or more easily available in Japan; the basis of the rite is the rarity and high value of the tea itself, which results in a kind of fetishism of both the herb and the objects surrounding its use.

The young man who will later enact the role of a guest in the ceremony tells us that before the *temae*, which we are about to see, the host will have sent an invitation to the guests and then on the day of the event will have hung on the wall of the tea room—a special small rustic building with a low door that supposedly reduces everyone to an equal, humble position because of the physical necessity of stooping to enter—a scroll selected especially for the main guest, for that one day's Tea. The only other object in the room besides the tea utensils is a flower arrangement—unlike the formal, artfully arranged *ikebana*, the Tea calls for wild flowers, plucked fresh and arranged in a way that looks spontaneous.

After the guests have drunk and admired a cup of hot water from a mountain spring or a "good or famous well," greeted the host, and consumed a meal and a lot of sake, the host prepares thick green foamy tea. This is the *temae*, the climax.

The twenty-minute rite at Japan House is repetitive but quite complex. The exact number of bows, the way the utensils are wiped clean with a silk cloth folded in a certain manner, the way the cup is turned a certain number of times before handing it to the guest or back to the host, the procedure of rinsing the tea bowl and bamboo whisk with hot water and then adding the powdered tea and more water, the exact position in which the water ladle is placed on the rim of the brazier, the prescribed topics of conversation and the pauses and exits and entrances would delight a semiotician. The caesuras between actions—like the *mie* in Kabuki theater—create frames, arresting moments in which attention is drawn to the action through its negation, a theme in Japanese culture that Alex Alland writes about in the current *Drama Review*. In the Tea the pauses literally make frames for the objects too, as the host rests his hand stiffly, like a pointer, against the tea bowl or whisk.

A tension is created between the slow, even tempo of the presentation (a stretching of time whose beginning is marked by the stretching of each side of the silk wiping cloth) and the pauses; between the way the pauses make each object luminous in itself, an item of appreciation, and the way the actions make each object disappear into its instrumentality in a social process. When the host flourishes the cloth (albeit understatedly) and covers the objects to wipe them, he reminds me of a magician concealing and revealing things; when the host leaves the room to let the guests scrutinize each utensil, there is a sense of wonder, of a search to uncover the mystery these objects contain.

Soho Weekly News, June 14, 1979

Unearthing Symbols

(Meredith Monk)

Meredith Monk's new piece signals a change in her work, as well as a peak of consummation in her skill as a maker of stunning theatrical images. Yet in many ways during *Recent Ruins* I was reminded uncomfortably of *Quarry,* Monk's last grand *Gesamtkunstwerk.* On a smaller scale in terms of cast size, though not in terms of conception or timing, *Recent Ruins* seems a repetition of *Quarry's* structure and rhythm—a thinner, self-derivative piece, although several of its parts are exquisitely crafted.

Monk's theater/dance/operas have always had a chunky, fragmented shape. This choice, as well as the choice to layer media in order to achieve a richly nonverbal world of feeling, sensation, sight and sound, corresponds strikingly to her subject matter. Like the surrealists, Monk is interested in plumbing the human psyche by finding ways of replicating unconscious processes in shapes felt outside the body. Many of her recent works have expressed themes of community and pilgrimage, and in *Quarry*—a lament for the victims of WWII and especially the Jewish community destroyed by the Holocaust—these motifs were concisely and poetically embodied.

The archaeological imagery Monk used in *Quarry,* or even before that, to suggest the psychoanalytic process (one of Freud's favorite metaphors, too) is made explicit in *Recent Ruins.* The second section of the piece is peopled by ten characters, simply called Archaeologists. These people are dressed in costumes from disparate generations, from two nineteenth-century women in gray safari hats, long skirts, and mutton sleeves to two 1970s campers with backpacks. They process along the borders of the stage space's long corridor, chalking cryptic ciphers on the floor. Two of them (Monk and Pablo Vela) sit at a table on a small proscenium stage at the end of the space, gently examining and reassembling a broken pot.

In this section a black-and-white film follows. Some of the Archaeologists reappear in what look like antique group photographs of immigrants at a dock. In the stillness of the poses one person suddenly brushes aside a strand of hair or turns her head slowly. The effect is uncanny. Gradually, the film begins to elaborate another theme: measurement. You notice the scale of the abandoned buildings these people walk through and pose in (Ellis Island, the film credits say, but you also remember that in the program note Monk talks about a bombed-out railroad station in Berlin). You watch as they are examined brutally by scientists in desolate, enormous rooms. Someone writes numbers across a closeup of a man's face, circles a woman's nose, writes Serb across another face. The film creates an ambiguity between the illusion that these acts are done to photographs and evidence that these are not photos but live human beings. And throughout the film striped measuring sticks appear.

The piece had begun with a choral section in a marked-off space, a circle of silver edged with silvery rocks. For Monk, who has been alternating vocal concerts with theatrical works since the early 1970s, this act of embedding one form within the other is a new synthesis that also succeeds thematically. It is as if the six singers—Monk, Andrea Goodman, Monica Solem, Robert Een, Paul Langland and Ray Morrison, with Een on cello as well—who sit gravely in their circle, making circular sounds that range from nasal twangs to bell-like, celestial tones, are mythical ancestors or demigods, consecrating a space that will be the subject of the evening's meditation.

In the third section, a yellow-clad woman repeatedly attacks/hugs a primal mother figure (Lee Nagrin), seems crushed lifeless then does it again. While Vela sits on the small stage and eats, a whole civilization of yellow-overalled creatures—led by Monk, who wields a measuring stick—talks in a strange sign language, plays, dances, works. The silver space is entered and—perhaps—the civilization is destroyed. The huge mother figure arises to fling pieces of wood and measuring rods from one end of the space to the other. A coda: in a strobe light, fabricated creatures—five large, white turtles, a huge ant, five gigantic flies, and three Sputnik shapes—appear and move inexorably through the space, borne by black-clad movers. I am reminded of the planes and clouds in *Quarry*.

There is much else to notice and ponder in *Recent Ruins:* the shower of sand in a column of light that serves as a marker between acts, between eras; the spoons that all the Archaeologists suddenly hold up in unison, freezing in poses; the maps and drawings an invisible hand (Carl Goldenhagen's) makes, that seem to be blowups of what Vela works on at his table; the coins the two women Archaeologists spill all over the floor; six enigmatic figures who dance with capes and objects; Vela's and Monk's short waltz together. And all the clear, striking imagery of the beautiful film and the richness of the vocal work.

Yet for me the work was lacking something. I don't demand that every work come with a moral attached, but Monk seems to be making a moral point here with her allusions to measurement, categorization, forced movement, enforced pilgrimage (rather than the spiritual quests earlier works suggested), broken objects, lost nobility and harmony. However, the very nature of her materials—the fact that she uses words least of all—deprives the performance of the kind of specificity one needs for moral argument. The refined distinctions between categories, which language provides, are simply not available, and the multivocal symbolism with which Monk so often creates magic in the guts of her spectators here dissolves into generalities, a very ahistorical way of looking at a historical process.

Soho Weekly News, November 29, 1979

Dressing
(Pat Oleszko)

Pat Oleszko's performance was billed as a "loose gesture of performance elements in a party atmosphere." But to me it was just another performance, and not all that much live stuff, mostly film. We got there 15 minutes early, and already all the grog was gone. So we settled in like the rest of the spectators in the polkadotted room that housed some of Oleszko's huge costume-sculptures, and the ordinary passive-active spectator-performer relationship prevailed.

To "Blue" Gene Tyranny's wonderful piano cocktail music, the show opened with Oleszko inside a construction of Picasso's cubist *Three Musicians*, which revolved and started to come alive and break down. About halfway through the evening, to Harlem 1940s blues, a chorus line of three black crows, about six feet tall with big orange beaks, swayed and "mouthed" the words. And at the end the statuesque Oleszko—hermaphroditically dressed in stylized clothing that made half of her body a man's and half a woman's—performed a partial striptease in mirror symmetry with her own filmed image.

The rest of the evening consisted of three films, made with David Robinson. All were based on the reconstitution and substitution of body parts. *Kneel and Dimples—Hon-Knee-Moon in Knee York* had two knees disguised as bride-and-groom faces and used low-angle camera shots to suggest the point of view of tiny creatures; *Footsie* opened with a pair of shod fingers disguised as two little legs, meandering along the landscape of a body—through a pubic hair forest, up a breast mountain—and continued with the manikin's further adventures, like walking through dogshit. The longest film, *Ashpattol—Lexicon in De Feet,* was a version of Cinderella peopled by Ubuesque stepsisters and emblematic Oleszko costumes, padded and puffy and sometimes adorned with multiple arms and gloved hands.

Like so much of recent performance art, Oleszko's favorite theme is glorying in unabashed, even impudent physicality. She has an especial, infantile delight in breast-tweaking, liquids and sludge, and in a polymorphous perverse confusion of body parts. Her concocted figures are either cunning minutiae or distended, corpulent giants, and their genitals are either huge or mysteriously obfuscated under shapeless coats. Yet, unlike the baldly outrageous humor of the Kipper Kids or the childlike gender confusion of Jill Kroesen, Oleszko's tactics, for all their bulk, are timidly arch. Whatever is interesting about her work relies on nostalgic quotation (fashion-as-art, the party tricks of *Footsie* and *Kneel and Dimples,* the Picasso shapes). While avant-garde performance often has borrowed from popular culture and entertainments, it usually rearranges the forms or comments or otherwise reframes them. Oleszko's unoriginality, combined with her insipid use of fashion and decoration, makes her performance fatuous rather than funny.

Soho Weekly News, January 3, 1980

First Intermedia Art Festival

The First Intermedia Art Festival was an ambitious undertaking. Performances, seminars, panels, presentations, and workshops were crammed into less than two weeks. Participants traveled uptown and downtown to hear and watch choreographers, composers, directors, video artists, and critics define the term *intermedia* in theoretical and practical sessions. The term never really got defined, though. Elaine Summers, director of the Experimental Intermedia Foundation, which sponsored the festival, proposed a very specific meaning: *intermedia,* she said, can only be applied to performances that incorporate film, moving bodies, and music. Critic and playwright Michael Kirby pointed out that poet Dick Higgins first used the term in the 1960s to refer to the gap between any two art forms. By the end of the festival it seemed to me that *intermedia* meant any instance when technology intrudes on performance.

Although its title suggests a whole series of future events centering on a new art form, by the end of this first intermedia festival I wondered whether it was the future or the past that the conference celebrated. Energy shortages, recent cuts in arts budgets around the country, the skyrocketing cost of film, and the perennial lack of space in New York City, where much intermedia work has gone on over the past 20 years or so, create a milieu in the 1980s that makes the technological experimentation of the 1960s seem an innocent dream. The conference reminded us again and again that technology has advanced to an astounding degree of sophistication over a mere two decades. But I missed discussion about how the arts will use technology now, after Three Mile Island. The dream has become a nightmare. Can the arts afford to keep sleeping? The festival brochure stated that one aim was "to develop a contemporary language for the study of Intermedia and the theory and criticism of this art form." Instead of engaging in boundary fixing and canonization, it might have been more useful to see where we go from here.

Seven workshops were given: autobiographical theater, videotape documentaries, dance and sculpture, mind-body training, video as sculpture, electronic music, and kinetic theater à la Carolee Schneemann. Eight performances were given at the Guggenheim Museum. The filmmakers Ed Emshwiller and Stan Vanderbeek presented programs of expanded cinema, composer Carman Moore orchestrated four "lecturing music makers," and *bricoleur* Ping Chong recreated his 1975 *Fear and Loathing in Gotham*. *Sames*, a 1965 performance by the late Ken Dewey, with music by Terry Riley and a film by Jerry Chalem, was reconstructed by Usco (Gerd Stern). Nam June Paik and Charlotte Moorman, dada vaudevillians, performed a retrospective of their "greatest hits."

Two of the performances moved toward the dance end of the intermedia spectrum. Elaine Summers's *Crow's Nest* (1979) is a landscape constructed from three elements: film images of natural phenomena, six dancers, and a chant composed by Pauline Oliveros. The screen on which the films are projected, a three-dimensional structure with hanging fabric panels forming a 10-foot square within a 15-foot square, was placed in the middle of the museum's rotunda. The audience was seated all around this screen, and four projectors simultaneously cast identical images on its four sides. The color images moved from birch trees, which seemed to be growing as the camera rushed downward, to a forest, an ocean, a desert, and a rocky stretch. The live dancers progressed very slowly through this illusionary moving landscape, disappearing behind one panel and emerging somewhere else, circulating inexorably in a counterclockwise path through the structure. They stretched and leaned, sometimes showing only fragments of their bodies as a head or entire torso vanished or a leg and an arm appeared. In their flesh-colored leotards they seemed almost like chameleons quietly lurking in these vast, unpopulated places. Once a dancer turned on her back and seemed to be drawn, floating, into a whirlpool of water and foam. But it was the one time the two planes of vision merged.

The chanting, a series of sustained tones that seemed to draw on a chance harmonic arrangement as each voice gradually inched up the scale and sandwiched itself into the other voices, emanated from singers stationed at various points along the museum's ramp, filling the rotunda with cathedral splendor. And yet the unremitting meditation on natural beauty began to cloy early on in this 25-minute work. Too often the films shone with a Hallmark card aura, and the dancing neither challenged that glossy image nor expanded it.

Like Paik and Moorman's performance, *Double Lunar Dogs* by Joan Jonas was a retrospective. It was even titled "Solo Hits" in the program notes. Paik and Moorman spent two and a half hours genially presiding over a loose format of events, with Paik donning and shedding workboots and sweatshirts, calling out to Moorman to hurry up with her costume changes, Moorman waving to a friend in the audience, and both often stopping between pieces to comment or explain. It was a leisurely evening that could have probably ambled on forever, except that the museum guards probably insist on locking up the building well before midnight. Jonas's evening had just the opposite effect. Her two hours felt packed with complex, demanding events, polished and theatrical.

The evening included fragments of the performances *Organic Honey's Vertical Roll* (1972), *Mirage* (1976), *The Juniper Tree* (1977–78), and *Upsidedown and Backwards* (1979), as well as a film by Richard Serra, another film by Babette Mangolte, and documentary footage of a volcano. Interspersed between the pieces and during *Mirage* were music pieces by Jon Gibson.

Jonas's performances are structured as series of images anyway, and in this anthology format it was sometimes hard to tell where one piece stopped and the next began. In certain ways her work is seamless, and yet in other ways it's not. Jonas is a wizard who reveals her techniques. She "bares the devices," as the Russian formalist critics put it. She fiddles with images, numerology, masks, repetitive movements (like rocking, stamping, marching, running, swaying hips, circling a ball in one hand and a mallet in the other, or spiraling a small mirror down and around her nude body).

She's interested in symmetries and reversals of colors and shapes: she paints a heart or face on white satin with red paint then on red satin with white paint when talking about the two children in Grimm's *Juniper Tree*. She holds a mirror up to her own face so that the audience sees a single face that is half-flesh, half-glass. She projects a slide of a strange dog's face, with eyes that seem to stutter—one double eye white and one black. Then she draws the dog's image and holds it up to the mirror, where it is recorded by the videocamera, so that in the end we see five images. Then she splits the video screen so that when she draws this same face in splintered fragments it coheres on the screen. She bangs a big spoon violently against the mirror, which lies flat on her small tilting stage (which is also a blackboard), and we see, on the monitor, the squiggly path of the spoon's invisible trajectory, suddenly made visible on screen. She bounces the back of her hand loosely against the surface of the stage, and, on the split monitor, she seems to be clapping, while we hear clacking noises that strengthen the visual illusion.

Jonas's work is sometimes irritating to watch. You want the images to hang together in some sensible way, especially in the two later works, which use fairy tales as content, and yet those images often seem deliberately obscure and disconnected. You are thrilled by the sudden sparks of magic when the concentrated moment ignites—when Jonas saunters down the ramp, dressed as a burlesque queen, to rock music that seems strange and powerful, for instance, or when she completes the video mirage, or when her reiterated motions take on an incantatory power. But the dialectic of illusion making and breaking never emerges as an explicit theme of the performance, which seems to waver between two poles. Jon Gibson's music took him on constant journeys along the ramp. Sometimes he clacked wood together rhythmically, deliberately; sometimes he played what sounded like gently bleating bagpipes then a saxophone. In the darkness and stillness and with the height of the rotunda, the music coming from all points did weave a magical spell.

For me the most valuable part of the festival was the historical documentation. Contrasting the sparse attendance at the panel discussions with the crowd at Billy Klüver's presentation and the sold-out houses for the performance reconstructions, I'd say the audiences were more interested in history than theory too. The part I saw of Robert Withers's film translation of Meredith Monk's 1966 solo *16 Millimeter Earrings,* reconstructed and filmed last year with Monk, was beautiful. But it was screened 20 minutes earlier than scheduled, and very few people saw it in its entirety. Klüver's slide documentation of *Nine Evenings: Theater and Engineering,* the 1966 collaboration between Judson Dance Theater choreographers, composers, Happenings makers, and technicians from Bell Laboratories, was exemplary as a documentation. Klüver talked about and showed slides of the beginning stages of the collaborations, including the artists' wishes and fantasies and formal planning meetings, the construction work—dancers crimping wires and testing machines—and rehearsals, as well as production shots. After familiarizing us with each of the ten pieces (by Steve Paxton, Alex Hay, Deborah Hay, Robert Rauschenberg, David Tudor, Yvonne Rainer, John Cage, Lucinda Childs, Robert Whitman, and Oyvind Fahlstrom) and explaining the rudiments of the technology, Klüver showed a short film Alphonse Schilling made of the series. Once we had rehearsed the structures and images of the piece, the film made it all come alive.

Dance Magazine, May 1980

Reading the Circus
(Ringling Brothers and Barnum and Bailey)

As a child, I couldn't stand the circus. It made me uncomfortable. There was too much to look at all at once, and yet all that looking never quite gratified me. It just made me dizzy.

Then Paul Bouissac turned me on to circus. Bouissac, who teaches French language and literature at the University of Toronto, has an irrepressible admiration for the circus and its artists. But, more important, he has a way of looking at and thinking about the circus that makes it all supremely intelligible. And when an art begins to make sense while continuing to surprise you, you get hooked. Bouissac's method of illuminating the circus is an analysis based on semiotics, the study of signs.

Bouissac and I sit at the Ringling Brothers and Barnum and Bailey Circus, watching the clown acts. Our conversation is distracted, punctuated with silent observations of certain details of the acts. I tell him about suffering from information overload. He nods sagely. "Circus is difficult to watch, and it is also very complicated, very precise. It's not like the theater, where the information is highly redundant. Here there are maybe 40 acts, only a few minutes long each, and within each act there are six or seven events. That's a lot of information to process."

We stop talking to follow an adventure, lasting maybe three minutes, involving a clown, a net, and a little dog's refusal to be caught. The dog constantly tricks the clown, running down his pants leg while the clown scratches his head and looks everywhere around himself, tearing away the seat of his pants, jumping into but then out through the net. Bouissac starts taking notes. He's interested in recording certain kinds of very specific information: the clown's costume, the kind of dog, the gestures and action, the instrument around which the action revolves, the musical accompaniment. All these elements—and all the sets of choices these elements imply (why a small dog rather than a large one? Why this type and size of net?)—are symbols in what Bouissac calls a "multimedia language." These symbols make up a code, a language, that conveys a message to the spectator. If a single item in the act is altered, the message can change enormously.

Bouissac tells me about a favorite dog act of his, which involves ten Pekingese. David Rosaire, the trainer, puts them through their paces and then leads them back to their bench, when a scruffy little mutt rushes out of a doghouse at the side of the ring and performs all the tricks they've just done but much better and much faster. The owner gets angry; the one-upmanship continues.

"I have seen this act around 15 times, in various countries, and it always meets with huge success. The audience claps and claps for Sheba, the mutt, who is a real hero. Now, it's interesting to reflect on the reasons for the success of this act. The Pekingese are completely useless dogs, the perfect product of culture. Their breeds have been fabricated artificially by humans. And opposed to this you have a crossbreed, an animal that has had to fight much more for survival, who has had to rely much more on smartness. The Pekingese just have to be pretty. There is an opposition between the smart mutt and the tame but unproductive Pekingese, but beyond that there is an opposition between the force and the sterility of culture and the energy, inventiveness, and creativity of nature."

Semiotic analysis begins with an examination of oppositions. By making certain kinds of choices, the circus artist manipulates a non-verbal language to construct acts of communication that are then unconsciously decoded by the spectators. The audience identifies the symbols, situations, and categories from its culture—the system of conventions in which we operate—like wild versus tame, big versus small, animal versus human, elegant versus sloppy, man versus woman, work versus play; or chairs, tables, spaceships, spiderwebs. And these items and categories are actualized in the circus arena—a "noiseless," hermetic space to which we can turn our undivided focus—in drastic narratives of survival and control.

Yet the familiar, or mythic, elements of our culture are not simply paraded out before us. The circus transforms and recombines them to create a "metacultural discourse," to help the audience gain temporary freedom to experience all sorts of transgressions of its cultural rules and operations. Culture is what separates us humans from animals. But in the circus animals act like humans—the polar bear waltzes with Ursula, his white-tressed trainer, and then kisses her; tigers walk on two legs or ride horses. Humans act like superior beings (acrobats, equestrians, tightrope walkers) or like inferior beings (clowns). Incompatible animals work and play together. Gravity is defied again and again. All the most fundamental themes of biological and social human survival—stories of control over the environment, over gravity, over animals, and over social interactions—are rehearsed successfully in their most extreme forms.

In certain global ways we all understand this function of the circus as a folk symbol for freedom and magic. We love it because it is associated with childhood. We think of it as a set of illusions. Yet Bouissac is indignant that the circus is usually considered the domain of small children who aren't culturally integrated enough to understand its profound lessons—and his analytic system is a very down-to-earth method of unpacking the metaphors for freedom that turn out to be full of meaning and quite logically ordered. Bouissac examines the deep structure of the circus by analyzing how every minute detail in a program contributes intentionally to a fantastically orchestrated complex of meanings, "a kind of mirror in which the culture is reflected, condensed, and at the same time transcended." The analysis begins with the behind-the-scenes training of the performer and the creative process of designing an effective act and continues with the programming of an evening—the system of choices, for instance, that puts a bumbling clown parody, the Clown Charivari, after a group of tumblers, the Charivari, and then moves the eye from ground to air with the aerialist Grantcharovi troupe—and even includes the posters that advertise the circus as texts.

As we watch the show, Bouissac gives me pointers for seeing everything more clearly. When all three rings are full, he advises, don't shift attention from one to another. Variations on the same message are being constructed in all three, so just pick one and stay with it. He tells me that the antics of the King Charles Troupe, a team of black basketball players who ride unicycles and dribble, pass, and shoot while interweaving chaotically, are minutely choreographed to look spontaneous—which, if you think about the speed and precision involved, makes perfect sense. To dissect this supercharged bit would require a lot of repeated viewings.

Bouissac knows certain tricks of the trade. He confides that the Georgiev, Polonia, and Korin troupes, who balance in vertical stacks on poles and on each other's shoulders, keep their balance by watching a point on the ceiling; this act would be almost impossible to do outdoors. Bouissac explains the basic structure on which all circus acts are built, though each has its unique variations and elaborations: the introduction, in which the artist is announced and enters; the series of actions, in which several problematic situations are created and successfully controlled, usually in an ascending degree of adversity, much like the trials of the folktale hero; the conclusion, in which the audience acknowledges the artist's triumph over all odds.

"Watch the Richter Family!" Bouissac urges. They are handsome, spirited acrobats from Hungary, who work with elephants in the first act and horses in the second act, mounting the animals while they flip from springboards, riding them while balancing in groups. "Notice how their act is built with all the best rhetorical devices, like poetry or music. Two systems are always at work. Technically, there are the problems of landing safely and in exactly the right spot on the animal's back after somersaulting in the air. But, as soon as they land, they assume a graceful posture, with the whole body perfectly controlled, even the exact position of the fingers." It seems to me that acts of this kind all look alike somehow, but Bouissac assures me that in the circus no two acts are exactly alike unless it is a case of quotation or plagiarism. How would you interpret the Richters' act? I ask. Bouissac shakes his head, overwhelmed. "Oh, that would take many more viewings, a very close analysis of all the variables. It would be impossible for me to say at this point."

I start noticing the canny appropriation of all sorts of current cultural preoccupations: the circus galaxy pageant, borrowing visual and aural themes from *Close Encounters, 2001, Star Wars,* and other science fiction myths; the familiar musical motifs that seed the soundtrack of the entire program; the references to kung fu; two motorcyclists racing inside a globe. It occurs to me that over and over we keep seeing families facing death-defying situations together. And I'm intrigued by the feminist tinge of the Guerrero high-wire act, in which Jenny Guerrero supports her brother on her shoulders while walking the wire—"For the first time ever, this stunt is done by a woman!" the announcer boasts. Bouissac tells me that in the circus *everything* is always done for the first time.

Paul Bouissac is a circus addict. He grew up in the southwest of France, where as a child he was taken to see European one-ring circuses. Studying in Paris, he managed to combine scholarly research with his passion; his master's thesis, in the department of classical languages, was on the training of performance animals in Roman circuses, and his doctoral dissertation, in semiotic measurement of gesture, was on the technical behavior of acrobats. During vacations from the university Bouissac worked in Firmin Bouglione's circus, cleaning cages, teaching Bouglione's children, and sometimes giving the spiel for the sideshow, which he unabashedly recalls as totally exaggerated, surrealistic, and poetic. His teachers have been the anthropologist Claude Lévi-Strauss and semioticians A. J. Greimas and Thomas Sebeok, but Bouissac's own approach is pragmatically eclectic.

Bouissac has written a book called *Circus and Culture*. With two partners—a lion trainer and a magician—he founded the Debord Circus, which toured Canada for two years during the 1960s, until "we lost our shirts." And he has two grand projects in mind that could each take several lifetimes. Bouissac wants to work with physiologists, medical doctors, and circus artists to make a full inventory of circus techniques and complete, scientific archives to preserve the circus art tradition— "not that the circus will be dead, but there are always some acts that disappear, since circus technical knowledge, as an oral tradition, is extremely fragile."

The other plan is more practical though no less ambitious: to produce a Circus of the Century, with not only the greatest circus artists but also the collaboration of the greatest visual artists, composers, stage directors, choreographers. "I'm very well aware that this was done for the ballet years ago, by Diaghilev. But, after all, Diaghilev tremendously changed the ballet! Imagine a composer like Phil Glass confronted with a circus act. I'm sure he'd come up with a wonderfully effective score. I don't want to criticize the way the circus is done now, but I think the best artistic genius could serve this sublime art."

Village Voice, May 26, 1980

Consciousness Razing
(Women's West Coast Performance)

Should a feminist feel guilty when she doesn't like women's art? This is not an idle or abstract question; I've been grilling myself all week. Am I a traitor to the cause if the cultural offerings of the cause disappoint? Or should I do backbends to see in failed art that nevertheless is politically correct some spark of pleasure—or at least of hope?

I really wanted to like Women's West Coast Performance. I mean, I came prepared to be bowled over. Despite my suspicions about rituals that are meant to create a sense of community rather than growing out of communal ties, I always liked hearing and reading about the adventures of the feminist performance artists in California. All sorts of things about it seem right to me. I like the notion of a public performance that slashes through pornography, that questions and confuses sexual roles, that grapples with the unspeakable—rape, incest, war. These issues are suitable topics for art. And, then, performance takes a certain kind of audacity. I'm pleased that all these impudent women are going around raising hell in public.

Performance art, that ill-defined mode of theatrical presentation, is the perfect arena for giving body to feelings and theories about identity. Performance art is a sort of natural clearing at the edge of all the arts. To make performances is to ask questions about conventions, forms, and appearances—to incorporate those questions, in the literal sense. And in some ways, feminism begins with theories about the body.

Until the 1970s performance art was dominated by men . . . like the other arts. We read that the Zurich Dadaists hung around with women who studied dance with Rudolf von Laban, and so on. New York Happenings were made mostly by men. The women who did intelligent, sensuous live art in the early 1960s were dancers, many of them forging a new movement aesthetic at Judson Dance Theater. Carolee Schneemann talks about falling between the two stools of Happenings and postmodern dance in those days, because the former camp considered her, as a woman, a dancer, while the dancers considered her, as a visual artist, a Happenings maker.

Moira Roth, who has written a history of performance art on the West Coast, traces feminist performance in southern California to the presence of a number of East Coast people—including Happenings artists Allan Kaprow and Claes Oldenburg, postmodern choreographers Simone Forti, Yvonne Rainer, Steve Paxton, Alex Hay, and Fluxus members Dick Higgins, Alison Knowles, Nam June Paik—and also to the nurturing feminist art community and the inevitable associations with Hollywood. All through the 1970s men and women contributed to a lively performance scene at art schools and in community art centers in Los Angeles, San Diego, and Irvine.

Now some of the original feminist performers have moved away from performance art. Judy Chicago, a guiding spirit at the Cal Arts Womanhouse, for instance, sought more sophisticated imagery in her own work and began her massive traveling exhibition *The Dinner Party* after 1972. But, although some of the feminist performance makers traded live art for objects, a new generation of women came on the performance scene. The recent series of performances at 626, curated by Bill Gordh, showed works by a number of artists of varying reputations and experience, all of whom are or were affiliated with the Los Angeles Women's Building, a center for feminism and art that opened in 1973.

An uneven sampling of ritual, comedy, storytelling, dancing, agit-prop, and technological manipulations, this program left me wondering about some of feminism's legacies in art. What happens when feminism collides with modernism in California? "The personal is political" becomes an excuse to put raw feelings on the stage; "correct" slogans are offered up as both substance and style.

Of the pieces I saw, only three transcended the banal. (I missed Denise Yarfitz's costume/sound/movement event and Tyaga's piece about incest survivors, performed by Mary-Linn Hughes.) Susan Mogul's *Design for Living,* Barbara Margolies's *Little Barbara,* and Martha Rosler's sketch for a performance about Yom Kippur and the Yom Kippur war of 1973 worked not because of their subject matter but because all three women are wonderful performers. You'd be entranced by their presence no matter what they were doing. But here their styles of being present—so different from one another—make their polemical messages vivid.

Susan Mogul makes a salad that gradually takes over the stage. She talks nonstop, impervious to the antics of Jerri Allyn, who rushes around her setting the scene, hanging strips of wallpaper, tying aprons on Mogul and taking them off, bringing out another table when the vegetables begin to fall off the first one, pouring out glasses of club soda, tacking vegetables to the wall, holding up small frames to turn objects and actions into Works of Art. In a Jewish *balabusteh's* sprightly accents, but peppered with a regard for fresh vegetables only a Californian could muster, Mogul rips through heads of iceberg lettuce, slices cucumbers, halves lemons, chops red cabbage, rattling on about the way iceberg waters down dressing, how she went out to buy clothes for this occasion and ended up dressed in a giant napkin (a white paper jumpsuit), what sucking lemons does to your teeth. Meanwhile, Allyn keeps bringing out color-coordinated decor as each new bag of vegetables reveals green, yellow, red. Mogul's timing, her expressive face and gestures, her single-minded concentration on her task despite Allyn's mad obstacle course, and her final plight—tacked to the wall herself by the apron strings—all added up to a comic brilliance that was intellectually refreshing and visually appealing.

Barbara Margolies is a small, slight woman, and, dressed up as "Little Barbara" in a short dress, anklets, and pigtails, she looks uncannily like a child. A video monitor produces an image of the grownup Margolies, in adult garb and neat hairdo. As the woman shows us snapshots of Little Barbara, reminiscing—as if about another member of the family—about her days as a sweet, good child, her live alter ego scowls and sneers. It's time for rebellion. She whines at her older self, making fun of her seriousness and uptightness. Margolies the adult smugly notes that she owes her success to feminism and psychoanalysis. Finally, Little Barbara wheedles her grownup doppelgänger into dancing with her, and the two disappear to wallow in fingerpaints together. A simple interaction, pulled off with technical finesse.

Martha Rosler, who works primarily with video to (as she puts it) "question the mythical explanations of everyday life that take shape as an optimistic rationalism and to explore the relationships between individual consciousness, family life, and the culture of monopoly capitalism," had planned to show *Losing: A Conversation with the Parents*. When she realized that her part of the series was scheduled for Yom Kippur, Rosler instead gave a solo live performance, a sketch to be further refined, involving taped liturgical music, slide projections, repeated lightings of Yahrzeit candles, and the reading of a text. Telling a story that begins with the death of a childhood friend who was nearly ten, Rosler builds a web of meanings that open outward, encompassing the grief and guilt of the friend's death, her relationship with her father and his death much later, her education in the yeshiva and a trip at 14 to Israel, her discomfort with Zionism, the mourning and suffering of the Holocaust, but also of the dislocated Palestinian people. Returning again and again to the friend Alice, to the card Alice sent Rosler on her own tenth birthday (and slide projections of that card), Rosler uses her life and memories as the unifying thread from which a complex fabric of moral and political issues spreads itself. Her patience was impressive—a generous sense of timing that let each segment of the story, each song, each image, appear gradually and fully.

In both Vanalyne Green's *Unmade Beds* and Micki McGee and Mary-Linn Hughes's *Getting Ahead,* crude Marxism, feminist cynicism about heterosexual love, and uninspired staging mingled somewhat awkwardly. *Unmade Beds* proposed new rock songs to more honestly express women's experiences, and *Getting Ahead* contrasted an artist's consciousness with her parents' bourgeois values. Jerri Allyn's *Laughing Souls / Espiritus Sonriendos* was an incantation of cultural and personal death rituals by a disembodied voice while Allyn lay still on a bier of red satin flanked by candles, pomegranates, apples, and dolls in black capes and later danced with some skeletal figures straight out of German Expressionism. Diane Holland showed out-of-focus films and simulated masturbation. Anne Mavor, nude except for a layer of silver paint, projected slides of classical sculptures on her body then danced and played with balloons. Katja Biesanj, a self-styled shaman, told neomythological tales.

Pervading every performance was a sense that its subject matter—women's experience, in one form or another—provided a basis for legitimacy. Perhaps this partly came from the framework of the series itself. Yet what would we think of a world in which painting only seascapes served as a criterion for artistic value? Sometimes being a feminist isn't enough.

Village Voice, October 1, 1980

Mother Wore a Tractor

(Early Soviet Fashion Design)

Lenin would have spun in his grave. Or maybe not—every Communist knows that capitalism can swallow even the prickliest barbs aimed to destroy it. Revolutionary art always ends up fetching high prices.

In conjunction with the exhibition "The Avant-Garde in Russia, 1910–1930: New Perspectives," which just moved from the Los Angeles County Museum of Art to the Hirshhorn Museum in Washington, a fashion show was presented the night before the opening. Could any event have illuminated the contradictions more clearly? A German design house translates Constructivist clothing, designed by Soviet women of the 1920s and intended as mass-produced items for working women, into silk and linen one-of-a-kind collector's items. One of the dresses, a long, tubular design with boat neck and sleeves, bordered with stripes and belted low, has been multiplied—well, not exactly mass made but repeated 149 times—and sells for $750. It comes with a scarf the museum is selling for $46.

It's ironic that the world of high fashion should so enthusiastically embrace an "ism" specifically aimed at destroying fine art as the world knew it in the nineteenth century, replacing elegance, decoration, and "beauty" with the efficient, machinelike beauty of a twentieth-century vision. The Soviet avant-garde artists turned from painting to photography, from sculpture to useful objects, from design to construction. The new art of the Russian Revolution celebrated the joys of collectivity, of learning, of forging a brave new world with new technologies and new social forms. To the fervent, young revolutionary artists of the 1920s—many of whom were women—life itself had become a joyous, brilliant masterpiece, and to enhance the daily lives of the working millions, to figure out the perfect form for books, buildings, chairs, teacups, clothing, was to be a true artist. No more dead masterpieces hanging in museums, accessible to only the privileged few.

As Mayakovsky wrote in *Mystery Bouffe:*

Why do folks go to museums, anyway?
All around us, treasures are heaped up high.

Is that the sky
or a piece of bright-colored cloth?
If this is the work of our own hands,
what door will not open before us?
We are the architects of earths,
the decorators of planets. We're
miracle-makers.
We'll tie rays of light
into bundles and use them as brooms
to sweep the clouds from the sky
with electricity.

For the Constructivists to reject the individualism of easel painting—
every artist creating yet another canvas on some well-known theme,
simply to decorate another private wall—was to plunge fully into the
modern world, to struggle with the realities of "materials, volume, construction," to put art at the service of the commune, and to achieve
"objectivity." In a society crawling out of the ruins of feudalism and the
bloodbath of war, in a world in which a mechanized life seemed to bring
only good things—food, clothing, health, warmth—a life filled with
mass-produced items, sleek surfaces, cogs and gears, and the rhythms of
repetition, was a splendid, not a bleak, vision.

So Tatlin's tower was a projected celebration that put mass media
equipment at its pinnacle. So various artists transformed trains and steam-
boats into posters, decorating their surfaces with agitprop imagery. After
the exhibition "5 × 5 = 25" in Moscow, Alexander Rodchenko turned to
photography and graphic design; Varvara Stepanova, Lyubov Popova,
and Alexandra Exter began to design porcelain, textile, books, and
dresses as well as theater sets and costumes; Alexander Vesnin collaborated with his brothers on architectural and industrial designs. In
1923–24 Popova, Rodchenko, and Stepanova worked as designers at the
First State Textile Factory. Their aim, wrote Stepanova, was to make
garments that were as practical, bold, and efficient as the factory a
woman would wear them to. "Aesthetic aspects must be replaced by the
actual process of sewing. Let me explain: don't stick ornaments onto
the dress; the seams themselves—which are essential to the cut—give
the dress form. Expose the way in which the dress is sewn, its fasteners,
etc., just as such things are clearly visible in a machine."

The fashion show at the Hirshhorn exhibited 12 designs by Popova,
Stepanova, Exter, and Nadezhda Lamanova, reconstructed by the Ger-

man fashion house Van Laack, under the direction of Erika Hoffmann-Koenige, an art historian and stylist. In a way, by showing only the designs by women, this show was a myopic view of the range of clothing design by avant-garde artists in the early days of the Soviet Union—Rodchenko's well-known worker's suit was missing, for instance, as were his costume designs for Mayakovsky's *Bedbug*. Tatlin sketched worker's clothing, and some of Vesnin's stage designs are positively space-age. The Russian art historian John Bowlt has pointed out that the prevalence of women artists in the early Soviet avant-garde is not a particularly strong indication of feminism. World War I had drastically changed the situation for women in most European countries. They had entered the work force, their social roles changed accordingly, and so did their clothing—it had to be shorter, looser, and simpler.

Hoffman-Koenige and her husband, Rolf Hoffmann, the director of Van Laack, originally put together these reconstructions for an exhibition in Cologne on "Women Artists of the Russian Avant-Garde," which accounts for the omission of male artists. But, while one eye stares at art history, the other is clearly focused on the market. The materials they've used—even if the volume and construction are right—are wrong. This is not historical reconstruction. These dresses are commodities.

Tall and gray-haired, elegantly dressed in a dark suit with a silk handkerchief printed with tiny hammers and sickles (a Popova design), Rolf Hoffmann provided the commentary for the show. (But only after a brief lecture by Abbott Gleason on the continuing themes of social meaning and spiritual content in Russian art since the nineteenth century gave the event an art historical seal of approval.) Hoffmann began his commentary with the observation that similar trends in fashion design were occurring in European design houses in the 1920s—the French *garçonne* look, for instance—but nowhere else, he said, were the radical changes in fashion so heavily theorized. He admitted that, in translating the Russian designs, his company used silk, silk wool and jersey, and linen, while the original designs—many of which were never realized—were for cotton or oilcloth. The manipulations of circles, squares, and straight lines that so preoccupied the Constructivists lose the stridency that is part of their peculiar beauty when translated into rich, too supple materials. These were the dresses that working women were to make out of simple fabrics from patterns published in magazines. In fact, Lamanova's design—a white shift with vertical black stripes of varying length, two of which are bordered in red—was meant to be made of two towels sewn together. One saw Popova's designs for *The Magnanimous Cuckold*—blue jumpsuits belted in red, in which actors could perform the director Meyerhold's system of acrobatic biomechanics, covered with a cape that looks like semaphore flags in red and black. One saw Stepanova's designs for *The Death of Tarelkin,* or, rather, Tarelkin's coat, a long, man-tailored shirt with horizontal and oblique sections of black and gray stripes, turned into a clinging dress.

Several designs used two contrasting geometrical prints in vertical panels, and in Popova's yellow coat with striped blocks for cuffs and pockets, worn over a striped dress, one could see the perfectly functional use of decoration—a graphic expression of the human body in motion and at work. According to Hoffmann, these designs were never really popular because they did not appeal to proletarian women, who much preferred a more blousy Popova design with a long flouncy collar and a soft scarf for a belt. Another, less rigorously geometrical dress was a pleated, long-sleeved, belted design with a white collar, made of a red print that on closer inspection was dotted with the hammer and sickle. It's a dress that looks perfectly up-to-date, and, Hoffmann announced wryly, Van Laack intended to put it on the market until the invasion of Afghanistan.

The revolution in dress design in the Soviet Union was short-lived. Popova died in 1924. Exter emigrated the same year. Stepanova and Rodchenko turned to photography. After Lenin's death in 1924 the Soviet values in art lumbered from abstraction to Socialist Realism. The avant-garde was no longer considered revolutionary but dangerously left-wing.

From the Hirshhorn fashion show one could catch only a glimpse of the passionate energy behind these designs. The models were the gaunt, pale corpses of today's haute couture, not the robust women of a bright, utopian society. The exhibition catalog quotes Stepanova on fashion: "Today's dress must be seen in action—beyond this there is no dress, just as the machine cannot be conceived outside the work it is supposed to be doing." Why not have the models doing biomechanics in Popova's jumpsuits? The background music for the show was muted jazz, a musical form popular in Russia in the 1920s but later repudiated as too Western and decadent. Why not show these dresses in movement, on people fox-trotting as well as shifting gears on a machine?

At the door to the fashion show the latest issue of *Interview* was distributed, including an interview with Hoffmann-Koenige on the Soviet designs. But, if you looked a few pages further, there was also a full-page ad for modern shirts and jackets by Van Laack, whose clothes sell at Saks Fifth Avenue. "It is fortunate, if people with money have vision and good taste as well," says the ad. I asked Rolf Hoffmann if he didn't think it strange to be adding a proletarian design to the Van Laack collection, if he didn't think it odd to be taking these simple, workaday dresses and turning them into silks. He assured me he did not. It is always the intellectual, he told me, who appreciates good design. The fashions of these visionary artists were not appreciated by working women (read: they were wasted on the lower class), and now they should be worn by those with taste, intelligence, and, well, yes, money.

Village Voice, December 10, 1980

Not Just Another Pretty Opera

(Victory over the Sun)

The laidback futurists from Los Angeles hit Washington recently to recreate a Russian Futurist opera called *Victory over the Sun*—a contemporary work dated 1913.

It seemed appropriate that they should arrive in the wake of the inauguration. The newly augured-in believe in the past and constantly harp on a vision of America's future that is part wishful thinking and part repetition compulsion. The Russian Futurists firmly believed in a total rejection of the old and in the novelty of a present bursting into the future. They passionately refused to be canonized, to become the "one-thousand-and-first ISM." Yet here they are, 68 years later, being recreated for an entirely sympathetic audience to whom, one must wonder, what could possibly be "new." Past future seems to be the new modality of our day.

But let us go back. 1913–1914 was the "golden year" of Russian Futurism. Rebellious young poets, painters, and musicians, they rejected any association with the Italian Futurists like Marinetti, who was given a chilly reception in Russia. Though they believed in the force of the city and the new "machine age," in its startling effects on perception and cognition, they were antimilitarists and artists of the letter. They held that new forms of art give rise to new forms of thought. Cubism had taught them that the fragmentation of the familiar led to the new and to hints of the future, and they proudly incorporated it into the name they gave their movement: Cubo-Futurism. During the year they succeeded in utterly scandalizing the bourgeoisie during a grand tour of 17 provincial Russian cities. They delighted in their own misadventures. When they arrived in Kishinyov—"damned town of Kishinyov," as Pushkin called it a century earlier—they hired 50 little boys to run through the streets shouting, "The Futurists have arrived!" Instead, the kids confused them with more popular heroes and chirped, "The soccer players have arrived!" (*futbolisty* in place of *futuristy*—a delightful if unconscious pun). Apparently, most of the Futurists' posters, which had been put up with a type of flour paste the local goats found irresistible, were eaten off the walls.

The same atmosphere of scandal and the unexpected animated the original production of *Victory over the Sun,* which was performed twice in Petersburg's Luna Park in December of 1913, back to back with a production of Vladimir Mayakovsky's magnificent autobiographical *Tragedy,* starring the future poet of the revolution as himself. The opera combined the unique talents of three of the most original members of the movement: the young "transrational" poet Alexey Kruchenykh, who wrote the libretto (admirably translated by Larissa Shmailo), the musician M. Matiushin, and the artist Kazimir Malevich, who designed the costumes and the background. Malevich, who died in obscurity and repression during the Stalinist era, has been recognized in the West both aesthetically and commercially (any canvas will fetch at least a million dollars) during the last 20 years as one of the great fathers of abstract art; he called his particular vision "Suprematism."

The opera was originally performed by poorly rehearsed students. The audition announcement read: "Actors, do not bother to come!" Professionalism was the last thing the Futurists needed. Of Matiushin's music the poet and author Kruchenykh was moved to exclaim: "Wonderful! Outstanding! That's certainly not Tchaikovsky!" Despite the incomprehensibility of the futuristic plot, the audience could not help but be outraged by the general ambience and the language of Kruchenykh's libretto. At times the latter is positively punk: "Scummed up everything even the bone puke." When an actor mistaken for the author yelled out, pointing at the audience, "Only gnawed-at skulls run on just four legs— likely these are donkeys' skulls," there were cries of "You're an ass yourself!" At the end of the first performance, in answer to the clamor of the younger members of the audience for a curtain call by the author, the manager of the theater shouted in disgust: "They've already taken him to the madhouse!" In short, *Victory over the Sun* was a *succès de scandale,* though its opening night was tamer than that of *The Rite of Spring* in Paris that same year, where a riot broke out.

The 1980 "reconstruction" of *Victory over the Sun* was originally staged in Los Angeles as a creative spin-off of the monumental exhibition "The Avant-Garde in Russia, 1910–1930: New Perspectives," organized by Stephanie Barron and Maurice Tuchman at the Los Angeles County Museum of Art. The cast and production staff are all students or teachers at the California Institute of the Arts (with help from noted specialists in Russian theatre and art like Alma Law and Charlotte Douglas). The Washington production (January 23–25) was presented by the

Smithsonian and the Hirshhorn; the show was paid for by the Shubert Foundation.

Not only the content of *Victory over the Sun* but—even more striking for our jaded late-twentieth-century eyes—its theatrical form are drastically forward-looking. A collision of color, sound, movement, smells, and the distorted shapes of human bodies, its disjunctive progression, sensory assault, and deliberate awkwardness foreshadow the avant-garde American theater and happenings of the 1960s and performance art of the 1970s. Essentially, all that happens in terms of plot is that the Futurists capture the sun, the symbol of the old aesthetics, and the world is "liberated from the weight of universal gravity." But such an event provides scenes that, with the simplest of means, create spectacularly stylized images of human emotional heights and depths.

The Futurist Strongmen (nicely played by Steven Breese and Merritt Butrick) lumber across the stage in their cardboard armor, powerful abstractions of beefy, muscle-bound warriors for the new. The world of the opera is populated by symbols of violence: Nero and Caligula (one figure), who eats "dog and white feets" and finally "goes off askance into the sixteenth century"; a Malevolent: a Fightpicker who performs a harlequinesque provocation reminiscent of Harpo Marx's mock efforts at violence; belligerent soldiers with serrated bodies who offer nosegays to the Malevolent, tempting him with the "old." There is also a Time Traveler who rolls around on wheels telling of the future: "There's no happiness there but everybody looks happy and immortal." The Malevolent picks off everyone with his rifle and performs a grim dance of victory, a kind of leaden Charleston. Three Pallbearers, drenched in red light, slowly whirl in a grisly burial rite, chanting of bloodthirsty turnips and insects.

When the sun is captured, the stage explodes in pink and green. A caricature of a capitalist in top hat and tails (played by the excellent Suzanh Hannon-Bookwalter) shrieks in terror, announcing the event over the telephone, and several Sun-Carriers lug in a box emanating suggestions of the sun's glare. In one of the most mysterious moments of the performance they break apart the box and carry the light out of the auditorium, along the very edges of the room's walls, chanting: "Our physiognomy is dark/Our light is within/We are warmed by the dead udders/Of red dawn/BRN BRN . . ." (As Bowie puts it: "I'm just the slave of a burning ray/Give me the night I can't take another sight/Please give me the night . . .") A dayglo skull and a Motley Eye skitter in, and

The New and The Cowardly wail about the new life without gravity, ambition, or push. A Fat Man (strikingly acted by Ron Boronkay), all aglow in peach light, renders a shattered speech with a voice that vibrates, stutters, and catches, on the physical constrictions he suffers in the midst of a constantly changing landscape—which also foreshadows the American complaints about the expansion and construction of the 1960s, to say nothing of its psychedelic cadences. Suddenly, with a burst of confetti (Futurist leaflets, no doubt) and a loud crash, the wing of an airplane and its stunned pilot appear, and the entire company dances in a chunky, robotlike celebration, singing a nonsense song of glee in scattered syllables suggesting victory, affirmation, and unrestrained joy.

For a reconstruction, *Victory over the Sun* was surprisingly lively, perhaps because director Robert Benedetti, inspired by the spirit of the original collaboration, encouraged his staff to think of the current production as a kind of second collaboration—between the authors and designers of the 1913 production and themselves. Because the Petersburg version now exists only in fragments—24 bars of music, Malevich's sketches for costumes and backdrops, the text, and scattered memoirs of the two actual performances—the staging had to be almost completely reimagined.

Most striking were the costumes, constructed by Martha Ferrara out of modern materials (including Velcro for quick changes, kung fu shoes, and painted gardener's gloves), bringing Malevich's primitive, bold sketches to life quite ingeniously. You see the themes projected as parts of the actors' bodies; the spines of the Sun-Carriers' backs like stylized drawings of sunrays; the depersonalizing helmets; the emphasis on hands, underscored not only by the oversized gloves and the choreography but also by the backdrop. Kruchenykh, who not only wrote but also directed the original production, noted the uniqueness of the director's and actors' dependence on the artist: "The costumes transformed the human anatomy and the actors moved, held and directed by the rhythm dictated by the artist and director." This obviously set unique demands on the choreographer of the re-creation, Larry Attaway, who subtly animated these redesigned bodies, setting them in stylized motion that only occasionally bursts into what you might call "dancing." Strangely, the set—a series of backcloths with reconstructions of Malevich's large abstract drawings in black and white—was overshadowed by the lighting and the movement of the brilliantly costumed figures.

The music was the most problematic aspect of this production. Jerry

Frohmader, who composed an entire score based on the surviving fragments of Matiushin's score, has given it a kind of gloss that seems
wrong. In this production the actors often sing in places where, apparently, they chanted in the original. And, while the off-key, untrained
voices of the actors only enhance the delightful, deliberate naïveté of the
production, the music at times glues the songs together with too much
polish.

Polish is the last thing suggested by Kruchenykh's libretto or by the
aesthetics of Russian Cubo-Futurism. The emphasis of the Cubo-
Futurists was on a jolting illogicality. *Zaum*, or poetry written "beyond-
the-mind" ("transrational" or "supraconscious"), is a type of verse that
attempts to shatter the usual connections between words and things. On
the basis of the internal structure of a verse—its sound repetitions, their
associations, grammatical disjunctions, neologisms, sheer sound—
concepts are conveyed transcendentally, as it were, rather than through
the facile mechanisms of normal (repressive) speech.

While the associative patterns of sound that create much of *zaum*
poetry are lost in translation, many of its direct semantic disjunctions
are striking even in English translation:

> I pick my way carefully
> Along the dark road
> On the narrow pathway
> A cow under my armpit
>
> black cow
>   cryptic sign
>   behind the silk saddle
>   is hidden a trove
>
> I on the quiet
>   Admire them
> In the silence a thin needle
>   Hides in the neck

This is in response to the sudden sound of a propeller, but its suggestive-
ness is hardly limited either by the context or its overt semantics. The
more associations that arise in the hearer's mind, the happier the author
will be. That "cow under the armpit" is not only a scandalizing image; it
is a seductive one. As for the "needle," the less said the better. . . . The
distance between Kruchenykh and David Bowie is not that great. Let us
recall Major Tom.

Victory over the Sun eloquently proclaims the ideal of man freed from the past: "How extraordinary life without the past is / Dangerous but without penitence and memories . . . / Forgotten are the mistakes and miscarriages that / tediously squeak in the ear today you are like a clean mirror or a rich reservoir in whose / clean grotto carefree little gold fish flick, their tails like Turks giving thanks." The LA futurists should not be blamed for the unfuturistic nature of their impossible task— "reconstruction"—or for the way their own traditions may have conditioned their interpretation of the futurist present, now past. It's indicative that in the last few years some of the most exciting events in performance art have been revivals. We are a generation that inherited the "tradition of the new"—and now, it seems, we are incapable of innovation.

Still, let us hope the LA futurists make it to New York. But, please, not Broadway.

Village Voice, February 11, 1981. Cowritten with Stephen Rudy.

Men Together / Bloolips

The persistent myth about the male dancer in Western culture is that he is gay. Sometimes the "myth" is true, and sometimes it isn't. Can you tell a person's sexuality by the way he or she moves? The standard stereotype ignores the fact that some of the strongest, most muscular presences on the dance stage in this century at least, have been men the public knew and knows are gay. And what about those still in the closet?

Ballet and modern dance have traditionally expressed human relationships in terms of heterosexuality. Although men have danced with men and women with women, not until recently has that partnering become explicitly erotic. Homoeroticism is still as shocking on stage as nudity was a generation ago. On the dance stage, to break that taboo is even more difficult than in film or drama. To talk about gayness is one thing: to express it bodily is quite another, because it is precisely at the overt physicality of gay culture that the straight world purses its lips.

"Men Together," a festival of gay performance organized by Tim Miller (November 14–16 at P.S. 122), explored a number of aspects of male relationships, bringing together diverse artists, not all of whom ordinarily deal with gay content in their work. For me the festival was striking in several ways. First, the artists were primarily young men of the post-Stonewall generation. Unlike past generations of gay men in America, they confront mainstream culture with a sense of pride, and they are aware of their shared culture and history. Still, the verbal and nonverbal signals a covert gay community developed out of necessity are no less vital for the current generation just because the culture has emerged from underground. Second, the styles and means of expression at the festival varied widely, even though all six items in the festival began with the notion of performance art as an arena stripped of theatrical conventions. Third, a sympathetic, often enthusiastic audience gave the event a sense of community involvement and validation of both content and intent.

John Bernd and Tim Miller collaborated on a piece called *We Had Tea. We Ate Cashew Chicken.* Bernd is a dancer who has been performing solos mixing dance movements, texts, and objects; Miller doesn't call himself a dancer, but he had just finished several months of weekly performances involving meditations on history, reading poetry, cooking, amateur arson, and some movement. Both men manufacture meaning obliquely, through correspondences and juxtapositions. Bernd and Miller met at one of the latter's Monday evenings and decided to make a dance together, which they originally titled *Post-Modern Faggot*. At one point during *We Had Tea. . .*, Miller (who is fond of writing on things with spray paint) wrote "F-A-G" in big letters across his chest. "I prefer the word *faggot*," he confided to the audience, "but it doesn't fit." Bernd obligingly took the can of paint and wrote the remaining three letters on Miller's back. The mixture of roughness and attentiveness matched the tone of Miller's erotic poetry, which Bernd read later.

We Had Tea . . . opened with the two men running in large circles in the vast gym of P.S. 122. Their black overcoats and pants gave them both an anonymous and an antique look. At times jogging together, at times overtaking one another, they set up an uneven rhythm of unity, leading, following, and gentle competition. They traded coats while running: gestures of sharing and aid. Bernd danced solo while Miller read from Proust about the beginnings of a friendship. Miller took his turn while Bernd read writings by Miller. Finally, the two again jogged together, this time along a diagonal, circling arms, advancing and retreating, talking about their own relationship in parallel, echoing phrases.

The two have similar movement styles: both hold their torsos straight, gesturing abstractly with the arms while stepping in easy rhythms. But Bernd has a chunky, solid quality, while Miller bounces and skitters, always veering off balance. The two made pleasing formal contrasts. "We had tea." "We had tea." "We ate cashew chicken." "Then we came here and did this dance." The collaboration, we came to understand, not only resulted in a product—the dance—but was also a process of two people discovering things about each other, becoming friends, perhaps also lovers. Threaded with ambiguities, the gentle dance transcended the personal.

(More) Short Lessons in Socially Restricted Sign Language, by Bruce Hlibok and Norman Frisch, was a parody of an academic lecture on "dirty words" in sign language that was witty, instructive, and quite moving. A tape-recorded, stuffy, male professional voice explained how limited the deaf person's acquisition of sexual knowledge can be—both because we learn about sex through various oral/aural communicative channels as well as sight and touch and also because so many deaf children are raised in institutions, where sexual expression

is suppressed. Meanwhile, Tavoria Rae Kellam, dressed in a man's suit, gave a simultaneous translation of the lecture in sign language. She gestured voluptuously as the voice pedantically described (with slide illustrations) the signs for sexual organs, acts, and positions. A slight change in facial expression, for instance, can transform the sign for *testicles* into *well-hung.* Small shifts of finger articulation make the difference between *breast, nipple, erect nipple.* In fact, an entire range of sexual expression, including gay and lesbian slang, can be communicated through signing.

During the lecture Hlibok, who is deaf, mimed a personal odyssey of sexual exploration, reading a newspaper, cutting out paper hearts, watching a film of men having intercourse. When the lecture was over Hlibok, Kellam, and Tom Schoenherr signed a taped conversation between a married couple and their marriage counselor/physician. In this section deadpan humor arose from two sources: the act of translation, which made the descriptions of mutual excitation purely clinical; the sexual role reversal, in which Kellam played the male doctor while the naive, bright-eyed couple was played by the two men. At the beginning and end of *(More) Short Lessons . . .* Hlibok performed a gestural dance to the song "Every Little Movement Has a Meaning All Its Own," a piece he has danced before with Remy Charlip. As Schoenherr sang the words, Hlibok signed their meanings. But the second time around his interpretation was spiced with the facial expressions and the full, lusty gestures we had learned during the performance. Suddenly it seemed that perhaps sign language need not be restrictive. And it had become clear that much sexual meaning is produced in the paralinguistic "grease" that gives nuance to any language.

The gay men's movement, like the women's movement of the 1960s and 1970s, has stressed a connection between the personal and the political. This idea was expressed in "Three Short Pieces in Progress" by the Philadelphia men's dance collective, Two Men Dancing, in two ways. One was that the very act of expressing one's sexual feelings in public—making oneself vulnerable and stating what is usually unsaid— is a political act of consciousness-raising. The second, related notion was that to reveal the process of a work of art—to show a work in progress or to talk about the making of the piece—is political in that it demystifies art, reducing the gap between artist and audience and thus erasing false authority.

Two Men Dancing now has three members—Michael Biello, Daniel

Martin, and Ishmael Houston-Jones. They were joined here by guest performers Warren Muller, Robin Epstein, and Charles Cohen. Biello's *Masked Mass* was a priapic ceremony that, for my taste, perpetuated negative, perverse stereotypes without adding any new insights. Martin's *Scenes from a Future Musical* was a sketch that suffered not so much from incompleteness as from poverty of conception. Can a banal soap opera about an adolescent leaving home, even when performed-tongue-in-cheek, be salvaged by the subversive plot twist that makes him grow up gay?

Houston-Jones's *Part Three—Friction. Friction* was more successful as a work-in-progress, partly because of the choreographer's own electrifying stage presence, which makes even a fragment compelling, and partly because the gestures in the dance were so graphic their shock value was immense, ultimately transcending the confessional tone of the piece and adding a note of humor. Explaining that he usually works improvisationally, Houston-Jones announced that he would tonight teach Biello and Martin a set movement combination. He demonstrated three basic, mimetic gestures, identifying each one by the slang words for fellatio and active and passive intercourse. The dancers ran through the combination until it reached a frenzied pace, appropriately enough to Martha and the Vandellas singing "Heat Wave." Later, Houston-Jones spoke about his adolescence, while Biello and Martin kissed and caressed for real. For the audience, transformed into voyeurs, this action was a shock—but transgression of the limits of sexual expression on-stage is certainly not restricted to gay art. Carolee Schneemann's *Meat Joy* of 1964 raised the same issues, and so, in fact, did Marius Petipa's smacks on the cheek of a Spanish ballerina in the middle of the nineteenth century.

The other three items in the festival were primarily text oriented. Jeff McMahon's *Smile at Knife,* a chilling stream-of-consciousness monologue about fear, crisis, and danger, was a dance of stillness. Riveted in his chair, face impassive except for blazing eyes and the moving mouth that rendered a multiplicity of urgent voices, McMahon's "active text" sliced like a blade, grated like a shriek. Its absence of movement—its utter rigidity—made this performance as eloquent physically as it was verbally.

The political meanings in "Men Together" were general and implicit: the freedom of expression of gay feelings—and of feelings in general—was the festival's central, cumulative, and often very touching theme. A range of movement styles, from gentle and tender to boldly lascivious, proclaimed a sense of liberation from stereotypes both of effeminacy and machismo.

Lust in Space, a drag show by the British group Bloolips (Theater for the New City and Orpheum Theatre), was political in another sense. Using androgyny as a vantage point totally outside straight society (straight in both senses—as opposed to hip *and* gay), these men take on the personae of female caricatures. Wearing gaudy costumes made of junk, sporting makeup and hairdos so stylized a Kabuki actor would do a doubletake, the Bloolips are not so much imitations of women as creatures betwixt and between sexual roles, free from social rules. Even their names are outrageous: Lavinia Co-op, Precious Pearl, Dizzy Danny, Bossy Bette Bourne, Naughty Nicky, and Gretel Feather. Clowns and tricksters, they dance outside social structure, commenting on and criticizing not only sexual roles and stereotypes, but also the arms race. American electoral politics, political repression, rampant consumerism, and an entire "parade of Western culture."

A plot of sorts is a loose skeleton on which to hang song and dance numbers that derive as much from the humor of British music hall traditions (including that of the heterosexual drag performer) as from the tradition of gay camp and the politics of gay liberation. The Bloolips group runs a laundromat that looks like a set for a science fiction film. The queen of England sends them to perform on the moon, hoping to outdo the Russians. While getting ready for the big night, the Bloolips run into an evil computer (at the local Lunar disco bingo) that turns people's minds to malleable mush. Luckily, they finally break its power.

Bloolips, a group of consummate performers, blends popular culture and reflexive meditations on performance to create a piece of show business that is flashy, entertaining, funny, and at the same time wryly agitprop. They subvert the banality of hit songs by setting lyrics that really mean something to familiar tunes. Some of the lines are old hat; still, one can admire the proficiency of Bloolips's turn of phrase, sense of timing, or tap dancing rhythm, along with its political wallop. In fact, all that entertaining singing and dancing, far from sugarcoating the message, speeds it along. And the dancing—not just tap but also bits of ballet, aesthetic dancing, cancan, girlie revue, Weimar cabaret, and floating in space—is integral to the production.

Presenting "Folk Dances from the Migraine," several Bloolips in peasant skirts and babushkas galumpf, brandishing scarves and singing about Soviet censorship. They discuss the possibility of performing *Swan Lake* on the moon (Aleksandr Godunov has sent them a request, written on a gargantuan ballet slipper, to stand in for him), but they decide that audiences would never stand for a plot based on ornithophilia. Still, they get away with a fragment of the four cygnets. They dress up as cheeses to disguise themselves as part of the moon's landscape. And, if they nearly blow up the world a few times, in the end we all survive—at least for one more show. Bloolips's anarchic black humor is a welcome anodyne in these dark times.

"Men Together" and Bloolips's *Lust in Space* pointed toward two tendencies in recent gay art. One is the acknowledgment that the body is both subject and purveyor of a social message. The other is a parodic thrust, from the vantage point of a subculture outside the mainstream, aimed not only at sexual mores but also the world at large.

Dance Magazine, March 1981

As, I, Like, It

(Tim Miller)

Some people think about history by personalizing it. Other people measure their lives by historic events. Tim Miller is one of the other people. In some way he makes performances about his life, but, inevitably, his autobiography resonates with the events he has felt compelled to witness or to cull from collective memory, and to make sense of.

In performance Miller's life and body become the arena where images of war, revolution, depression, and other political disasters rub against comfortable domestic images and ignite. In POSTWAR, a group performance, Miller reworks themes from his solo performances over the past year and a half: the baby boom, nuclear war, the Reagan administration, his parents' lives, calamitous dreams, hamburgers, lawn mowers.

Tim Miller was born in Los Angeles in 1958 (the year after Sputnik) but grew up in Whittier. Nixon was his first hero. By the time he was fourteen, his older brother, who'd gone to Berkeley, had turned him on to Trotsky. "This was all pre-politics," Miller explains. "When you have no information. Before you know how the world works. Being ten years old in 1968 was weird—old enough to witness but not to do anything. I remember being afraid of being drafted and killed."

From the age of ten, Miller considered himself a writer, producing books, journals, and plays. In high school he listened to Wagner for hours every day, learning both the German language and a consuming vision of art. He also belonged to the school film club and lectured on D. W. Griffith. And he took ballet classes and hung photographs of Martha Graham on the wall next to pictures of Napoleon. "I approached dance," he recalls, "as a mixture of Artaud, Martha Graham, and Peter Brook. Theater of Cruelty plus Modern Dance."

After high school Miller moved to Seattle, where he studied with Joan Skinner, the director of the American Contemporary Dance Company, who had worked with Martha Graham in the 1940s and Merce Cunningham in the 1950s, and who developed the Skinner Releasing Technique. "My time with Joan was the only time I submitted to someone I considered a master, with everything that implies—passion, commitment, an altered sense of my ego. It's absorbing work, a thorough pedagogy developed out of a neurophysical connection, a complete daily process. But it has its limits; that work doesn't explain certain other phenomena—like madness or World War II."

In Seattle Miller also danced with Mangrove, an all-male Contact Improvisation group, and studied with Douglas Dunn, Steve Paxton, Nancy Stark Smith, and Deborah Hay. There he became fascinated with the work of Merce Cunningham and in 1978 made the pilgrimage to New York to study with him. But in New York his activities shifted to performance art. His first year in New York, he remembers, he was obsessed with Jerzy Grotowski and Allen Ginsberg. He began working with Peter Rose, who was also influenced by Grotowski, and with Charles Dennis, who had been active in Robert Wilson's Byrd Hoffman School. The three led open movement sessions at P.S. 122, a carry-over from the Byrd Hoffman open houses and from events Miller had organized in Seattle, developing "basic issues of community/event/participation/ritual."

Miller's solo performances mix his peculiar, skittery style of dancing—always seeming to career out of control, yet calm in the center—with storytelling, iconic gesture, bombardments of sound and video and slide imagery, cooking, amateur arson, spray paint, undressing, incanting chronologies. Making things, destroying things, putting things in order. Images of tenderness, of violence, of hope. And honesty. In an Avant-Gard-Arama organized by Dennis at P.S. 122 in 1980, coincidentally held on the anniversary of the Stonewall uprising, Miller petted a chicken he had rescued from a downtown poultry store and talked about gay politics and past loves, recasting personal history into political wisdom.

Increasingly fascinated by the Russian poet Vladimir Mayakovsky, Futurist, comet of the Revolution, and suicide, Miller performed a series of Monday night events for nine weeks in the fall of 1980, titled *PAINT YRSELF RED/ME & MAYAKOVSKY*. At first he worked directly from Mayakovsky's life and writings but soon broadened the material to include Dostoevsky, revolution, and other Russian images. One night he brought 30 pounds of potatoes into the space at P.S. 122—which he used differently each week—and balanced on them, spat on them, all the while drinking vodka. One night he bundled all the spectators into the tiny kitchen off the gym space and cooked potatoes, traded clothes with Beth Lapides, set paper on fire inside a cupboard, and spoke about the Russian Revolution. The fires, he says, began from the desire to burn what he had written—to read something and then have it immediately disappear. Spray-painting his name in block letters on his chest—by now a Miller trademark—began as a reference to the Russian Futurists and to Burlyuk's manifesto on painting oneself. Miller's collages and posters, in the same block letters, plaster downtown walls.

"I wanted to be performing in an ongoing process hopefully more like real life," Miller wrote to me. "like going to church. like a tv show. or something. like *real* research . . . in beginning this on my birthday began working with my connection to the soviet poet mayakovsky and on the first performance dealt with the details of my birth in s. california 22 yrs ago and mayakovsky's suicide in 1930. that weird point of personal identification with historical event and personality, esp. personality, that has formed my life probably more than anything else. this is real interesting to me. bits of memory. a book. 20th century. yeah. dead poets. my big brother. potatoes. 1917. pasadena ca."

By spring and a second series of Monday night performances, the imagery had opened up to include material on Nixon, a lawn mower dance, war. In one performance Miller seated the audience around a dinner table on which he cooked hamburgers, danced, and crawled in a pile of plastic silverware, while the spectators were surrounded by the sounds of bombers and images of dirigibles.

"When you set the table, certain things go in certain places. There is a kind of order to things that people try to maintain," Miller writes of a performance he did on the day Reagan was shot. "Like my grid [projected over a photo of a Danish woman checking out the wreck of a German zeppelin in 1915]. That grid fit over that disaster. It made it a little more orderly. 1915. 1916. 1917. 1918. 1919. 1920. 1921. 1922. 1923. But Ronald Reagan was going to live and the doctors put things back in order and I tried to set my table and make some hamburgers for a few nice people. It isn't unreasonable to just want a little order in your life. But sometimes that's too much to ask for and you just have to sweep everything into a pile and forget about things making sense or fitting together. Maybe this is where faith or something comes in. Or maybe you just get your brains blown out by a big gun."

With Charles Dennis and Charles Moulton, Miller now codirects the performance space at P.S. 122, programming the weekly series, and meeting with other groups in the building and in the community around First Avenue and Ninth Street. In the fall of 1980, Miller organized a festival of performance by gay men, drawing enormous crowds to witness what Miller refers to as the second generation of gay artists—not mainstream artists who have come out as gay men but artists who are attempting to make avant-garde work with specifically gay content. Last spring, for example, he collaborated with John Bernd on *Live Boys*, in which the two men brought their relationship as lovers and partners in art directly into the ten performances, with the audience as witness. "That was good, dangerous, weird," Miller recalls. "We were happy."

For Tim Miller performance is about being yourself in public, but it is also a moral act, the carrying out of necessary action. And necessary action encompasses love, the making of communities, and the discovery of grace as well as danger and violence. Especially violence, because it is so much a part of American life "and yet we know so little about it." Last fall at the Kitchen, Miller performed *SURVIVAL TACTIC*, a solo that gets reworked into *POSTWAR*. "It all comes down to the big bomb question," Miller explained. "It's a question of survival, of our government, of being Americans. Of how to not simply make images of memory, danger, and apocalypse, but of direct action. How to find the hopeful geranium. How to do something and not despair."

Village Voice, January 27, 1982

Let There Be Dark

(Eric Bogosian)

Eric Bogosian's *Men in Dark Times* reworks themes and materials that have appeared in his solos and group works over the past few years. It also raises serious questions about performance art, its means and its subjects, by treading the blurry border between performance and theater, between aggression and satire, between outrage and social criticism.

The evening is what Bogosian calls an "amplified solo." A string of 12 vignettes presents images of men ranging from a terrorist to a TV talk-show host. Although Bogosian is joined by four other performers (Joe Hannan, Grethe Holby, Jeff McMahon, and Marcelino Rosado), his own presence dominates the work. The piece is also amplified in the sense that the action goes beyond the physical body to include taped voices, live and taped music, and slide projections.

The Kitchen is shrouded in black. Bogosian's voice is heard calling for lights, and he is suddenly seen standing in a cone of light at one edge of the space. Dressed in a dark suit, he is elegantly unctuous, an oily version of Rod Serling as he greets us and tells us to "Relax—have a good time." There is something ominous in this message, underscored by Bogosian's half-lit face. His patter then his gestures slither into the spiel of a maniacal circus barker boasting of his freaks. As he exits, the lights come up on the other side of the space, where Hannan plays piano cocktail music and McMahon croons a 1940s-style love song whose lyrics also seem ironically to describe a very contemporary sense of global depression. Bogosian reappears as Ricky Paul, his TV host persona, to trade quips with straightman Hannan about rock stars and mass murderers. After a burst of rapid-fire anecdotes, Bogosian breaks into a smile and Hannan plays a few chords. "Crooked senators, mass murderers, Las Vegas entertainers—they're all just people!" Ricky Paul exclaims, launching into song. "People . . . people who need people. . . ." Next Bogosian becomes a wild-eyed terrorist holding a woman hostage while demanding free food and electricity, an end to nuclear armament, and "no more nightclubs." He sits at a desk, talking about the power of light, like a two-bit evangelist, and then reads a poem about children getting lost in the dark. He plays a middle-aged Italian day laborer reminiscing about the old gang, a teenage punk miming a guitar player to the sound of the Ramones, a go-go dancer, a sadistic army officer, a bum, and, finally, a clean-cut political speaker who is transformed into a satanic demagogue. The other performers come and go, playing foils and partners, as the action moves around the murky space, suddenly illuminated by a point or slash of light.

Bogosian's brilliance as a performer has been his ability to switch gears instantaneously while operating at the highest pitches of intensity. His personae are so various, each with its distinctive accent, pacing, and vocabulary, that one marvels, first at the speed and pliancy of the voice itself and at the facial expressions and bodily gestures that plastically express the states of that voice. Then one marvels again at the crash-speed hairpin turns voice and body take as they careen along the grotesque landscape of masculine identity. He's like a man possessed, a medium, a schizophrenic. That terrifying, violent tension between control and loss of control, a favorite American theme played out in spheres as diverse as the religious cults and possession films of the 1970s and real-life politics in the 1980s, is the true subject of Bogosian's performances. And this is the brilliance of Bogosian the scriptwriter. The characters are chilling not only because of the intensity of performance, not only because of what they are as slices of behavior, but mostly because of the formal dissonance that comes from their scraping together. Bogosian structures the work more like music than like drama, and it is this approach that pushes his pieces more toward performance art than theater.

But there is another kind of dissonance—a raw cognitive screech—in the work. And that is in its sexual meaning. In religious cults and in possession films it is usually a woman or a child who is invaded by multiple voices. Bogosian doubles the tension produced by the notion of control by making men the instruments of fear and dominance.

In *Men in Dark Times,* as in *Men Inside* and *That Girl,* two solos by Bogosian that use some of the same material, there are several kinds of characterizations. One is the familiar, superordinary, even slightly stereotyped figure—the middle-aged Italian worker, the soldier. One is the criminal or the outcast—the terrorist, the bum. A third category is the constructed, artificial persona ripped from other performance modes—the circus barker, the TV host, the politician, the preacher. These form the nucleus of the work, and they are, I think, its real source of interest—as well as its source of darkness. Here again lies an important boundary between theater, through which Bogosian creates impeccable character sketches, and performance art, through which he not only dazzlingly imitates other modes of public action (performance in its broadest sense) but also subverts those imitations.

When I saw *Men Inside* as an intimate barrage of shattered monologues in a crowded Club 57 a few months ago, I thought Bogosian had found the perfect vehicle for his acceleration-performance. Without special costumes, without added theatrical trappings, the contortions of voice and body were right there, raw, extreme, aggressive. The work struck out at the spectator just because it was so fast, so close. The nightclub venue was plumbed then turned inside out. The concision of the piece sharpened its slicing edge.

It seems to me that the "amplification" of *Men in Dark Times* dissipates not only its effect but its meaning. As the piece unfolds in time and space, a certain spring, a certain irony, is lost. As with some kinds of punk music that claim to criticize violence but only seem to imitate and valorize it, Bogosian's performance flounders in ambiguities. The sexual, ethnic, and racial jokes previously undercut by structural fragmentation linger here. And, like the often sinister images of the men Bogosian creates, they demand a critical commentary.

Village Voice, March 30, 1982

In the Still of the Night

(Chris Burden)

Like many artists in the early 1970s, Chris Burden, trained as a sculptor, moved from making objects to making situations. Never entirely forsaking the gallery setting, the people who made body works commented on the rules of the art game by questioning the fetishism of the art "product" and the social relations among artist, spectator, and gallery owner. Using the human body as art material, they asserted the artist's physical presence in the work and amputated aesthetic distance. The antiseptic gallery became the arena for aggressive corporeality. But, ironically, the attempt to demystify the art process, to present it as activity or sometimes simply as work, tended to turn the artist's body into yet another object.

Burden's work over the past 11 years has paced this uneasy terrain at the edge of art, raising deep questions about ethics as well as aesthetics, and not only confronting the immediate participants in his pieces but also, through documentation and the use of mass media, extending the work's implications geographically and chronologically. A lot more people know about *Shoot* (1971), in which Burden had a friend shoot him in the arm, than could have witnessed it, and 11 years later people still talk about it. In several works Burden has bought commercial time on TV to present images or make statements. The problem of the artist's role and identity is a theme basic to his work, and to list his performances is to find a catalog of possibilities: worker, saint, spy, citizen, inventor, voyeur, philanthropist, exhibitionist, servant, prisoner, demon, smuggler, prophet, counterfeiter, traveler, child, entrepreneur, jailer, God, teacher. . . .

In *Working Artist* (1975) Burden set himself up for three days in a gallery hung with documentations of past works and furnished with office equipment and furniture and "attempted to conduct my affairs as if I were in my own studio." In *Coals to Newcastle* (1978) he used model airplanes to fly American-grown marijuana to Mexico. In *Garçon!* (1976) he served coffee to the visitors of a San Francisco gallery for a week. In *Diecimila* (1977) he printed an Italian 10,000 lire note. In *Full*

Financial Disclosure (1977) he displayed his 1976 canceled checks and tax forms. He has invented the B-car (a cross between a bicycle, a lightweight airplane, and a car that carries one passenger, travels 100 miles per hour, and gets 100 miles to the gallon) and the C.B. TV (Chris Burden Television, a primitive mechanical system for transmitting images that duplicates a 1915 forerunner of modern electronic TV).

A lot of Burden's pieces satirize or subvert American myths and icons: the sacrosanct TV, telephone, car, dollar bill. But others have more specifically religious, almost mystical overtones. In *White Light/White Heat* (1975) he stayed on a shelf ten feet off the floor of the gallery for three weeks, invisible to gallery visitors, and claims that "during the entire piece, I did not eat, talk, or come down. I did not see anyone, and no one saw me." In *Transfixed* (1974) he was crucified on a Volkswagen. In *Oh, Dracula* (1974) he spent a day suspended in a white chrysalis on the wall of a museum, in between two religious paintings of the Renaissance, with two candles in front of his body. *The Visitation* (1974) set up a subterranean confession booth, lit with glowing coals, in which Burden received one visitor at a time.

In a number of pieces Burden seems to quote from accounts of the suffering of Christian saints—being kicked down a flight of stairs, being set on fire, being shocked with electric wires, crawling on glass splinters, being punctured by pushpins, breathing water, fasting. The imagery is violent but also mysterious, even beautiful. Taken out of a religious ceremonial context, certain kinds of Christian behavior become unacceptably sadomasochistic. Yet our repulsion in the face of these works is also shot through with a measure of attraction, as Burden scrapes one of the deepest nerves of our culture—the split between body and spirit.

Burden's performance/action in Washington last weekend plays on many of these themes. A cavernous space, painted black, is filled with gently swinging objects—doors, windowpanes, tables, a pair of wooden chairs, a metal ladder, a dusty hand truck. Small votive candles dot their surfaces. In the soft glow you can navigate between the moving corners and discern the figures of the other spectators, some talking in clusters, some threading their way through the ghostly landscape. Burden and several assistants unobtrusively make their rounds, pushing the objects and replacing the candles as they melt down. Most of the articles hang parallel to the floor, suspended with three or five ropes at levels rarely exceeding human height. As Burden and his assistants push them in different directions, their asymmetrical suspensions give them each a distinctive, shifting oscillation. The ropes creak. People come and go. Some give a door or a table a push, but for the most part the spectators limit their activity to walking through the installation. As time goes by, some sit to observe and some go up to find a new vantage point in the lighting booth. After two hours Burden and his assistants put out the candles, and the few remaining visitors are plunged into darkness. After a moment the lights come up, giving the furniture, with its dust and candle drippings, the appearance of a stage set or nightclub the morning after.

Though simple in structure, Burden's piece resonated with rich layers of fluctuating meanings. The setting at times seemed like a church or a distant landscape—at Lourdes, perhaps—peopled with pilgrims carrying tapers. Then it seemed suddenly like a cocktail party, with its clumps of people standing and chitchatting in candlelight. But next it took on the gloomy semblance of a catacombs, all the more so because Burden himself seemed like a ghostly visitor in his own performance. If not a catacombs, perhaps a wake. Then a sense of festiveness returned— you suddenly felt you were in a gaudy amusement park. Viewed from above, the scene resembled an airfield at night or a harbor filled with the lights of floating boats. Suddenly the place became a dingy attic with paraphernalia that unaccountably migrated to midair. But when the candles were blown out, the image was that of a child's birthday party.

By calling the piece a performance/action rather than an installation, Burden set a time frame that permitted and encouraged spectators to stay in the space for a long span. The act of naming transformed the act of viewing from gallery scale (a few minutes) to theater scale (two hours). Yet the viewer's role became less passive and more active, nearly indistinguishable from that of the performer. The situation of duration prompted a satisfying stream of protean images. And the metaphysical connotations of those images of memory, travel, childhood, holiness, and death prompted a structure for experiencing them that seems to replicate meditation and to behold life's awesome mysteries in serene repose.

Village Voice, April 6, 1982

The Tradition of the Old

(Bob Berky, Fred Garbo Garver, and
Michael Moschen/David Warrilow)

If the sociologists are right and virtuosity is replacing identity as a key
value in American culture, then performance art surely reflects our times.
Since the nineteenth century avant-garde theater has been precisely that
place where inspired amateurs from any field could *act,* in the fullest
sense. Kandinsky moved his ideas about painting from the canvas to
furniture, clothing, books, and the stage. The Happenings of the 1960s
were public extensions of the Abstract Expressionists' freighted gestures.
In the 1970s Stuart Sherman borrowed a magician's stance, making a
different kind of magic through an obvious and deliberate antitechnique.
Through performance art the skills and procedures of traditional high art
theater as well as popular entertainments have been foregrounded, made
the materials and the subject of an art form. One way to focus on technique is to "make it strange"—to be a bad actor on purpose or to act in an
inappropriate style. The denial of technique can paradoxically make the
spectator contemplate the nature of that which is absent. The gap between end and means resonates with a tension that supplies an ironic
distance, a subverting edge. A purely excellent performance tends not to
assert itself as an instance of reflective mise-en-scène but, rather, to work
seamlessly into an illusion.

In the 1980s performance art seems to move in another direction.
The demystification of virtuosity has been played out, and technical
brilliance takes center stage. As the avant-garde borrows more and more
directly from circus acts, TV variety shows, stand-up comedians, and
Shakespeare, it becomes harder and harder to draw the line between the
critical commentary on a thing and the thing itself. It's no surprise that
in times of economic insecurity even our aesthetic appreciation becomes
parsimonious. We thriftily demand art that we can count on, that's
worth something. So we now find in all the arts not only a new conservatism in terms of style but also an overemphasis on technical proficiency
and historical authenticity. It almost doesn't matter what a work is
about, as long as it's done perfectly and fits securely into a tradition. If

the turn of the twentieth century inaugurated an age of innovation in art in the Western world that correlated to accelerating economic and geographic expansion, the turn of the twenty-first century seems to signal exhaustion. As we deplete our resources and our political power, the act of conservation looms wiser.

In *Is 60 Minutes Enough?* Bob Berky, a mime, Fred Garbo Garver, a clown, and Michael Moschen, a juggler, presented a variety program that was a chamber version of a circus or vaudeville show. The evening began with a skit for the three men as aviators, dancing on, off, and around the stage wielding gaudy plastic airplanes. Garbo made juggler's pins sit up and jump like three dogs of different sizes; Moschen dazzled the audience with subtle manipulations of a Ping-Pong ball that seemed to travel around his body on an air current; Berky played a Californian surf-bum communing with the ocean but struggling to change into bathing trunks in public; Moschen and Garbo teamed up to act the role of classical musicians whose "instruments" turned out to be juggler's pins. The two closed the show with a flame-tossing exhibition.

Although the skills of these performers are impressive, the evening itself was strangely unsatisfying. The material didn't hold up to the physical feats. Berky's impeccable timing and sense of character made for moments of hilarity, but you could see the "punch line" of his routine the instant his swimsuit fell out of his towel. The choreography for the three aviators could have come straight from "Saturday Night Live." The juggling duets were standard circus fare, including musical selections, costumes, and gestures of presentation. The size of the theater forced the acts to be less spectacular than they normally are in the circus, not only because the audience sat close to the performers and thus watched a smaller picture but also because the diminished space allowed for fewer objects and less room in which to throw them. In an hour-long performance there are fewer contrasts of themes and skills. Moschen's solo stood out especially because it was detailed and small-scale, more like a magician's act planned for a tiny stage than a juggler's act in a tent. The "revolutionization" of traditional circus acts, rather than freeing these three adepts, often seemed to shackle them instead.

David Warrilow's evenings, *Moments in Classical Literature*, were essentially dramatic readings of *Hamlet*, Jules Laforgue's "Essay on Hamlet," Samuel Beckett, the Song of Songs. What made it avant-garde? Warrilow juxtaposed his elegant oratory with the banal lyrics and jittery ebullience of a New Wave band, whose members—Johann Carlo, Henry

Stramm, Michael Butler, Bruce Cross, Vincent Gallo, and Val Kilmer—are also actors with whom Warrilow recently appeared in Minneapolis production of Liviu Ciulel's *As You Like It*. Warrilow doesn't need to substitute virtuosity for content. His texts themselves shake the soul, but his eloquence makes them live even more profoundly. The juxtaposition of punk and classical styles added humor and another kind of virtuosity, and, rather than subverting the actor's role, set it off like a jewel.

Performances like these raise new questions about how we judge avant-garde art. Should we have the same standards for a chamber version of a circus, seen in a downtown theater, that we have for Ringling Brothers and Barnum and Bailey? If so, won't the chamber version inevitably fall short, simply on structural grounds? If what the audience in downtown theaters wants is virtuosity, why not buy tickets to see Ringling Brothers and Broadway plays? Can transferring the classics to new venues give old traditions new values?

Village Voice, April 27, 1982

In Search of Illumination

(Curated by Ann Magnuson)

For four Sundays now Ann Magnuson has been producing afternoon variety shows that mobilize scores of participants around religious themes. First, there was "The Word," on Easter. Then "The Flesh," "The Fracas," and, finally, "The Light." Magnuson says in her publicity that she planned these programs because the world's attention has turned to religion again and that "given the national and international realities (Moral Majority, dissent in the Catholic Church, the crisis in Poland, and the ever present threat of nuclear atonement), many performance artists are exploring themes of a religious and/or political nature"—a departure from the autobiographical and reflexive performances of the 1970s.

Now this might sound morally stern and didactic. But it's hard to take such statements seriously, since the press release also promises a crossover between performers in the art world and on the nightclub circuit that "extends itself into the realm of Neo-Grooviness." Most of the performers in the series are not, in fact, making works about religion, and the only one who did on last Sunday's program was from neither the art world nor the entertainment world; she was an honest-to-god religious fanatic. You don't have to be religious to find it strange—depressing even—that spiritual faith has become just one more mode of entertainment for us jaded New Yorkers.

But, in fact, the levels of piety in "The Light" fluctuated wildly. The afternoon began (an hour after its advertised curtain time) with a lovely piece by Toby MacLennan called *Singing the Stars,* originally performed in Canadian planetariums. In the opening image a woman dressed as an ocean entered, wearing a bonnet that looked like a rock and a voluminous skirt à la Marie Antoinette, that later, when she pulled a lever, dropped torrents of teacups. The lines she recited, and a film and two texts that followed, developed a mythology of a people whose boundaries and categories are more fluid than ours, who take objects into their bodies with their eyes the way other people eat, who make holes in space for objects to move into and thus invent airplanes, especially one that is made to look so exactly like the night sky that it disappears into it. This is a musical race that can put a staff over any object and "sing" it, and in the final scene a series of wooden staffs—on slender tree trunks, on a gigantic wooden cut-out of a deer, on a helmet, and on a bed that revolved—let two singers, a cellist, and a xylophonist make celestial music as they read the stars projected over the backdrop.

The second presentation was a slide lecture by Mary de Blassio, a woman from Bayside Queens, who works with Veronica Leuken, aka Our Lady of Bayside, who has been experiencing visions of the Virgin Mary and other saints since 1968 and, since her relations with the Catholic Church are not so great, holding vigils in Flushing Meadows Park. De Blassio showed us photographs taken of the statue of the Virgin Mary during the visions, deciphering for us the various messages manifested in squiggles and beads of light that marred every slide. Apparently, the Virgin is as upset about the length of women's skirts as she is about rampant homosexuality, abortion, rock and roll, satanic cults, communist infiltration of the Catholic Church, UFOs, the peace movement, and a variety of other contemporary problems. At first the spectators giggled and coughed during de Blassio's lecture, but, as time wore on they hissed and straggled out. The performance seemed excessively cruel on both sides: de Blassio ranted in her homey way for over two hours, losing the patience even of those who might listen out of curiosity about such folkways; but, also, she apparently didn't realize until the moment of performance that her role was that of laughingstock rather than proselytizer.

De Blassio was a hard act to follow. As Fran Lebowitz pointed out, *she* had no fashion tips from God. So she read from her novel *Social Studies* and answered questions, mostly about working for *Interview,* with quips on a limited number of themes: how she'd like to earn lots of money and find a good apartment. As she put it, her philosophy is one of unenlightened self-interest. Her cynicism is a comic act that not only seems old-fashioned—a brand of male Jewish neurotic stand-up humor popular in the 1950s and early 1960s—but that soon wears itself thin with its own ennui. Far more interesting, on the cynical side of faith, was Marty Watt, reading/chanting/singing poems of failed love with an electrifying, slightly nasty demeanor.

Kazimir Passion, a collective of Russian emigré artists (A. Drewchin, H. Khudyakov, A. Koslapov, V. Tupitsyn, and V. Urban, curated by M. Tupitsyn), made a powerful spectacle with their *27th Congress of the Communist Party*. A model of Malevich's coffin, a suprematist artwork he designed himself, stood silent witness center stage while people marched with banners and gave rabble-rousing speeches on the political function of art and on a mythical Russian hero, Kazimir. Patriotic music and the applause of a crowd blared, and socialist realist posters flashed behind the speakers' podiums. Finally, a man in bathing trunks and a mask of Brezhnev, wielding a hammer in one hand and a sickle in the other, danced a clumsy, haunting step at the coffin's side and led the others out.

The two other numbers on the program—Magnuson's *California Now!* a satire on 1960s folk-rock groups, and Kenny Scharf's *Hanna-Barberic Cavalcade*, a dance parade of 12 performers wearing cartoon character masks—were downright silly. Maybe the point is that we can come out the other side of dumbness to enlightenment. I find this hard to believe and wish "The Light" had offered more than its scant glimmers.

Village Voice, May 11, 1982

The Long and the Short of It

(Robert Longo / Dan Hurlin)

Robert Longo's performance work transgresses boundaries in many ways. In terms of form performance is an appropriate medium because it is all-inclusive; sculpture, opera, film, still photography, dance, band music, sound and light shows all mix, without clear borders. And this causes some cognitive uneasiness to begin with.

Sound Distance Part I is Longo's 1978 work *Sound Distance of a Good Man.* On the left two bare-chested men (Eric Barsness and Bill T. Jones) wrestle in slow motion on a revolving pedestal. The imagery wobbles between the cruel, the powerful, and the erotic. The revolving platform supplies a sense of clinical but voyeuristic detachment. It also situates the action somewhere in the realm of sculpture rather than theater, since it allows the spectator to "walk around" the static event and inspect it from every angle. Unlike sculpture, the wrestling constantly changes shape, but, unlike drama or an actual wrestling competition, the energy remains steady and evokes an illusion of stillness. On the right a woman in a long white dress (Peggy Atkinson) sings an operatic aria to recorded music. She stops and starts, while under her voice the music goes on, and other voices occasionally join her. Again, the dynamics make the event hover in time, rather than rush to a conclusion. The melodic structure makes the aria always seem incomplete, as if Atkinson perennially began and ended in the middle of a phrase. Things that ordinarily progress in time go nowhere. The third element is a film, projected on a large screen between the two live tableaux. It consists of only one image: on the left, the profile of a stone lion; on the right, and lower in the frame, a man in a hat looks upward, his back to the lion. If film consists of changing images, is this a film or some variation on still photography? These three elements, individually lit in their separate spaces like objects in an exhibition, continue for about 15 minutes and then stop.

Sound Distance Part II is a new work, *Iron Voices.* In the center screen another black-and-white film shows people walking along a sidewalk. They are uniformly glum, and they avoid looking at the camera as they enter some unspecified public place. Flanking the film are two men in uniforms, illuminated in red, who perform a military drill, shouldering arms at first in perfect synchrony and then in canon. The film ends, and the screen is raised, revealing a deep space backstage. A loud, high-pitched, machinelike roar floods the theater; one feels trapped in a war factory. Five saxophonists in black uniforms form a phalanx that marches down the black runway in the center of the space. Reaching the audience's knees, the musicians stand at the edge of the runway in columns of light, adding a layer of cacophonous sound to the continuing roar. A trumpeter enters, then a line of three drummers, then four bass guitarists. The sound (by Peter Gordon) escalates in texture, volume, and disorganization. But the image remains relentless and unmoving.

Longo's images of power, dominance, and eroticism are bathed in a chilly, classical, polished style that is frightening, not only because of their immediate connotations but also because they are reminiscent of the art of fascist Germany and Italy. The cacophony of *Iron Voices* functions not as a criticism of these assertions of monumental control but as a kind of inexorable, destructive, crowning glory. If *Sound Distance Parts I & II* flirts with fascism, it ends up celebrating rather than "deconstructing" a political system that can only be repugnant. And this is the deeper way in which Longo transgresses boundaries.

Immediately following World War II the horror of Nazism left the world in silence. In the 1960s and 1970s Europeans began to examine the sources of this dark side of their history, producing films and artworks as well as political analyses on the subject, and this compulsion spread to America as well. The past decade has seen books on Nazi art and films, and this week Albert Speers's best-selling memoirs were broadcast as a five-hour television series. A film like Syberberg's *Our Hitler* purports to criticize fascism but equivocates in its elegant, often seductive depiction of German nationalism.

The artists of Longo's generation, all born long after the war, have grown up seeing Syberberg and Riefenstahl and hearing the debates about fascism's fascination. In a sense by choosing this particular subject matter they are treading on some of the most explosive territory of our times. In an art world that seems to have exhausted the possibilities for originality, few rules are left to be broken. By violating most of society's values about fascism, they make themselves outsiders, on a par with motorcycle gangs who sport Nazi regalia. It's one way to be avant-garde. But, in light of the current political climate, it's a way that seems unpleasantly amoral.

Dan Hurlin's performances were diametrically opposed to Longo's in that they celebrated the funky, the humble, the small-scale. His *Small* began with eight tape recorders strewn along the floor. The lights came up, Hurlin plugged in a master plug, and began a series of solo antics that included a dance of flashlight signals, conversations among the various tape recorders (all issuing Hurlin's voice), a parade of Barbie and Ken dolls, and monologues taken from the Bible and Nancy Drew. *Beds*, with text by Laura Ernst, was more of a conventional play (performed by ensemble no. 3), with four characters unable to leave their beds, meditating on the most banal and the most profound questions of existence. In each performance a down-to-earth quality was literalized by placing all the action on the floor. Hurlin's own presence was a riveting factor not only in his solo but also as the nurse—in a mental hospital, perhaps—of *Beds*. He has an earnest energy that is unassuming but refreshing; his vision of the world may be small-scale, but it is generous.

Village Voice, May 18, 1982

More than Human

(Bruce Schwartz / Manteo Sicilian Marionette Theater)

Americans tend to dismiss puppet theater as kid's stuff. Perhaps it's because puppets seem to fall in the same class of objects as dolls, or perhaps it's because the kinds of things one can do with puppet actors (beat them mercilessly, for example) make them the perfect medium for infantile, aggressive action. Or maybe it's simply that the art of puppetry has never been well developed here and, as with so much of children's art, we relegate what's second-rate to kids. The cartoon violence of a Punch and Judy can be as satisfying to adults as it is to kids, but, also, the mystery of how an inanimate object seems to quicken in gifted hands might be even more wonderful for grownups. Why don't we appreciate puppets the way the Japanese, Greeks, or French do? Maybe there aren't enough gifted hands around. Besides, movies and television have upped the ante. How can live spectacle be as spectacular as what can be accomplished through camerawork and editing?

Bruce Schwartz is one of those rare performers who remind us that one of the most spectacular acts we can witness is the naked power of human presence. Through his puppets Schwartz plays many roles, transforming himself into an old woman, a devil, a young woman, a ghost. There is something very modest in the way Schwartz asserts his versatility as actor/dancer/singer/musician, as if the puppets provided a screen behind which his own persona becomes impersonal and neutralized. When he emerges from the body-theater behind which he manipulates his hand puppets, or when he stands behind the table where he moves his rod puppets, we are amazed that so much power and so many voices could emanate from such a quiet, unassuming presence. He seems, like his puppets, a vessel for a range of emotions and experiences beyond the ken of any single person. And, as he closes his eyes and dances the rod puppets into life, he seems animated, in turn, by some larger force.

Schwartz uses the two different sorts of puppets for two different styles of theater. The hand puppets, tiny but meticulously detailed, and their gaudily striped body-stage, rising to a ribboned turret and leaving only Schwartz's legs visible, are modeled after Elizabethan prototypes.

Here we encounter the characters, plots, and style of early European folk drama; elements of Shakespeare, Boccaccio, Chaucer, and medieval morality plays mingle in these roisterous episodes. The evening begins with a live recorder duet by a man and woman puppet, each wielding a tiny recorder and playing it with lively nods of the head and motions of the hands. I still haven't figured out how Schwartz, who, as anyone could see, has only two hands, handled puppets and recorders all at once. In *The Rat of Huge Proportions,* a hefty matron, Dame Eleanor L'Amour, adores cheese but her fiancé detests it. He poses as a rat to scare her out of her passion, she poses as a lady rat to blow his cover, and a real rat seduces her and comes to blows with the unfortunate fiancé. Dame Eleanor, thinking him dead, forswears cheese (the plot is a pretext for all sorts of verbal play with names of cheese, in rhymed couplets), and, of course, her man comes back to life. In the second half of the program Dame Eleanor appears in the title role of *The Farmer's Cursed Wife.* She plays a shrew who is taken to hell by the devil but so pesters the demons there that Satan brings her back to earth. Schwartz effects scene changes by turning his back to the audience; we hear Dame Eleanor, backstage, commenting on the play's progress and goading us to clap louder. Schwartz invests these tiny creatures with such highly articulated gestures and with such comic timing that by the end of the evening we've come to love Dame Eleanor's familiar primping of her gray strands of hair, the way she plumps her sagging breasts and spreads her skirts, her sideways glances, her homely, distinctly ratlike features. The plays are perfect mixtures of ribaldry and sagacity.

The other kind of puppet Schwartz uses prompts a different kind of theater. The rod puppets he has made, with their white faces and white slender hands, their halos of frizzed hair, their floating bodies, are like Victorian china dolls. The automaton-ballerina leaps and poses with an uncanny grace, her long spindly arms fluttering gently as she lingers in the air—as if she were the spirit of Romantic ballet and the human ballerinas merely imperfect copies of perfect dancing machines. In *He Moved through the Fair* Schwartz sings a melancholy Scottish ballad about a young woman who is visited by her fiancé's ghost, while he enacts the narrative of the wan woman remembering, grieving, and collapsing, and then her ghostly lover entering her room to caress her. In *Toritsukareta-Mai* a Japanese dancer commanded by the emperor to dance with a lion mask is possessed by the spirit that inhabits it. There is a pierrot, a Chinese figurine-automaton, a woman composer writing her last letter to her egotistical artist lover. Like a Japanese Bunraku manipulator, Schwartz is visible as he works these puppets, and in a meditative state that seems almost trancelike. At times his presence intrudes like a fatal deus ex machina, as when his hand enters the puppets' world in *Her Last Letter* to rip the tiny letter in half or when, in *Toritsukareta-Mai,* the stroke of his hand over the dancer's head as she lies face-down fastens the demon's mask on her face and effects her transformation. These are not only figures but also themes from a theater tradition that is esoteric and erudite, and Schwartz is as capable of moving us to tears with the antique, dreamlike dignity of this world as he is of moving us to laughter with his neo-Elizabethan antics.

To compare Schwartz to Manteo Sicilian Marionette Theater is to compare apples to oranges. Schwartz is a chamber performer whose work depends on intimacy, a complex range of expression, and a finely articulated set of moves for his puppets, the multiple aspects of a solo self. The Manteos are not only an ensemble, they are a family. Their performances—from a repertory that consists of 394 episodes of the epic poem *Orlando Furioso*—are folk expressions both of and for a community. Their aim is not range, subtlety, and complexity but boldly direct, graphic legibility and an excitement that both carries the plot forward and fans the flames of ethnic pride.

The Manteos' nearly life-size marionettes are too large-scale to gesticulate and tremble. Their legs remain firmly planted apart; their arms swing as they march along, brandishing swords and shields; their faces are large featured and brightly painted. In battle scenes they fly into collisions, and their heads and arms are detachable for gorier moments. An integral part of every performance is the Manteo family emerging at the end of the play to introduce themselves and to show how the puppets work. Each marionette is manipulated from above by one person who practically wrestles his or her character through the action. (In this performance Tony de Nonno's film *It's One Family—"Knock on Wood"* preceded the play with an account of the troupe's history, the way the puppets are made, and the role each family member plays in the productions.) The puppeteers are hidden behind the curtains of the miniature proscenium stage. The puppets stand in front of scenery painted in deep perspective and, as in grand opera, remain motionless while their lines are declaimed. Instead of arias, most scenes are punctuated with battle scenes in which the puppets swing into action, arms flying and armor flashing.

In this performance Roland the Furious (a knight in King Charlemagne's service) meets Alexander, another Christian knight, who is in love with a pagan princess, Viviana, and who has fallen in combat with a pagan courtier who has abducted Viviana. In the six scenes of the drama we move from forest to pagan court to a tournament in the public square to the forest, as the events leading up to the meeting between Roland and Alexander are explained. The lovers are finally reunited.

Although the Manteos' activity is endlessly fascinating as a set of folkways, as art for a general audience it is problematic. *Orlando Furioso* is an epic poem, not a drama, and it is hard to sustain theatrical interest with a plot that strings together military encounters but that lacks character development. Unlike opera, the fact that the text is in Italian is not compensated for, in the case of those who don't understand the language, by the coloration and variety music can provide. And the visual arias—the battles—are also invariable. Taken out of its ethnic context, the bold simplicity of this theater soon changes from novelty to monotony, and unfortunately a great deal of its meaning is necessarily lost.

Village Voice, June 8, 1982

The Politics of Performance and the Performance of Politics

(Dinosaur / Marshall Reese, David Bowman, and Nora Ligorano / Tim Miller)

As the performance art world moves away from the visual arts toward the realm of rock music, cabarets, and fashion, performances have often threatened to degenerate into light entertainment. The fashion show Richard Foreman scripted for a Soho antique clothing store a few years ago foreshadowed the shift in both the artistic and economic topography of Soho—while the number of new galleries has stabilized, every week it seems there's a new expensive restaurant or clothing store. Soho and Tribeca became fashionable because they were centers of art world activity, but now artists can't afford to live, eat, or shop in their own neighborhoods. In this milieu it's not surprising that the pressure is on to make art that keeps up with the changing fashions.

I almost didn't go to Dinosaur's *Fallout Fashion* because I didn't want to see yet another trivial exercise in glamour, this one on a political theme, no less. But what a relief it was to see a group of artists attack the upper crust of American politics and the clothing industry by subverting the fashion show format with intelligent wit and a funky style refreshingly devoid of pretensions.

"Why change your world when you can change your clothes?" the honey-voiced commentator (Bruce McNally) cooed as Nancy Reagan doubles, dressed in glitter and crepe de chine that looked like it came from the local thrift shop, processed down the runway. American icons from football to jogging to sunbathing were paraded, each with its bitterly ironic function in the post–nuclear holocaust age. Gerri Jones modeled a wedding dress ("for the fall bride") that unfolded from white to black, doubling as a funeral frock. Frieda Dean wore a dress studded with baggies—"for survival of the fattest; didn't you know that diets are practice drills for postblast starvation?" Kim

Knowlton, dressed in skintight "solid lead" jeans, closed the evening with a rap.

> These pants are built to withstand destruction.
> You can write 'em off as a tax deduction!
>   When the music stops and the phones are dead,
> You'll still be pulsing in your jeans of lead.
> "Get his silo superhardened with your EMP."

The Dinosaur fashion show was a collaborative effort by over 20 artists based in Ithaca. Some of the entries leaned more toward the poetic, some more toward the serious. It seems to me that the entries most successful as trenchant political commentary were also those flaunting the blackest, grisliest humor.

Marshall Reese, David Bowman, and Nora Ligorano's *Dyslexiology* is a performance concerned with education, or, rather, miseducation. It begins with two white-shirted readers seated stage right. They might be teachers; they might be students. Stage left a man plays a synthesizer. In the center an oversized notebook symbolizes a classroom. Lessons—words and combinations of words—are spoken in monotone rhythms over the music and also flashed in green computer-type calligraphy above the giant notebook; letters are traced with a colossal pencil. The scene is a combination of schoolday memories and a sci-fi rendition of school. About midway through the piece, however, the lessons go awry. Words like *egg* begin to be correlated with the wrong images—bombs and other goodies of the military-industrial complex. Here the reference to cognitive psychology in the title doesn't indicate phenomenological and personal preoccupations, as it would have in the work of various performance artists of the 1970s; instead, the notion of an educational disability is a metaphor for social criticism. A fictional student, Johnny, comes of age and becomes an ad man or a politician. He speaks behind masks in a Peter Lorre whisper, turning questions of social concern into nonsensical tautologies that uphold the status quo.

In some ways *Dyslexiology* is like Peter Handke's play about Kaspar Hauser, another tale of the debilitating effects of language learning. Both pieces share the somewhat questionable premise that language is the source of all evil. Taken literally, they raise conspiratorial thinking to the heights of paranoia. Read more charitably, both pieces can be seen as symbols for educational regimes that pervert reason for the sake of social domination. In this regard *Dyslexiology* is an example of an increasingly political tone in performance art that I find salutary.

But *Dyslexiology* has some major aesthetic problems. It sets out its theme too slowly and introduces the political content too late. This diffusiveness, added to the performance situation, made most of the Danceteria audience lose interest early on. But, also, I wonder why the group didn't exploit the syndrome of dyslexia more specifically. The particulars of the disability—right/left confusions, letter inversions, inabilities to tell time—could have added a wealth of word wit to the flagging introduction.

Although *Dyslexiology* was a performance that used music as an integral component, ironically its format seemed ill suited to the Danceteria situation. Performance audiences at art galleries are trained to give the live act the same rapt attention they would devote to an inanimate artwork, and the artworks of the 1960s and 1970s have taught us to commit our minds as well as our eyes to the object at hand. Audiences at music clubs have a different orientation. They want to split their attention between listening, dancing, watching, drinking, and talking. And it's usually possible to sustain multifocus concentration when a band is playing loud music that washes right through you and people are dancing all around. If you miss a few words here or a step there, you still get the message. *Dyslexiology,* however, suffered in this situation. Although patterned after rap music, its meaning was based on verbal detail, some seen, but much of it heard. It was hard to hear the piece clearly, so the first few "lessons," which were not particularly engaging visually, were unable to keep the audience's attention. People gravitated to the bar or sat at their tables and talked. The loss of spectator concentration affected the level of the performers' concentration. So, although the piece itself accumulated density and meaning, the performance never really accelerated. It was obfuscated by its own conditions.

Tim Miller is a performer who compresses the energy of a rock band into one body. Maybe that's one reason his performance at Danceteria "read" so strongly. While *Dyslexiology* was confined to the small stage on the first floor, Miller and the seven men he performed with commandeered the entire dance floor on the second floor. You didn't have to work at watching this performance; it surrounded you.

Miller has evolved a recognizable style and format for his performances that mix free-associative autobiographical musings, documentation of political or social crises, slide projections, loud sounds, movements that seem dangerously on the edge of losing control, and a boyishly brash presence that makes you care about the childhood memories and dreams he recounts and that supplies the glue to make all the disparate elements not only cohere but take on deeper meaning. His works are not only about the literal subject of the moment—losing one's balance in a dream or, in this case, flying—but also plumb the metaphoric connotations of that subject. They are about how difficult it is to find one's equilibrium in a world full of disorienting events like wars. They are about how difficult it is to grow up in a world bereft of heroes or hope for the future. If Miller's past performances stressed the gloomier aspects of our chaotic lives, the current work suggests a gleam of hope, an ecstatic vision of redemption.

Six men in bathrobes and sunglasses run and fall to the sound of an amplified voice repeating, "I'm flyin'!" The Peter Pan imagery is completed when Miller and Barry Davison jump off chairs in a childlike imitation of flying, while Mary Martin's voice sings the rest of the song with booming orchestration. Miller tells about his childhood desire to fly, then about his recent skydiving lesson, recounting in detail—in words and gestures—the various sets of safety procedures. A second theme—suicide—is introduced in a slide of a clipping that tells about a boy who has killed himself because he had "stopped growing." Davison swings on a long swing suspended from the ceiling, and Miller runs in his trajectory, repeatedly escaping crashing by a hair's breadth. The chorus of men turn the skydiving Emergency Procedure Mode into a loud chant and a dance: "Look, look, grab, close, punch!" They attach Miller to a pulley and hoist him up to the ceiling, where he undergoes an epiphany and announces excitedly, "I don't have to commit suicide; I can fly; I want to live!" The six men jump and fall into duck and cover positions.

The evocation of bliss in Miller's performance stems from the childhood iconography—specifically, that of a Disney utopia. It is interesting that Steven Spielberg trades in similar imagery in his two recent films, *Poltergeist* and *E.T.* But, unlike Spielberg, Miller uses this imagery in an overtly political context. He acknowledges the political horrors *Fallout Fashion* and *Dyslexiology* describe but is literally transported to an overarching, transcendent vision that suggests not only means (learning survival techniques and forming communities) but also rapturous forms of salvation.

Village Voice, June 22, 1982

Making Worlds Alone
(Martha Rosler/Stephanie Skura/Jeff McMahon)

The solo performance is a remarkable form. There are so many things a single human presence can say. The body bristles with associations, and what it speaks of ranges from the private to the globally political. It ought to give us some kind of faith in the world and in human action.

Martha Rosler's performance was part of Dance Theater Workshop's series "Manifesto! New Investigations in Political Performance." It was a performance, in fact, designed to elicit such faith in the world while expressing political rage, but it was so misconceived and misguided that one could react only with anger toward the artist. If this work pretends to be an analysis of American culture and ideology, if, as Rosler's program notes state, the work is an argument for critical consciousness in which "we . . . link the politics of daily life with those of the public world and regain a sense of history to achieve the activism the current situation demands," then our political art is in as sorry a state as our national government.

Watchwords of the Eighties was in two parts. The first, a 30-minute videotape, juxtaposed a conversation between mother and child with a radio talk about 1960s art on the soundtrack and cultural images (snapshots, ads, bank logos) from North and Latin America with running subtitles on the visual track. The separateness of these components at first made the tape painful to watch, but, as the image track repeated itself, it soon became clear that what seemed difficult to catch and comprehend was in fact almost simple-minded. The "analysis" in this tape is simply a string of radical clichés—"The controlling class rules culture and its ideas"; "The news is a bland curtain of excuses"; "Here [in the U.S.] we are sleeping with our eyes open"—the image of a Bank of America sign flashes on. Such rhetoric is not analytical but exhortatory. We're meant to shout "yeah!" when we hear it, not stop to think. Rosler's inclusion of every hackneyed maxim currently fashionable among academic Marxists reminded me of a rally I went to last May Day when a tired crowd of die-hard anti-imperialists absentmindedly cheered each item on a laundry list of demands, including "U.S. out of the Falkland Islands!" Although Rosler's late-night audience consisted primarily of sympathetic political artists and critics already familiar with her rhetoric, the pointedly one-to-one correspondence of images and commentary seemed designed for first-graders. To this introductory lesson in ideology the soundtrack added Rosler's two additional points: in a world where people are struggling against domination, the family provides solace; the art world does not. The first point was probably inadvertent, but the second was intentional.

The second part of Rosler's presentation was a series of slide projections punctuated with her appearances and a "pseudo-rap song." As newspaper clippings about El Salvador and Reagan's policies and other political horrors flashed on screen, Rosler ran in and out of the space, dressed as a street kid and carrying an enormous, foam-rubber "box." Every time she entered she wrote a word on the screen, "defacing" both the wall and the image with magic markers. Her list began with ruling-class watchwords—*quality, elegance, cutbacks, repression*—but gradually, as the slides began to show images of marches and rallies, the words in the list became altered in subversive ways: *cutbacks* turned into *giveback; repression* into *concession; quality* into *equality*. Occasionally, Rosler tossed off a few dance steps or pushed the box across the floor with her head.

I found this section of the evening worse than banal—in itself it was an example of cultural rip-off. The graffiti writer Rosler portrays is a figure she obviously knows nothing about. Her shadowy impression of black and Latin street culture is insulting as well as naive. She says that she draws on the sounds and images of popular culture, but her rap song has the cadences and content of a 1960s folksong, rather than the syncopated egotism of a Kurtis Blow cut; her dancing is more like that of a Jules Feiffer modern dancer than electronic boogie. And certainly the messages of real graffiti are political only in an implicit way. The competition cast in terms of style and celebration of the individual has nothing to do with writing political slogans on subway walls. It's true that such a competition reflects the alienation of our city's kids from mainstream culture. But that alienation in the 1980s leads to mainstream ambitions, to dreams of bourgeois success, not to revolutionary anger. Rosler seems to be stuck in a 1960s fantasy that these kids will rise up angry to join the white middle-class marchers in her snapshots.

Rosler's performance was particularly disheartening because her intentions are good. She sees the present time as one of change, and she wants to make political, critical art that will help people resist Reaganism by taking control over their lives and over society. "I want to help add credence to people's life experiences while suggesting their susceptibility to change," she writes. Yet her art is not popular art. It is shaped for educated, elite audiences, not for mass presentation. Its forms are not revelatory. Its content is so global, so all-inclusive, that it ends up saying nothing.

Two performances at Franklin Furnace, much more modest in their claims, shed more light on the human condition in their own small ways. Stephanie Skura's *Some Kind of Dance* was a "baring of devices," a commentary on the life of a performance artist and the making of a performance. For Skura the creative struggle is inevitably embedded in the social struggles of everyday life. Part of making the work is the mundane, unromantic detail of arguing with friends, explaining one's marginal existence to loving parents, earning enough money to survive, doing one's own shitwork, going home alone when the performance is over. Skura shows these facets of the-artist-as-ordinary-person-and-worker with a dead-pan wit and appealing sincerity.

The evening is structured as a series of vignettes, some taking place only as disembodied sounds (on tape) in the dark, some as pure movement, some as poses, some as moving and talking. The vignettes, Skura explains, are actually ten beginnings, five middles, and six endings, because, once she had dreamed up these various beginnings, she decided that it would be too bad to throw any of them away. And the same with the middles and endings. She cleans the floor. She writes in her journal. She tries to explain to her mother what sort of place she performs in—further off Broadway than off-off. She appears in the doorway in a sweatsuit wielding a huge soup spoon. We hear her play the piano. We hear her mother's voice describing a diet she must follow. Somewhere in the middle of the piece is a virtuosic outburst of monologue in voice and gesture—an ego dance, in which Skura rages, "I am the duck! I am . . . the milk! I am . . . !" And threaded through is some low-key, casual movement, its understatement and serious, inward focus a pleasing contrast to the other sections.

Skura is not making explicitly political art. Yet there is much in *Some Kind of Dance* that comments on the political situations of artists and of women, bringing it all home with a human sensibility.

Jeff McMahon's *Rate of Exchange,* like *Watchwords of the Eighties,* mixed video imagery with the solo presence. Yet his approach was directly opposed to Rosler's. Where Rosler sought fragmentation, Mc-Mahon designed a unity of effect; where Rosler undermined the graphic simplicity of TV with an intended complication of audio/visual channels, McMahon let the simplicity of video condense the meaning of his performance. *Rate of Exchange* is both austere and obsessive. It's like a long, low shriek against the distortions of modern life, the shortages—as the title ambiguously suggests—of money and of human energy.

McMahon sits in a chair stage right; behind him the kitchen in Franklin Furnace's performance space forms a kind of scenic backdrop. Stage left, an Advent screen shows us the same image we see live: the performer's face, staring impassively then blinking and shifting eyes from side to side. "Get moving! Get moving!" a video voice hisses. McMahon stands and, in white T-shirt and khaki shorts, begins tossing a basketball from one hand to another. The voice relentlessly continues its driving, rhythmic patter. "What are you thinking about? What are you thinking about?" The patter includes answers. "I'm thinking about work. I'm thinking about you. I'm thinking about fame. I'm thinking about me. I'm thinking about making love. I'm thinking about the critics. . . ." "Doing one thing and thinking about another." McMahon's movements become a kind of dance, a set of limited variations on the incessant tossing of the ball back and forth, with an occasional duck of the body under the arm to turn around, a dance of nerves, of rising tension. The mood changes as he croons a 1940s love song over a recording smoothly secure. But then a metronome appears on the screen, and the sound of its rapid tick renews the sense of edginess. The ball tossing, the litany, the pacing begin again. "To bed to table to work to love. . . ."

A separate text in the program notes echoes the paranoid, insistent tone of the piece and concludes, "no more no more there is a limit there is a point where somebody's got to say no somebody's got to say stop stop stop." In the performance McMahon himself seizes the moment, pulls open the shutters on the long window facing the audience, and stands silently before an eerie landscape—crooked tree flooded with nighttime light—opening a feverish mind to the world. The performance creates a monotone image of a restless, driven persona—but, oddly, shows us only its structure and not the subject of its obsession.

Village Voice, October 26, 1982

Dream Time in a Warehouse

(Robert Whitman)

Robert Whitman's Happenings of the 1960s were like fairy tales for Americans. In them the most quotidian objects and images—pieces of cloth or plastic, balloons, ropes, people picnicking or taking a shower— were alchemically combined and transmuted into improbable, fantastic events. Using immense spaces or (as in *The American Moon*) partitioning the space into tunnels for the spectators, Whitman made strings of actions that coursed along like a boat down a river. His use of film that rhymed with live actions confounded the spectator's sense of scale and depth. His mixtures of biological references (as in *Mouth* and *Flower*), geological elements (the constellations, water), primary colors, and social activities, as well as his combination of qualities—crude, homemade objects and smooth technical feats—gave his events a magical, mythic aura.

In 1976, Whitman presented a retrospective of his Happenings and created a new work as well. A generation of spectators who had never seen the originals became familiar with his work. Since then Whitman has been presenting new works occasionally. *Raincover,* which took place in a ground floor warehouse near the West Side highway, was clearly a continuation. The liquidity both of time and of the world around us has been a constant in Whitman's work. *Raincover* was an evocative, poetic meditation on water and on its opposite, fire.

The space is divided into three parts: stage left, a chair stands in a corner; stage right, a huge cloth ball is suspended from the ceiling. In the center of the space is a wall made of men's shirts, and behind the wall—visible to the audience via a mirror set at an angle above the wall—is a rectangular space. A woman dressed in white ignites a frame in this space behind the shirts; we see this action from above, in the mirror. Next a huge drum of liquid is rolled out on a hand truck, and liquid spouts from it, spilling into the rectangle, which we now perceive is a huge, shallow pool. The largest part of the performance space, then, is visible only from above and indirectly; the rest of the action occurs on a shallow, almost flat area that spans the width of the immense room. A film of indistinct blue and red shapes pans the shirts and settles on the ball. The ball magically lowers to the ground, and the film projects enormous images of body parts: a finger, an eye, a mouth. The ball opens to reveal a screen, on which we see a portrait of a clean-shaven young man in a suit. The man in the film portrait appears in the flesh. It begins to rain on the stage, on the man who stands expressionless.

The man picks up a glass and holds it out to the side. As the "rain" fills the glass, we see that it is a bright yellow opaque liquid. The man turns his head slowly several times to look at a pile of cloth stage right. Each time he turns his head, the bundle glows with a bright yellow light. Gradually the man moves—or rather, is imperceptibly *drawn*—to the chair stage left. He sits down in the chair and ignites a stream of flame on the wall behind him. The white wall burns, the pool of water is afloat with small flame-boats, and the wall of shirts is a screen for a film of fires.

Later the stage is divided into two parts. On the right a man carries boards bathed in a gleaming orange aura and deposits them in a garbage can. On the left a screen has been erected, and a fluttering film of the New York City skyline is shown. The man carries out a cardboard box; attaches it to a hook, and hoists it aloft. After a few minutes red fabric is pulled out of the box by an invisible pulley. As storm noises are heard, the left-hand screen shows trees then flames; on the right the red rectangle becomes another screen, now bearing the image of a flaming frame.

In terms of its formal correspondences and oppositions, *Raincover* is one of the most tightly constructed of Whitman's theatrical events that I have seen. It uses several of his favorite elements—water, cloth, wood, rope, the primary colors. But it uses them in patterns of repetitions and rhyme schemes. The rhymes are visual (the flames, the red cloth, the glowing boards), aural (the sounds of a storm on tape, the spouting liquid, the falling yellow rain), but they are also verbal. Although no word is spoken during *Raincover,* the images prompt labels, and the most prominent images in the event include the pair flame/frame. On the other hand, all sorts of oppositions form contrasts to the rhymes and repetitions. Not only is there fire and water, but there are all sorts of downward movements in the first half of the piece, which are finally answered by the rising of the flames and of the red fabric at the end.

Part of the unearthly beauty of *Raincover* (and of Whitman's work generally) comes from a deadpan flow of images. Things that are extraordinary are presented as if ordinary, and the mundane and the astonishing mix without warning. As in a dream, all sorts of things from daily life combine in impossible ways to create rich metaphors. We half-recognize various images and respond with varying emotions, but in Whitman's events the images are cool and affectless. And, as in a dream, our experiences of time and space are disoriented—we continue to hear and see the water spouting from the drum long after we know it should have emptied. Yet Whitman's work is even more marvelous than dreams, since his images live outside of consciousness; they are real events, concrete arrangements of things, taking place in time—gliding by our wide-open eyes.

Village Voice, November 23, 1982

The Text of the Matter

(Bradley Wester / Peter Stickland and Fiona Templeton)

In certain respects performance art is like theater with the priorities reversed. The text recedes or disappears altogether, while the supporting elements of ordinary theater—the acting style, the gesture system, the sound, the lights, the mise-en-scène—emerge singly or in combination as the focus of attention. Perhaps for this reason, one is often tempted to notice the formal elements in performances and to treat the content as secondary. But, since in performance the meaning of the work also seems to make itself apparent in bits and pieces, across various media or channels of information—because the text itself is not the main thing—the content of the work is often fragmented and elusive. The spectator has a psychological as well as an aesthetic motive for noticing the spectacle at the expense of the content of the work. (The formalist, descriptive criticism surrounding the performance art of the 1970s reflects this bias.)

The performances by Bradley Wester and by Peter Stickland and Fiona Templeton, though entirely different in theme and in style, shared one problem: both were impressive as spectacle but weak when it comes to sense. Yet both had intellectually fashionable pretensions. Wester's *Re:Gender(Scape)* revolved around the ambiguities of sexuality, with nods to Jean Genet, Jean Cocteau, and Roland Barthes or—as the blunt world of rock puts it—the subject was gender fucking. *Against Agreement: Duel Duet #4* was a mental battle along the lines of a chess game, with a prearranged substructure of rules and strategies for agreement and disagreement.

Wester's performance was so technically smooth and visually striking that it slid directly into one's sensations. He entered the dark space framed in a rectangle of light and dressed in a dark suit. Facing the back wall, partially obstructed from the audience by a screen, he created a double layer of physically ambiguous imagery (pain / pleasure) as he writhed in a chair while dissolving slide images of him in similar poses suggested a dance. Later the slide images created a new ambiguity, male / female— and Wester appeared in a red satin dress and elegant makeup to recite a honeyed, poisonous text punctuated with stylized gestures. Wester's verbal imagery, jewel-like, splintered, and violent, rather than subverting sexual stereotypes, seemed to turn them into fetishes; his invocation of Hitler's name seemed a calculated attempt to be modishly wicked. The final visual tableau, in which Wester-as-woman stood behind a glass frame and spray-painted it so that its opacity caught the filmed image of Wester-as-man in a gloomy forest, left the audience cheering. Yet when the dazzle wore off, what remained? Simply a high-class drag show, decadent in its duplicity, in its own posing as a theoretical gloss on the profound complexities of gender. Rather than challenging stereotypes, Wester made of his womanly transformation the same set of uninteresting clichés you can see at any sleazy barroom drag act.

Against Agreement didn't aim for technical polish, and its funkiness was one of its better qualities. In ways that the performance makers probably could not have foreseen, the performance's bar venue took over this work, reducing clarity and legibility but enhancing atmosphere. Stickland and Templeton arranged themselves at opposite ends of the red formica bar that dominated this otherwise white room. On the wall was a black-and-white drawing that included images of a woman eating a slice of pizza, King Kong and the Empire State Building, and Kandinsky's Blue Rider figure. As Stickland and Templeton played out their verbal duel, the distance between them was peopled by a "scenic metronome drunk" and a "rhythmic metronome barmaid," as well as by a chorus of three men and three women who sang, argued, climbed up on the bar and fell off it, and looked like punk extras in a film noir in shades of white, gray, and red. The red bar itself was so long and the room so crowded that you could only see and hear parts of what was going on. The chorus had an advantage in terms of visibility and audibility by virtue of sheer numbers. Anna Köhler, as the rhythmic metronome barmaid, worked her way from one end of the bar to the other, mixing only red drinks, balancing lemons on her head, pouring ice cubes everywhere, cleaning, sliding glasses down the bar, and rocking, smoking, and humming (things like "Hernando's Hideaway") with metric intensity. Her performance—apt, exaggerated, concentrated—was brilliant. In the end what was lost was the text read by Templeton, which was the crux of the work's idea. I suspect that the text would only have detracted from, not added to, the vivacity of the group's antics.

Village Voice, December 7, 1982

Barefoot in the Gym
(Anne Bogart)

Women and Men, a big dance is a big dance in the way that life is a big dance, moving between love and death. It is a dance in the broad sense—its imagery comes out of gesture. And "the dance" is the perfect metaphor for the world Anne Bogart describes, the world of adolescence, where the dance party is the arena for playing out desires and anxieties. The private is forced to become public because, in the adolescent world, unlike the adult, one has no room of one's own. Issues of bodily control and pleasure become excruciatingly paramount. At the party dancing is the form in which physical and social relationships take place. Bogart makes that form expand and reverberate.

The auditorium at P.S. 122 was the right setting for *Women and Men,* a big gym in which the atmosphere of a high school dance was easily suggested. Twenty-six young men and women saunter slowly into the space to pair off and walk away in couples. The music (from Philip Glass's *Glassworks*) and the soft lighting give the scene a stylized, antique air, as if it were a photograph in an album. This group, "the club," functions as a chorus that frames, watches, or moves around the "core group" (John Bernd, Jim Diaz, Laura J. Hoffman, Brian Jucha, Kevin Kuhlke, Susan Milani, Janet Murtha, and Gayle Tufts). Lit in white fluorescent light and arranging themselves on a small stage at the far end of the gym, the core group makes moves of hesitant, awkward flirtation. A boy turns his back on a girl and bites his thumb; another boy steals a kiss from a girl, who slaps him. With Frank Sinatra crooning "What Is This Thing Called Love?" and its 1940s costumes, the scene is at first a touchingly humorous pantomime. But then the entire series of gestures is repeated in sequence several times; the actions become abstract and larger than life. The accumulation of gesture and the tension between verisimilitude and abstraction become the organizing principle of the performance. Each scene is more like a song (and songs accompany most of the scenes) than like a drama: they don't develop but, rather, iterate statements until they become patterns. The result is a sense of distance that allows for a powerful effect without sentimentality. The images lose their specificity and gain the scale of a zeitgeist.

The core group moves down to the dance floor, where they jitterbug and slow dance. The club, frozen in dance postures, watches as the four couples touch, partner, and then hold one another with mounting urgency. When the dance is over both the format and the theme of the performance split open. The couples grow up: they come out one by one to make pronouncements on womanhood and manhood then help their partners change into dark, adult clothing. They line up to recite fragments of text all at once that bleed together, a collage of World War II images. They fight, love, manipulate, separate, and begin the patterns again with new partners. Their male/female roles have hardened and imprisoned them. When a woman and a man exchange lines or when two women enact the motions of a physical dialogue that moves from tenderness to brutality, the incongruity turns the stereotypes inside out.

The war images expand. The emotional tangles of adolescence have threads that lead out into the world to form a complex web of violence. Bernd and Kuhlke have a fist fight that looks for real, as other boys look on and intervene and the girls watch from across the space. Later, the crowd of men falls into formation to shoulder arms with sticks for rifles. People speak of bombs and concentration camps. Later still, the women mass on the opposite side of the room, miming the rhythmic gestures of an assembly line, their hands implacably smoothing, patting, pulling, picking, pushing. The two groups have been standardized and dehumanized. Once again they dance but this time like zombies. The club, no longer dressed in party clothes but in overcoats, has become an ominous mass. They dress the core group in overcoats too. They rush in waves to the very knees of the audience, falling dead as the lights flash on momentarily. And now, when the core group reassembles on the white-lit stage and Frank Sinatra sings the same love song, the same gestures look entirely different. They are no longer gestures of flirtation but of a mixture of despair, displacement, loneliness, and both fear and hope for the future. The word *"love"* has taken on an entirely different meaning.

Women and Men was stunning in more ways than one. As a visual spectacle, it was impressive: the groupings of the young cast (of all sizes, shapes, and characters), the use of space, the lighting effects (designed by Carl Delo). The massive scale of the piece exerted its own power. But, also, the breadth and depth of Bogart's vision, her ability to concentrate and extract the most basic and profound things that both shape us and move us, struck directly to the heart.

Village Voice, December 21, 1982

Truth in Advertising

(John Malpede / Eric Bogosian)

Both John Malpede and Eric Bogosian create characters onstage. In this way they differ from a monologist like Spalding Gray, who adopts different styles of performance but remains himself, telling stories and reacting to the different characters in his stories. The texts in Malpede's and Bogosian's pieces are treated dramatically. But these pieces depart from conventional drama in their structure—in both cases, radical juxtaposition, or a list rather than a development.

Malpede's *No Frills* has two subjects—one aesthetic, one political. On the one hand it is a performance about performance art, its styles and conventions, and also the stereotyped characters of popular media. The art of packaging. On the other hand it is about our disintegrating economy and its psychological effects. The sociology of packaging. We laugh when Malpede promises "a good, basic performance at an affordable (?) price." But it is a laugh tinged with hysteria, because Malpede has hit the nail on the head beginning with the conception of his piece. We look for ways to cut corners financially in every area of our lives these days, from groceries to art and entertainment. We want more for our money, we want satisfaction guaranteed, and why not, since our money is worth less than ever.

It's one thing for the packagers of generic cola to promise satisfaction, however, and quite another thing to guarantee a no-frills performance. There's a formula to making cola taste like cola, but the question of taste in works of art is a more elusive matter. I'd say Malpede pulled it off. He began by explaining what, in fact, generic products are: they provide substance, nutritional value, and calories . . . and they fulfill your expectations. We would, he promised, get all the basic ingredients of a performance—except that he would not get undressed. Like a talkshow host, Malpede told us what to expect for the evening, promising two guest appearances and interlacing it all with wry jokes about unemployment and bullet-proof fashion. After some handplay with three croissants and a toy gun (manipulating objects) he gave us a quiz (audience participation) to prepare us for his first guest, the Professor.

Shaking hands with himself, he switched voices and sat down in a comfortable chair to be interviewed by himself about his new book, *Packaging and Self-Esteem.* Of course, whenever his pedantic descriptions of his subject threatened to become lucid, he stopped short to say that he didn't want to give away the whole book, which the viewers should go right out and buy. The secret of the book was to show how to raise one's self-esteem through proper packaging of oneself.

The second guest, Malpede dressed in a set of slicker coveralls, was the proprietor of a carnival game, Sink-a-Sucker/Dunk-a-Dope. He explained that he sits on a contraption with a target and a trap door and lets the customers get out their aggressions by throwing baseballs at the target and thus dunking him in a tub of water beneath the trap. He pointed out the line of baseballs at the edge of the audience, stationed himself on his contraption, and began to tell a hard-luck story about how he came to open this business after losing jobs and suffering accidents at work and in his car. But, when a member of the audience came up to throw the balls at the target and made bull's-eye every time, the tables were turned and the customer became the sucker as Malpede continued to sit imperturbably atop the thing and heckle. Malpede's accent and the details of the story made his character waver between black and Italian, but the self-loathing, generated in a society that creates economic outcasts and then victimizes and stigmatizes them, came through loud and clear.

As a performer, Malpede is gentle and genial. You trust him immediately, and that's part of the reason his host and professor characters, though ironically limned, worked so well. His more violent character, more removed from the audience spatially as well as culturally, was not as strong as he should have been. Still, the three characters, presenting three facets of Malpede's double theme, provided a satisfying array of perspectives on some knotty issues.

As we walked from Malpede's performance to Bogosian's, my friend said, "You know, Malpede should have gotten Bogosian to play his bad guy." Bogosian's *(devil's) Advocate* continues in his recent mode. It is a list of about a dozen characters, all culled from outcasts worse than simply down-and-out-murderers, torturers, psychopathic doctors, and evil faith healers. This performance went beyond previous monologues in showing slides and films of the most horrific and degrading human experiences, including child pornography and war crimes. More than ever, it made me wonder why Bogosian refuses the distance and criticism necessary to presenting such material. True, we can read about such things daily in the tabloids, and we see these images on TV, but performance is never mere reportage. Its intensity supplies it willy-nilly with a point of view. In this case Bogosian's own charisma and control make the monologues take shape not as a string of facts but as privileged, thus sympathetic, interior views. The material demands an editorializing component that can't be left up to the viewer.

Village Voice, January 4, 1983

A Couple of Grays Sitting around Talking

(Spalding Gray)

Spalding Gray is a storyteller par excellence, but it's not just his intense style of narration that makes his monologues so compelling. We laugh at the anecdotes the way we would at a comedian's, but Gray draws on a greater range of expressive effects than comic. The way his stories animate each other, added to the momentum of the narrative, makes us think as well as laugh. His evenings are surrealistic epics of the American cultural landscape, in which all the absurdities and banalities of our lives rub together to create a kind of metaphysical rush. All the world, even what is most normal, looks strange to Gray, and, when he recounts how he constantly embraces the world in all its strangeness, his very quest unites a bewildering multitude of events, quirks, and temperaments and makes them utterly logical.

In Search of the Monkey Girl and *Interviewing the Audience* were the two final episodes in Gray's recent retrospective of eight monologues. They represent a turning point in Gray's work for several reasons. For one thing, *Interviewing the Audience* is not really a monologue but a series of dialogues with audience members that in turn gives each guest the opportunity to launch into his or her own monologue. Both of these performances also make use of specific themes that Gray favors in the other monologues but which are condensed into organizing metaphors for each program.

In Search of the Monkey Girl plays out in a new key Gray's fascination with both the oddities and the universality of the human body and the experience of physicality. On the one hand, it is a description of the freak shows at the carnival Gray visited with a photographer for the specific purpose of documentation. On the other, it is about the issue of abnormality itself: not only the mystery of physical aberration and the twin feelings of fascination and repulsion it provokes but also the inevitable parallels between physical and spiritual grotesqueness and, finally, the question of how human norms are set and where the lines are drawn.

Spalding and Randy, the photographer, pose as carnies in order to gain an inside view of the sideshows at the Tennessee State Fair in Nashville. Randy's quest is to finally photograph Priscilla the Monkey Girl and Emmett the Alligator Man, the only living sideshow freaks who have eluded his lens. Spalding wanders through the rides and the sideshows, recording the spiels, talking to the owners, noting the disappointed grumble of the crowd, moving from sensory overload to carnival addiction. He visits Tiny Tina, the miniature horse; the Pickled Punk Show, with its images of deformed babies; he befriends the son of the freak sideshow owners, who wants to stop working in the carnival and major in philosophy. For solace Gray watches the farmers and cows in the agricultural barn. And he meets Maurice, Ellen, Baby Ian, and Pierre, who opened an oddly moralistic geek show featuring a supposed dope fiend and two pythons in order to carry out a crusade against drug addiction.

The material itself is riveting. We become voyeurs with Gray as he inspects the exhibitions in the carnival and becomes increasingly intrigued by them, just as Maurice and his family, despite their moralism, increasingly move toward becoming actual geeks. But, also, Gray's performance is a brilliant replication of the carnival rhythms, a creation in style as well as content of the blaring rides, the excited kids, the glib barkers, the atmosphere of display, raunchy physicality, and perverse allure. He speeds up, slows down, gestures, runs his words together in a single breath like a child who can't get his story out fast enough. As he describes with both words and body a python's gerbil dinner, which he, Randy, and Maurice and Pierre witness while Ellen cooks hamburgers for their own dinner, the full irony of the carnival as a barrage of physical contradictions becomes visible in Gray's sideshow of the mind.

The intimacy of the monologue situation and the personal nature of Gray's material sometimes make his performances resemble psychiatric confession. There were audience members at the opening night of *47 Beds* last year who were so unaware of any aesthetic distance between Gray's emotional entanglements and his talking about them in public as performance that they seized on the post-performance question-and-answer session as a way to offer personal advice. *Interviewing the Audience* drew on this ambiguous boundary between private and public inherent in much performance art and close to the surface in all Gray's work. The interview situation—in which each chosen spectator sat with Gray, cut off from the rest of the audience by blinding lights, and subjected to probing, often personal questions—added to the image of the psychiatric visit. Yet the equally strong image of Gray as a TV talk-show host, interviewing ordinary people rather than stars, made the performance become an event that refused neat categorization.

Gray opened the evening by talking about what had happened to him on the way to the theater and, in his typical style, spiraled into a free-associative chain of memories that included being kidnapped by Hasidic Jews to clean up their synagogue while strolling among the prostitutes down the Bowery one Sunday morning. The Grayism—the underlying, irreconcilable clash of worldviews—was that he thought they wanted him to perform unspeakable sexual acts, while they thought he was a derelict.

He then called up a series of spectators out of a number of volunteers, asked them what they did on the way to the theater, where they lived, whom they lived with, how they earned a living, and so on. In the least interesting of the encounters the interviewees answered in monosyllables, but Gray's pensive, gentle, at times awkward attempts to draw them out still held one's attention. In the most interesting dialogues—and the night I went there were three, all with men—there was a chemical spark that lit up, a cooperative effort, as if Gray were able to generously impart to his guests the same meandering, curious, candid, organizing wit that seems to generate and focus themes even as it proliferates good stories.

Village Voice, January 18, 1983

Zaloom Vrooms

(Paul Zaloom)

Paul Zaloom would be a great carnival barker, with his booming, quick-fire voice, his flexible face, and his semaphoric gestures. In fact, his performance technique is deliberately modeled after a mountebank's. But Zaloom works the other side of the fence, educating rather than hustling. His shows have a politically astute cutting edge that is tempered with comic irony and swift timing. They're not only effective agit-prop; they're remarkably funny and entertaining. Zaloom's humor adds subversive power to his political attacks.

Each of the three shows in *Crazy as Zaloom* is based on a popular form of entertainment or communication. "A Day in the Life of Senator Punch" is a modern-day Punch and Judy show, performed in a gaudy puppet booth. Punch is a corrupt southern senator who propositions his secretary, murders his wife, and takes a bribe from an Arab oil sheik. He's collared by an FBI agent but murders him too. He gives political advice to General Someother Bozo, South American dictator and American puppet. Taking questions from the audience, he adroitly avoids social security, the Middle East, the MX missile, and economic trickle-down with blustering double-talk. In between the puppet episodes Zaloom's head emerges from behind his puppeteer's curtain. He looks like Abe Lincoln, talks like a cross between Colin Clive and Claude Rains, and, in a lampoon of the Gettysburg Address, frames the antics with omniscient narration. "Clap if you think Senator Punch will be caught and punished for his corrupt ways," he instructs the audience. And when a single pair of naive hands responds, he nods sagely: "Ah, I see the bus from Disneyland *did* arrive." In the end, though, Punch meets his just deserts—not by the hand of the government but in the gullet of a vacuum cleaner monster.

"Do It *Now!*" is a parody of the 1950s civil defense films that nonchalantly taught us how to duck and cover or build a bomb shelter. Dressed in coveralls plastered with CD badges, Zaloom plays an enthusiastic survival buff who shows us, with the aid of a cranky paper "video," just how easy life will be during and after the nuclear holocaust. Using current Crisis Relocation Planning documents, Zaloom summarizes basic tips for cheating radiation death by emergency evacuation: what to pack, what to do with your pets, how to deal with traffic, where to go. And for those who can't get away, how to build a fallout shelter—for instance, a model whose roof can be used as a patio or an economy version whose roof is your car. Failing a fallout shelter, you can always completely cover your house with dirt. Diagrams show how to throw burning furniture out your windows in the 30 minutes between the flash of the explosion and the onset of fallout. Don't worry if fallout hits you, the manuals advise. You can wipe it off, just like dust. And Zaloom demonstrates just how effective is the recommended gas mask—a handkerchief folded six or eight times. What's more, we are shown a book for children that comforts by explaining how to abandon your family and friends in order to survive at all costs.

Both "A Day in the Life of Senator Punch" and "Do It *Now!*" have fine moments but at times ramble and drop in energy. "In the News," however, a cross between a TV news broadcast and a children's cartoon, shows Zaloom at his best. He's not simply playing a role here but also creating the action and the sound effects. The stage is dotted with mysterious packages covered with plastic garbage bags. Zaloom enters, dressed in an iridescent sharkskin suit. "Brought to you by satellite!" he shouts, and, grabbing a wall clock with gold-plated rays, he makes it careen in orbit. "And by your cable TV network!"—he rushes to the opposite side of the stage, picks up a bundle of foam-rubber cables, and makes one of them into a square that frames his face. "This is the evening news!" He stands behind a table where he dumps the contents of the mysterious packages, keeping up a running patter that turns the flood of cheap objects into metaphors. A pile of plastic cigars stands for the first session of the 1983 Congress. The politicians jostle, mumble, debate, and decide to adjourn for lunch. With a sweep of his hand Zaloom knocks them to the floor and goes to his next episode: ugly tacks fall on a nice mountain landscape (a flowered shower curtain), and a black piece of plastic creeps in to cover the whole thing. "Acid rain," Zaloom comments. A doctor finds a new medical breakthrough—more money—after he checks out his patient's lungs (cigarette butts) and liver (empty liquor bottle). The Falkland Islands (two rocks), populated only by sheep (a box of cotton balls is emptied onto the table and begins to bleat), is attacked by plastic forks. The Helen Hayes Theatre is knocked down to clear the way for the Portman Hotel, AT&T tries on its antitrust suit, Diane von Furstenburg shows her latest line of slacks. And, finally, in the sportscast two big plastic bombs named Johnny and Ivan, one in a baseball cap and one in a fur hat, knock each other out. Zaloom is like a delighted infant turning his toys into soldiers, animating them not only with his hands but also with the steady stream of surprising bleeps, buzzes, blams, and vrooms that issue from the same mouth that produces a serious news commentary. The collision of objects creates a string of concise visual metaphors, while the collision of personae makes our current events as absurd as child's play.

Village Voice, February 1, 1983

Music to Play By
(David Van Tieghem / Performances from the 1960s)

For David Van Tieghem, making music is "playing" in both senses. Van Tieghem is a percussionist who turns every conceivable object into an instrument to be played; he coaxes sounds from things with a childlike spirit of delighted discovery. In fact, *Message Received . . . Proceed Accordingly* is part of Van Tieghem's series (ongoing since 1977) called *A Man and His Toys. Message Received . . .* was an hour and a half of pure pleasure, given form by a vague narrative based on science fiction film clichés. The narrative disappeared during virtuoso rhythmic digressions—the fragmentation became part of the pleasure, an overtone of mystery.

The evening began with the screening of a videotape, *Ear to the Ground,* by John Sanborn and Kit Fitzgerald, which featured Van Tieghem roaming the city and, with his drumsticks and his rangy pace, turning the urban landscape into a one-man percussion orchestra. He beat the bars of metal fences, sounded glass panes and concrete pavement, stopped in a phone booth to make the telephone ring in time to the beat. When the tape ended, Van Tieghem stepped onto the stage, dressed in white overalls, to begin an odyssey that traced a path among the multifarious things piled on long tables on the stage. He whirled bull-roarers, played bowls of various materials, set toys walking and whirring, talked and joined himself on tape creating audio illusions. And he danced. Van Tieghem can use his feet and his lanky body as effectively as any instrument. He parodied a Spanish dance, quoted Fred Astaire's famous firecracker dance, and did a little breakdown on plastic bubblewrap. Loping along the floor, he did a perfect imitation of an ape and then, as *Thus Spake Zarathustra* thundered over the speakers, created a new gloss on *2001* as he discovered—and gradually mastered—a pair of drumsticks.

Although Van Tieghem's inspiration is the child's polymorphous perverse pleasure in sounds, shapes, and textures of all kinds, his performance was anything but primitive. Commanding the proscenium stage at an uptown theater, he reveled in a sophisticated, high-tech riot of huge speakers and Las Vegas lights. Part of his humor comes from the incongruity of the childlike antics in such an adult setting. Part of it comes from his impeccable timing, and yet another part comes from the constant stream of surprising objects set into play. And mixed with that wit is a confident, generous presence that shares with the audience an expansive sense of wonder and—new for Van Tieghem—the elusive suggestion of a coherent storyline.

The past few years have seen a flurry of reconstructions of dances and performances from the recent past. Maybe it's the acute historical consciousness of the current generation of spectators, critics, and even artists; maybe it's the conservatism of the times that has brought so many best hits back from the past. I'm glad all the reconstructions are happening even though they can lack the evanescence and vitality crucial to the time arts. I was especially glad to see "Performances from the 1960s" at P.S. 1, curated by William Hellermann, which made me think a thing or two about the 1960s. They were also, many of them, impressive performances in their own rights.

People talk about performance art as having moved from the art world to the music world over the past decade. Yet the P.S. 1 reconstructions showed a long-standing emphasis on sound that ranged from Malcolm Goldstein's thoughtful interpretations (on violin) of pieces by John Cage, Philip Corner, James Tenney, Christian Wolff, and himself to John Giorno's chanted poetry to Simone Forti's dance that is an accompaniment to music by La Monte Young. Ed Sanders, one of the memorable Fugs, sang his earliest composition—William Blake's "Song" set to a humble tune—and one of the Fugs' notorious songs, "My Baby Done Left Me (And I Feel like Homemade Shit)." He also performed some more recent songs of his own, including a protest against nuclear reactors and a moving plea against getting burned out—"Nolti in Spiritu Combueri," as it translates into Latin.

Almost all the pieces also incorporated the body in a way that reminded me how physical the arts were in the 1960s. Carolee Schneemann's *Noise Bodies* (originally performed with James Tenney, here with Bruce McPherson) was part fight, part loveplay between a man and a woman decked out with metal and ceramic attachments. As they "attacked" each other with sticks, they played music. The process didn't turn them into disembodied musical instruments though, but amplified their physicality and sexuality. Corner's *Pulse* dictated a musical tempo set by the performer taking his pulse (Goldstein explained that, since he had a fever that day, the piece would be exceptionally fast), and Cage's

Solo for Violin I called for grunts, breaths, and other sounds produced by the musician's body, besides those made on the violin. Sanders played his songs on two homemade instruments, one of them a synthesizer that involved passing the fingers through beams cast by flashlight bulbs to create musical notes. Giorno's "Suicide Sutra" involved the audience in a physical experience of being uptight. And Simone Forti's two dances, *Rollers* and *Accompaniment to La Monte's "2 sounds" and La Monte's "2 sounds"* were simple but profound experiences of the body in action. In the first, six volunteers from the audience pulled the two performers (Forti and David Appel), who sat in two wooden carts, around the space. They seemed almost like small vulnerable animals as they were pulled to and fro, their chants expressing mounting anxiety as the pullers whipped them around the space. In *Accompaniment . . .* , Forti stands in a rope loop, wound and suspended from the ceiling, and slowly revolves until the loop hangs straight; Young's piece is composed of the scraping of ashtrays across a mirror, amplified. It was remarkable in its understatement. Forti's concentration is like no one else's. As she turned in a slow-motion pirouette and, finally, just stood there in air, listening to the crashing sounds, her silent there-ness became radiant.

Village Voice, February 15, 1983

Laurie Anderson's Disjointed "States"

Like its subject, Anderson's *United States* is monumental (eight hours long, BAM Opera House, heavy technology) and frequently dull. It has its funny, clever, and breathtaking moments. But its epic proportions, its ambition, and its publicity make you expect more. It raises the old question: does a novel about a boring life have to be boring? Must a performance about a trivial culture—or the trivial aspects of a very complex culture—be as shallow and pretentious as the life it describes?

In fact, Anderson doesn't seem to intend her form to so neatly fit her content. Part of her pomposity is a deliberately profound stance. Every song is an epiphany. And the revelations embrace all the serious sides of life: work, religion, politics, love (a little), and, especially, language. It is the semiotic gap that lies at the root of many of Anderson's story/songs—the multiple ways our verbal language, gesture codes, and other sign systems either misfire or are misunderstood, so communication jams. There is, for instance, the vacuous chatter of "New York Social Life," in which artists never have anything more to say to one another than "Hi! How are ya? Let's have lunch, maybe next week." There is the interrogation of "Steven Weed," in which two FBI agents sit to Weed's left and right, so that by looking at them as they alternately fire questions, he is always, in effect, saying no. There is the impossibility of understanding Parisians in "Beginning French." All of these situations have their moment of truth, but, as Anderson reels them out endlessly, her mock-dumb astonishment at cognitive dissonance ceases to seem sophisticated. You see the punchline coming as soon as the situation is set up.

In a broader sense Anderson's songs reveal a persona who—like Spalding Gray—travels incessantly, on a latter-day pilgrimage, but who finds everywhere only the absurdities of human life. Yet, unlike Gray, who revels in unexpected behavior and delights in solving the mysteries of unfamiliar social rules, Anderson is repelled by the strangeness of how the world works, by other people's habits. Her pilgrimage is a lonely one; the landscape she discovers is alien and desolate. Not until part 4 is a single song concerned with love (since Anderson's performance emulates that of a rock singer, the absence of love as a topic is both striking and distinctive), but, when she does sing about it, love is also either something foreign people do, as in "Hothead (La Langue d'Amour)," a parody of an anthropological film; or something perverse, as in "Song for Two Jims," about an incestuous Appalachian family; or something to be repudiated, as in "I No Longer Love Your Mouth." The photographs and films often depict the American landscape as an ominous setting for a science fiction film.

"Big Science" could be seen as Anderson's theme song, a pun that mixes futuristic musings about technology with projections of street signs. Like the Pop artists of the 1960s, Anderson borrows both the mindless content and the slick style of the mass media. Her images come from televisions and computers; her voice is electronically altered in various ways, but even naked it sounds like the voice of a microchip. But Pop Art, with its gaudy colors, huge objects, and rich textures, celebrated American life even as it poked ironic criticism at U.S. politics, economics, and popular culture. There was a vitality in the Pop Art images that came from all sorts of bodily references. In Anderson's work the body is etherealized, made miniscule by costuming (black), the unimaginative use of space and lighting, the amplification of the voice, the slide and film projections, and the insistence on language. The references to popular culture are eerie and empty, rather than vibrant. They desiccate, rather than vitalize, the world they describe.

Yet some of the most powerful songs in *United States* quote from 1930s culture, rather than 1980s. The big band sound, which appears more often in parts 3 and 4, is impressive (David Van Tieghem's drumming is a major contribution here) in such songs as "Example #22" and "Blue Lagoon," both of which also feature saxophones (Chuck Fisher, Bill Obrecht, and Rufus Harley), OBXa and Synclavier (Ann DeMarinis), and the voice of an elegant soprano singer (Shelley Carson). Graphic imagery from the 1930s crops up throughout the four sections. Some of Anderson's appeal has to do with her technology/futurism hype, but some of it also has to do with depression nostalgia.

The question of Anderson's appeal has become an important one because she is the first performance artist to hit the big time, with Warner Brothers recording *United States: Parts I–IV* and Harper and Row publishing the text. Other performers have worked on a scale as large as hers—everyone who's appeared on the BAM Opera House stage, to name a few—and other performers mix musical savvy with high-tech visual media. But Anderson trades on the intersection of several factors. The more her act resembles a rock band, the easier it is for her young audiences to love (and it has grown more and more like a rock band). The subjects of her songs *are* our real and present concerns. And the ambiguity of her stance toward these topics (half-embracing, half-censuring) lets you make whatever you want of what she has to say. In the end she says nothing, but in such a seductive package.

Village Voice, February 22, 1983

Motions: Eccentric and Burning

(Pooh Kaye / Joan Jonas)

Pooh Kaye and Joan Jonas share certain strategies as performance makers. Both use a variety of means: task activities, objects, dancing, film. Both are interested in magic and in mythic structures but locate these themes in specifically urban, modern cultures. Yet the meanings of their two recent performances could not be more distinct. Kaye's work is all about sensation; Jonas's is about perception.

Kaye's concert consisted of her solo, *Homelife of a Wildgirl,* a new group piece, *Eccentric Motions,* and a film-in-progress (with Elizabeth Ross), *Sticks on the Move.* The "wildgirl" is Kaye's stylistic hallmark—a combination infant, kitten, and rodent, who wriggles, clambers up a small brick structure, spits, spouts water, builds pathways, stuffs bricks into a pouchlike T-shirt, and watches films of herself burrowing into a mattress at double speed. Like a child, she is curious about the textures, smells, and movements of things around her; like an animal, she savors her sensations untrammeled by social rules. Hers is a preverbal, paradisaic universe in which communication takes the form of squeals and grunts (in the film, by Jana Haimsohn). *Eccentric Motions* spreads these images among a group: Yvonne Meier, Brian Moran, Nelson Zayas, Susan Brown, M. J. Becker, and Kaye herself. Where in the solo one sensed a narrative building from the actions of approaching the brick structure, playing in it, pulling it apart, and leaving it, in the group piece the action is less logical and more diffuse. The performers (one could think of them as players) manipulate wooden posts in a variety of ways. Yet their range of actions transcends, for instance, the factual manipulations of the analytic postmodern dancers and the related down-to-earth, anti-illusionist objects of the Minimalist sculptors. The posts are not simply structural devices. As the piece opens, two men, in the dark, hold two posts that are smoldering with burning embers. That light, in the darkness, creates a sense of mystery and then danger. Later, the entire group gnaws the huge sticks and spits out splinters. The motions are eccentric, but they are the motions of a community, albeit outcast, not the motions of aberrant individuals.

Sticks on the Move is simply a delight. It is a trick film in which the outdoor light changes rapidly from day to night, people chase sticks and sticks chase people, and, finally, the humans and the objects team up for uncanny feats of locomotion. As in Kaye's short, pixilated wildgirl films, speed creates humor, but here that effect is amplified by a sustained sense of the mystery of things themselves.

The opening film in *Homelife of a Wildgirl,* showing a brook in a forest where Kaye bounces erratically, sets the scene for the live action, and the second film, in which Kaye scurries around a New York loft, transfers the action from a natural setting to a cultural one. Thus, Kaye creates a salutary overlay of the holistic environment that serves as compensation for the spectators. Her red grass skirt may hang on the Kitchen's white column, but through the performance we can see that column as a tree. Joan Jonas's use of recorded images, on film, and closed-circuit video, have the opposite effect; rather than creating an imaginary environment, they build a mental space, and they subvert images by artificially constructing and deconstructing them. Jonas, too, shows us a film of a forest, this time with a lake. But, as the film changes from black-and-white to color, what we are privileged to sense is *that we see.*

He Saw Her Burning continues many of Jonas's favored themes: the problems of perception, memory, and the symbol-making processes of the mind. Thus, one powerful difference between Kaye and Jonas is the latter's use of language both in terms of text and in terms of verbal images. Kaye emphasizes the sensory qualities of her objects: their texture, weight, smell, sound. Jonas not only emphasizes the most intellectual of the senses—vision—but also uses her objects as things saturated with cognitive and social meaning. We are shown these objects at first bereft of context, but, as the fragmented narrative progresses, we fit them together like pieces of a puzzle and triumph as we endow them with sense. A huge red fan that Jonas slowly moves and the diaphanous red dress Y Sa Lo wafts around her as she turns in place become, by the end of the hour, metaphors for "fanning the flames." These are only two in a complex stream of symbols that Jonas generates in the course of her movement through the real space, through that space as re-perceived by us on the video monitors, and in bringing to the space two other performers seen only on the video screen. *He Saw Her Burning* is based on two recent news stories. In one an American soldier steals a tank and wreaks havoc in the German city of Mannheim, before he and the tank topple into the river. In the other a woman spontaneously bursts into flames and burns to death, while a witness watches from his car. The actions and words of the man and woman (Shawn Lawton and Y Sa Lo) on the video screens make the stories resound and overlap. "If each one witnessed the other's crisis, which came first?" Jonas asks at one point. The alluring mass-media presentation of the man and woman as key witnesses, newscasters, commentators, contrasts with the low-key live presence of Jonas, whose persona (often masked) is part storyteller, part charlatan. She shows us pictures: "What does this remind you of?" she asks, but as we watch each picture breaks apart to become something else. And we see these images seeming whole over the video screen even as we can watch the mechanics of her sleight of hand under the video camera right in front of us. She builds mysteries for us to puzzle our way through, made vivid by "clues" like the brightly painted cutout tank and car, her dances with gold clubs and flags, the fragments of intense, often festive music, a story about a hunted seal. Ultimately, the subject of Jonas's performance becomes its very form. *He Saw Her Burning* is not so much about the incidents it describes but about their theoretical implications. Where Kaye gleefully presents the mysteries of the human body, Jonas meditates on the mysteries of the mind.

Village Voice, March 8, 1983

Sentimental Journeys

(Peter Rose / Vanalyne Green)

Halfway through *Berlin Zoo* Peter Rose sings a spiritual, "I Am a Pilgrim." That moment sums up the theme of Rose's performances, yet his pilgrimage is anything but traditional. His way is neither docile nor well traveled but a quest that mixes headstrong curiosity with willful outsiderhood in quite unsacred places. In a manic, anecdotal monologue Rose recounts his (mis)adventures while looking for a place to spend the night in Berlin, beginning with his being booted out of the theater he had hoped to perform then sleep in, and continuing with a circus, an empty lot that serves as a memorial to would-be escapees from East Berlin, a Salvation Army hostel, a jail. He interrupts himself to illustrate the narrative or comment on it with songs, with readings from James Joyce and Georg Büchner, with a dialogue between himself and the theater manager outraged by Rose's props, with another scene, between himself and the cops who arrest him for stealing his landlady's Volkswagen, with spirited dances in a faintly Yiddish manner. And throughout he accompanies his narrative with simple, graphic gestures underlining the meaning of his earnest, propulsive patter.

Rose's earnestness is both his strength and the source of the flaws in his performance. In *Berlin Zoo* the literal gestures are motivated by the subject: Rose's difficulty in making himself understood in a foreign culture. Yet the gestures soon became a cloying mannerism. As Rose experiences his Jewishness and the memory of Nazism, through the Yiddish songs he becomes a yeshiva boy, his arms dangling from a skinny torso that dips back awkwardly from the pelvis. In the songs and the dancing (the musical accompaniment is by Noah Shapiro), Rose sparkles.

Like the pigeons Rose watches throwing themselves against the glass dome of the railway station or like the hero of Büchner's novel, Rose is split between seeking salvation and beating his head against a wall. He looks for love, freedom, and the rootedness of history in places mired in hatred, repression, poverty, and the memory of suffering. His ecstasy is pain transcended, and in performance he stands witness, his vision so clear and bright that he reminds us of a Dostoyevskian "simpleton" who alone understands what is good.

Vanalyne Green's *Trick or Drink* is another kind of testimonial, about a childhood scarred by alcoholism. She stands at a microphone coolly describing scenes of her parents' violence, physical illness, and deterioration then analyzing the effects on her body and soul. As slides flash by on the screen, we see how Green's adolescent obsession with dieting was not that of the average American girl of the 1960s but a neurotic by-product of her mother's alcoholic obesity. Gradually, she discovers that her obsession is turning into a full-blown case of bulimia and that she could cause her own death by suffocation, ironically the cause of her mother's death, although brought on by exactly the opposite problem.

In the course of *Trick or Drink* Green talks about attending meetings for relatives of alcoholics and the therapeutic value of confession in those meetings. The performance is modeled so closely on that mode of confession that it is almost unbearable. On the one hand, the material is devastating. On the other, Green's coolness seems phony and, rather than distancing the material and (for instance) making a generalized political statement, she creates a mood of self-pity that is undercut by the evidence. As Green complains that she has no family, no experience of love, no hope for the future, we see her before us, good-looking and confident. We see the slides of her beautiful loft and her handsome boyfriend, who helped her put on this performance. Her childhood was an especially cruel and violent one. But her sense of loneliness is surely not unique. If Rose, stepping outside of society, becomes sentimental when he finds redemption always shining through the rubble of urban life, Green becomes sentimental in another way, insisting that society has stepped away from her and making that complaint her salvation.

Village Voice, April 5, 1983

Body Talk

(Luigi Ontani / Cheri Gaulke)

Human presence is the crux of performance art; the human body *is* presence. Both Ontani's and Gaulke's works centered on the meaning of that mysterious, inescapable, polysemous entity—the body. But, unlike much body art of the 1970s, these performances were not intended to demystify corporeality by, for instance, making physical demands on the performer or presenting physical feats in a matter-of-fact way. Rather, both Ontani and Gaulke used their bodies as the foundation—in a literal sense—on which to construct a set of metaphors about physicality. It was not the body itself but ideas about the body their performances displayed.

After nearly half an hour's wait in a crowded vestibule, the audience was admitted to Ontani's tableau vivant, Bal'occhi. He lay on a circular ground, its borders marked with rocks. His body was covered with Balinese masks. One was on his face, a long-nosed red visage with lips that clacked with the regularity of a metronome. But the rest were on less conventional sites. A foot and calf were covered by another red mask that was half-boot, half-house. Another foot became the pale face of a creature that seemed like a water nymph. Ontani's breathing animated the mask that covered his belly and extended downward to act as a codpiece.

On two opposite sides of the room enormous slide projections showed two identical eyes in black and white; the reflections of light in their gigantic pupils took on the shape of a room with windows. Smaller slide projections circled the outspread figure on the floor and embellished each white column flanking the central tableau. These images changed every few seconds, showing delicate drawings of figures and emblems, often expanding the symbolism of the masks. After about ten minutes the slides ended, the lights went out, and the performance ended.

Ontani's performance was intriguing, even though it was flawed. Some of the problems had to do with its presentation. There were no chairs in the room, yet most viewers sat down on the rim of the circle. But, since the tableau was both stationary and circular, the seated audience could get only a partial view. Yet it was impossible, for those of us who wanted to circumambulate, to get close enough to the slide projections to incorporate their significance into the whole piece. Perhaps the piece should have been scheduled as an installation, with fewer people viewing it at one time and encouraged to walk around and through it. The imagery of the masks was powerfully suggestive, recalling the odd, symbolic disguises of certain Italian Renaissance parades, entries, and ballets. Yet it needed to be buttressed by systems of imagery more assertive than the flowery drawings—physical action, perhaps, or competing sets of masks—in order to develop its complex metaphor of the body as house/window/eye/image. In fact, the title, a series of puns on the Italian words for *eye, dance, toy,* and *pretty* (and, perhaps, *Bali*), suggests that antic movement could have enriched the associations.

Gaulke's piece, *This Is My Body,* was a series of eight tableaux. Four wooden shelves were attached to a white wall, roughly forming a cross. With the help of a ladder and a hooded assistant, Gaulke in different states of dress and undress climbed onto the shelves, to fit into a series of images projected on the wall with slides. Title slides with quotations from the Bible and from feminist literature and a taped score of autobiographical and other readings as well as popular, religious, and ritual music, all supplied a context for the tableaux.

As she entered, in turn, a fifteenth-century Flemish painting of Adam and Eve, a photograph of herself at four years old in church with her minister father, a seventeenth-century engraving of a public hanging of witches, or a Botticelli *Pieta,* Gaulke became a series of incarnations: a serpent, Eve, a child, a preacher, a witch, Christ. In an imagined correspondence with her father, as well as in the changing visual settings, she obsessively explored the guilt-ridden connections between her own religious and sexual feelings. The body, of course, is the central mystery of both those systems.

Gaulke's tableaux each used body movement or appearance to underscore the uncomfortable presence of the body in Christian theology. As Eve, she bumped and ground her hips, while she lustily ate from two apples at once. As the serpent, she wriggled in the tree and later, in the final tableau, became a kind of belly-dancing Middle Eastern priestess/serpent, fanning branches with convulsive arm movements. As Christ, she writhed on the Cross, tore at her skin, then became healed as the old woman rubbed her supine body in the *Pieta.*

Gaulke's performance was skillfully done. The blending of live and projected imagery and the way the shelves fit into the different pictures were striking aspects of her stagecraft. And, of course, her subject was an explosive one. Yet the juxtaposition of elements never cohered; the autobiographical obsessions never took on the historical scope demanded by the texts (both visual and written); the didactic tone never came to focus on any clear lessons. The piece often seemed to build toward a repudiation, but whether it would be of religion, of heterosexuality, or of male culture generally was never resolved.

Village Voice, April 19, 1983

Stuart Sherman's Good Time

An entire genre of performance art is devoted to the manipulation of small objects by solo performers, with varying effects and meanings. Paul Zaloom manically piles and pitches toys as his rapid-fire monologues add political commentary. David Van Tieghem joyously teases sounds of all sorts out of toys, bowls, bottles, and other things. Stuart Sherman's operations are much more concentrated and controlled than Zaloom's or Van Tieghem's. The power of Sherman's images lies in an odd friction between the completeness of their patterns and the unexpectedness of their links. All three of these performers share an infantile pleasure in the surprising capacities and hitherto unthought-of uses of everyday items. Sherman adds an obsessive note to performance style that is midway between childlike absorption and scientific experiment.

Yet, as he sets up his blocks, sticks, ribbons, boxes, and grids on his small black collapsible table, puts them into surprising relationships, and then unravels the image he has just built, Sherman, unlike a scientist, has achieved no product. That he does complicated maneuvers only to undo them, that he labors seriously with no material result, and that these connections between categories appear both compulsory and arbitrary, all give the performance the look of a game, a ritual, or a magician's act. But, of course, it is not exactly any of these things. Unlike a magician, Sherman doesn't mask his maneuvers, smooth his gestures, or pull sleights of hand. In fact, his mundane, perfunctory way of doing things paradoxically adds to the sense of wonder he generates. All the materials for a particular image are there from the start; there are no hidden compartments, false bottoms, or sudden appearances. And yet out of these materials a series of associations is built that casts them in a new, intriguing light. Unlike a ritual, Sherman's segmented, symbolic behavior effects no social transformations.

Sherman's *Thirteenth Spectacle* is "about" time in the broadest possible sense. Symbolic images refer to processes that manifest the passage of time: eating, shaving, walking, traveling, building, weather. As in Sherman's films and other spectacles, the images arrive through a series of abstractions, acausal associations, correspondences, and miniaturizations. Sherman opens a flashlight. Instead of a battery, out falls a smaller version of the flashlight. When he opens this flashlight, we're primed to expect a tinier, third flashlight, but, instead, a wooden match appears. In another vignette he opens what looks like a travel alarm-clock case. Inside are five concentric squares, orange on one side and green on the other. He sets them up in a graduated order, opens an orange placed next to them, reveals a green apple inside it, and turns each square around. Now a green orange encloses an orange apple. Sherman takes out a Hershey bar and bites into it. Now the entire sequence is repeated with black squares and fruits. Finally, he coughs and then sneezes. The chain of events gives the impression of cause-and-effect, but the logic of causality has evaporated.

In one of the loveliest sections Sherman turns his table so that its orientation to the spectators is perpendicular. Across it he sets out a set of black sticks, a set of clear Plexiglas rods, and two cutouts of a house. He "builds" the house, inserting the sticks and rods into holes in the cutouts, which are now held apart. Sherman puts a tape in the cassette player beside him; the sound of rain is heard. He opens the umbrella over the house and lifts it. The clear rods slip down, like needles of rain. A new tape plays the sounds of wind. Sherman places a tiny image of the house atop the umbrella. As in a verbal metaphor, several meanings are condensed into a single object; the sound of rain lets us see the rods as both walls and raindrops.

Part of what is gamelike about Sherman's performance is his use of implements used in games. He throws small cubes covered with patterns of black or red whorls as though they were dice. But they have identical digits on all six sides, and later he uses them like jacks. A grid like a checkerboard has numbers on some of its squares and small red cars on others. Gamelike, too, are the arbitrary lists of numbers, times of day, names of food, snatches of songs in the various sections of the work. Perhaps *puzzle* is a better word to describe the images, for in them everything seems to interlock, both literally and metaphorically, as objects enclose other objects, items fit snugly into cutout shapes, and symbols meet up with their referents.

The thorough, symmetrical patterns and the economy of means are extremely satisfying, and the subtle wit of the images, their absurd logic, and their brisk resolutions all add to the pleasure. Sherman's concision was especially evident in his *Portrait of John Cage*. He set up a tape recorder and turned on the microphone, laid out a paper keyboard slotted with narrow holes, marked the slots, cut strips of magnetic tape to fit the slots, lifted off the keyboard, and, with a stopwatch, "timed" each strip. And that was that.

Village Voice, May 3, 1983

Housebroken

(Nightfire Theater)

The program notes tell us right away that *Obedience School* is an analysis of control whose elements are "training, decision making under pressure, fear, sex, and devotion." With that said, you don't have to search too far for the meaning in the string of images presented through live action, architecture, recorded voice and music, and video. In fact, the program notes seem redundant, even condescending, since every image is so tightly focused and simple to read. The meaning floats on the surface of the work.

The piece begins as the audience is seated in a steep bank looking down on the playing space. On several video monitors, high above the stage, we are introduced to the characters—a model (Deborah Myers Marcom), who puts on red lipstick and smiles, and a pilot (Bill De Young), who checks his blood pressure. Both the characters and their actions have the smooth, seamless, fictitious look of advertisements. But then the houselights dim, and the same figures, with their illusion of perfection, appear live onstage. Both characters live out their lives on a light-studded runway. The pilot taxis a toy plane down it; the model, brandishing her flawless smile, paces it herself, posing, turning, and gesturing with perfunctory chic. Later, in a bathing suit as red as her lipstick, the model mixes drinks, grills a hamburger, and feeds her husband—the pilot—on a little square of Astroturf. They drink, dance, and smile with the mechanical poise of Disneyland robots. Then they become robots out of control when she stuffs the half-cooked hamburger into his mouth, as if their humanness could only be expressed by their most bestial appetites.

The model has three dreams, indicated by abstract imagery and video game signals on the monitors. All of the dreams tell how the model tried to build the perfect house but failed. She wants to settle down and have a baby. She is afraid her husband's plane will crash. He wants her to be his beautiful showpiece. She takes a shower, and he, disguised with a dog's head, rapes her. Their rift widens as they argue, she thinking the attacker was a stranger. He plays the concerned husband and buys a watchdog. She protests that they already have a dog, that it was just an accident, that it won't happen again.

At other times the video monitors show actions taking place in a larger, real-world place, while the actors use models of objects (airplane, house, dog) to simulate those actions on a miniature scale. Ironically, their "model" lives on television are fuller and realer—even though we know the information on the videotape is artificially constructed and canned—and the live action of the performance becomes either false, distorted, or symbolic.

There is a third actor in the performance, the Technician (Ray Myslewski). As his role suggests, he is a nearly invisible presence. He keeps things going. He helps move the scenery, including not only the runway but also two futuristic ziggurats and free-standing venetian blinds that cast an ominous striped shadow during the rape scene. (Brian Mulhern designed both sets and lights.)

In terms of its production *Obedience School* was impressive, even though many of its elements were reminiscent of the work of other performance makers, from Richard Foreman to Carolee Schneemann to Spalding Gray and Elizabeth LeCompte. But where, for instance, the nudity and deadpan voices in Foreman's work rub against complex verbal play, manic action, and visual imagery that ranges from the obsessively elegant to the funky and grotesque, and thus accrue powerful meanings, in *Obedience School* they simply seem to be theatrical devices.

Is it that very impressiveness that may be *Obedience School's* fatal flaw. It is as cool, self-contained, and forbidding as its hero and heroine. There is no thread of subversiveness. Thus, it seems less a *study* of control—which would imply a critique of the systems it employs—than a surface-level display that takes no stand. The fears and desires of these Disneyland creatures seem trivial, like the emotions in True Romance comics. Whatever control they exert or submit to lacks power. In a sense this is a Pop Art performance. But in the context of the 1960s that imagery pulled many punches. In the 1980s it simply seems an anachronism without affect.

Village Voice, June 7, 1983

Strong and Sexy

(Trix Rosen)

The men in the audience press closer despite the stuffy heat. The women are more reluctant, fascinated in spite of themselves, looking and not looking. With the setup on the ground floor of Danceteria badly equipped for theatrical events (i.e., there's a raised stage but no seating), the sweating, impatient crowd has become animalistic even before the spectacle begins; one can't help thinking of ancient Rome.

Onstage a group of young women take their turns posing and dancing. Dressed in scanty bikinis, each one creates her particular character within the conventions of a highly formulaic performance. All the women proudly face front, show their backs, lift one leg then the other, lunge, lift an arm, roll their hips and bellies. But, depending on the mood of the musical accompaniment and the nuances of energy, gesture, and facial expression, this one is innocent, this one shy, this one lascivious, this one mysterious, this one a jock. And yet . . . the more one watches, the more the differences seem merely superficial. Only one image is created in the course of this evening, in this peculiar form of performance that has ensconced itself somewhere in between go-go dancing, aerobics, beauty contests, and athletic competitions. These are women body-builders, the subject of Trix Rosen's book *Strong and Sexy*. And, although they wear the psychological trappings of diverse characters, each one is ultimately there to represent herself as an embodiment of a new idea of femininity: both muscular and seductive.

At the performance and in the book Rosen tells about these specimens of a new breed—about their daily exercise regimens, their diets, their jobs, their love lives, and their unabashed pride in their self-made bodies. The author fashions a philosophy for an entire lifestyle by fusing feminist and capitalist rhetoric and using it in its most shallow sense. For instance, one of the epigraphs in the book quotes Harriet Hosmer, a nineteenth-century sculptor and mountain climber. "I honor every woman who has strength enough to step out of the beaten path when she feels that her walk lies in another; strength enough to stand up and be laughed at if necessary. . . . But in a few years it will not be thought strange that women should be preachers and sculptors, and everyone who comes after us will have to bear fewer and fewer blows."

Although women like Hosmer, Isadora Duncan, and others may have fought for and practiced physical liberation as an integral part of women's social, psychological, and political emancipation, certainly they did not mean that the key to that freedom is to be literally (physically) strong. By allying her subjects (and herself) with the feminist movement, Rosen claims an entire network of social gains. But that logic is flawed; a thing isn't necessarily good just because a woman succeeds at it, nor is a woman better just because she does something (anything) women don't usually do. The premise behind *Strong and Sexy* is yet another example (like women corporation executives) of feminism backfiring. The only thing it shows about women is that they are as capable of narcissism, hedonism, and acquisition as men are.

In a way body-building is a perfect reflection of the American dream, of the Horatio Alger myth—and of an attitude toward physicality that marks the 1980s. If in the 1960s we wanted to free the body—to let go—today we are no less obsessed by our anatomy, but our approach is just the opposite. In an age of economic expansion one could afford to drop out; in these hard times no one is embarrassed by ambition and control. One of the cheapest and most convenient things to master is one's body. So it's not surprising that, contra the "natural" beauty of the 1960s, current fashion demands an appearance that is fully constructed, a body that is reimagined, padded, dyed, trimmed, molded, decorated, and pumped up. The quintessential rhetoric of body-building for both men and women, moreover, promises that, just as you can make over your own body, you can attain any goal you set your sights on. Or vice versa. "Go for it!" screams every movie, magazine, and TV show, as if one could overcome the knots of human social relations by gritting one's teeth, in exactly the same way one achieves one's thousandth sit-up. You can literally shape your own destiny, the body-building system vouches; you can start out with just the same resources as the next person, and, if you work hard enough, you can collect sets of muscles and invest in them until you become the physical equivalent of a millionaire. And, what's more, you get a high that's better than drugs.

In the 1960s and 1970s everyone started looking for ways to be physically fit. But body-building pushes exercise beyond its salubrious functions, turning it into yet another specialized, competitive profession. The gym absorbs one's entire life. "I live in a world unto itself," one of Rosen's subjects exults. Perhaps only a dancer spends as much time and sweat in the masturbatory preoccupation with the body's condition and appearance. But the dancer's obsession is the unfortunate by-product of a larger artistic goal. What makes body-building so narcissistic is that the self-absorption it requires doesn't go anywhere; its end *is* its means.

As befit the political temper of the 1960s and 1970s, a tendency toward androgyny gave men feminine attributes like long hair and a gentle demeanor. The androgyny of the 1980s inspires women to cut their hair short and look big-shouldered, rough, and tough. Is that what feminism has won for us? Body-building is a way for women to "get hard," just like a man. But I suspect, given the reactions in the Danceteria crowd, that, the pseudofeminist rhetoric notwithstanding, it's just a 1980s piquant version of the come-hither.

Unpublished, June 1983

New Primitive Mysteries

(Ellen Fisher / Diane Torr)

These performances had so much in common that it seems an entire genre is upon us. Both Ellen Fisher and Diane Torr used cabarets as venues, although Fisher had cleared out the tables at Plexus to use the largest possible space to move around in, whereas Torr capitalized on the cramped, seedy stage and runway at S.n.a.f.u. Both projected a romantic-atavistic vision of female sexuality. But a more fundamental common thread, as place and theme suggest, was the mixture of "low" and "high" art, not only in terms of subject matter but also in terms of style and form—in the use of popular entertainments from go-go dancing to television to circus, recombined in a new context. References to punk style underscored this mix.

In *Spectre Nymph* Fisher appears as a kind of dayglow yellow fawn, with antlers, red lipstick, a halter top, pedal-pushers, and long gloves that turn her hands into hooves. She prances into a pastel landscape of yellow and pink chicken-wire clouds and a bright-green fake grass rug. She gambols to the sound of pygmy flutes, a cross between Bambi and Nijinsky's Faun. Suddenly, she becomes aware of a large noose that hangs from the ceiling. It works on her like a magical fetish, drawing her out of her narcissistic fascination with her own body and enticing her to play with it. The music changes to a percussive beat that builds excitement. As the Spectre Nymph contemplates the seductive noose, she stands, glows, and seems to grow into a powerful, muscular superhuman. She dances in awe around the rope and, after a few false attempts to enter the loop— once it takes her around the neck and almost strangles her—she mounts it authoritatively and rides it ecstatically, swinging and flying and twisting as she barely grazes ceiling and floor. Her gyrations are a source of both delight and terror for the viewer, as every shift in her position seems to threaten a fall and every new oscillation, a crash. But for the Spectre Nymph the ride is pure, peaking pleasure and at last, sated, she dismounts. Perhaps the noose worship dance went on too long and smacked too uncomfortably of pseudoprimitive posturing. But the odd mixture of the other elements in *Spectre Nymph*—the transformation of character from animal-child to intergalactic Spectre Woman, the tongue-in-cheek eroticism, and the homemade circus act that was just as dazzling as the real thing—made it both unpretentious and pleasurably ambiguous.

Fisher's second piece, *Living Set,* begins with a cartoon horror film. The film draws us closer and closer to what seems to be a haunted house. Just as the camera eye is about to enter the house, Fisher draws aside the curtain it was projected on to let us inside the "real" house. There, a punk housewife, she slithers over the furniture, violently arranges her plants, and watches a TV that casts out not only light but some kind of malevolent force. Fisher grimaces, shrinks, and crumples with such magnified, melodramatic facial expressions that you can almost see her hair stand up on end. Finally, the spirit of the TV takes over and Fisher enters a nirvana-like state of possession, sitting atop the set and serenely rippling hands and arms into sequences of mudras. As in *Spectre Nymph,* Fisher creates a sci-fi world in which objects have animistic powers and people are only one minor element, but there the intimations are paradisiacal, while here the interaction between objects and people chills.

In *Amoebic Evolution* Torr creates a different kind of fantastic biology. Dressed in a suit and lit in green, she slithers from the door of the bar and climbs up to the stage. She is a macho businessman, a travel agent, posturing and rolling a toy airplane along his desk. The man takes off his jacket and, as he slumps over his desk, a film projected on his white-shirted back shows a tiny dancer swirling her white dress into shapes à la Loie Fuller. The man recounts how, one day, he was so hot he surprised his secretary by taking off his jacket, then his tie, then his shirt, then his pants—and Torr disrobes as (s)he narrates. Dressed now in a gold lace evening dress she continues the narration, explaining that she changed from a man into a woman. After a belly dance atop the desk that scatters all the business accoutrements to the floor, she transforms again, nude except for golden straps circling her body, into a pregnant warrior-huntress. She dances and, reverting to total mammality, gets down on all fours to crawl away.

Go-Go World is a trenchant view of the profession of go-go dancing. Her body grotesquely padded with bright pink hips, breasts, navel, and labia, Torr gives a simple breakdown of how the sexual come-on in a go-go dance works. Reminding us to tip go-go dancers because, like waitresses, that's how they earn a living, she gives a quick rundown of the political situation in Europe, comparing each country to different kinds of go-go dancers—from England, who won't admit she is one, to Germany, who when she isn't onstage spends all her time in the toilet but somehow ends up with the biggest tips at the end of the night. In *Go-Go World* Torr is both funny and serious, seductive despite her absurd attire and down-to-earth about sexual entertainment as work. Her dancing is, in fact, very good; her analysis is even better.

Village Voice, June 21, 1983

Thought for Food

(Paul Schmidt)

Good Writing about Good Food was the final installment of the Manhattan Theatre Club's Writers in Performance series this season. Knowing Schmidt's work as an academic and as a translator from French and Russian, I expected a tasteful selection of extracts from those literatures: a good reading of good writing, and so on. I didn't know, but learned from the performance (and from Stockard Channing's friendly introduction), that Schmidt is an experienced actor and director, a good cook, a discriminating gourmet, and a reader of cookbooks. His idea of good writing about food embraces not only the great books of the West (from the Bible to Greek mythology to Tolstoy, Dickens, and Carroll) but such authors as Escoffier, Emily Post, Joan Crawford, the wives of U.S. congressmen, and poet Joe Brainard; his commentaries on the texts and on food and eating include nods to Barthes, Lévi-Strauss, and Foucault. But this was more than an intelligent, catholic reading. It was, as the program promised, an entertainment—witty and wise in both word and deed, a performance that gave body (appropriately enough) to descriptions of and instructions for eating. For of course, as Schmidt makes clear, eating is not something natural but an activity that our culture trains us to do—and often in ways that, given the distance of time or an aesthetic frame, look exceedingly strange.

Schmidt entered, a commanding, elegant figure in a white chef's uniform, complete with fluted hat, brandishing a silver carving knife. Recalling the story of Cain and Abel, he pointed out that food has long been associated not only with life but with death—in fact, with the first murder. And why, he pondered, did God accept Abel's offering of game instead of Cain's gift of fruit? Simply because of His bad luck in the past with that family and apples? He reminded us of Tantalus, punished by the gods for dismembering his own children and serving them up as a divine banquet, and sentenced to an eternity of finding his favorite foods just out of reach. Beckoning to his assistant (Bob Mellon), dressed as a waiter and carrying a silver-covered platter, Schmidt took a volume from the stack of books that proved hidden on the plate, and read us Escoffier's recipe for Turtle Soup, a gruesome enough account of dismemberment.

And yet there are recipes that are nonviolent. From the *Congressional Cookbook* came the directions for making Corn Pinwheel, which began, "Open a can of corn," and somewhat later instructed, "Open a package of frankfurters." Or Joan Crawford's recipe for wilted lettuce salad: "Add hot oil and vinegar until it sags." At least it avoids the knife.

But for Schmidt such recipes are the exception. Cooking usually involves some measure of violence, which, however, is justified because it is a means to a higher end: human communion. And here he read about two sorts of gatherings for dinner—those in restaurants, exemplified by the contrast between Levin and Oblonsky as they dine together in the restaurant to celebrate Levin's engagement in *Anna Karenina,* and those at home, illustrated by two passages from the 1924 edition of Emily Post's book on etiquette. The first was a dire fantasy of what might befall a young bride if she dared to give a dinner party without sticking to the rules and firmly overseeing her copious but inexperienced staff (i.e., social chaos); the second authoritatively laid down one small set of rules—those for setting the proper table. As Schmidt gave instructions, down to the number of candy dishes and vases of flowers, Mellon officiously furnished a perfectly set table for a formal dinner for one. And this was the setting for the second half of the show.

Dressed this time in formal dinner wear, Schmidt sat at his place at the table and mused on the grammar of the menu (from eggs to apples, even since Roman times), on the eroticism of oysters, on the way we "read a truffle like a text." If in the first half Schmidt played the role of chef/director, here he was pure performer, a charming, erudite dinner partner who gave the impression that every spectator was seated with him at an intimate table. A passage from *Brideshead Revisited* poked fun at those who value atmosphere and appearances in a restaurant over the taste of the food and thus, like the snobbish cousin in Waugh's novel, can't trust their own tastebuds to tell them the austere restaurant a poorer relative has brought them to is the best in Paris.

Here and in his reading of the Cratchits' goose dinner in *A Christmas Carol*—followed by a gloss on how that innocence and sense of family love would be ruined if the Cratchits earned more money, so that instead of sharing the work the servants did it, even down to the baking of the Christmas pudding—Schmidt became downright sentimental and romantic in his notions of class and taste. But a brilliant reading of the Mad Hatter's Tea Party more than made up for that, and when Schmidt returned to his opening themes—describing in gory detail the brutality involved in pressing a pressed duck and meditating on all the figures of speech in which ducks are victims, and, finally, in a truly moving double monologue, becoming Abel and Cain making their offerings and showing us how Cain's gift was refused because to grow fruit is to become too godlike—the evening felt satisfyingly full.

Schmidt's reading of food and eating takes a decidedly Europeanized, upper-class point of view, even though he often satirizes the elitist rules of the dinner game. This is obviously a tradition he can satirize because he knows it well and loves it. If he were to recount the "odd" eating habits of other cultures, perhaps he would only sound xenophobic. I'd love to hear a second installment with more robust passages, a more Gogolian perspective. (I think for instance, of the *nyanya* at Sobakievich's dinner in *Dead Souls*—sheep's stomach stuffed with buckwheat, brains, and trotters, served with cabbage soup.) But that would be an entirely different kettle of fish.

Village Voice, July 5, 1983

Bits and Pieces of Bogosian

(Eric Bogosian)

The dividing line between performance art and theater blurs when it comes to Eric Bogosian's work. This season you read the review of his latest piece, *FunHouse,* in the *Voice* theater section; last season you read a review of *Advocate* on this page. So I asked Bogosian to talk about what distinctions he sees between his work and the work of the dramatist. Is it the place that makes the difference? The length of the run? The structure of the "play"?

"I think for some people the difference between performance art and theater is a bigger question than it is for me," he mused. "I'm a performance artist, but now I'm performing in a regular theater, the Public Theater. One thing that means for me is that I can repeat my text and learn something about it. I was tired of doing something someplace once, then having it be over. Or even performing it one weekend. Now I've performed *FunHouse* four times, and it's just the beginning.

"I think of myself as an artist but an artist who makes constructions with theatrical tools. I'm not like the guy who writes a play that someone else can perform; *I'm* the one who goes through a series of personalities. But also, even though these personalities have a variety of points of view, the text isn't really a debate between different philosophies—otherwise, I would just write a play with characters and dialogue. My characters are there as context."

FunHouse consists of new characters as well as some from earlier Bogosian monologues, including a rubber fetishist, a man who paces back and forth on the street with the problems of the world weighing on his mind, a dad encouraging his son to stick it out on the football team, a paranoid maniac, a leader of an aerobics class, and an agent describing a new TV sitcom. "One big difference between my format and theater is that there's no 'line-through,' no pretense at continuity or causality. The meaning comes out of the juxtaposition of the segments. But also, the meaning comes out of something much more gigantic—the enormous amount of information assaulting us every day. The audience already knows the story of every character I present. So that lets me do something else—I'm playing off that, letting the audience watch the part itself *and* me playing the part.

"Brecht says, 'If you present the pros and cons of the character, the audience will make the correct choice.' I don't have to make commentaries on my characters; I think that if I put out the hypocrisy of a TV evangelist right there on the stage, it's plain to see. People don't lose their mental posture in the theater the way they do when they watch TV, and I believe in the communal function of the theater.

"But then, the question of performance versus theater is an economic one as well. In the world of performance art there's no place to go. The performance spaces have very little money, touring is difficult."

For years Bogosian has been in the forefront of the movement of performance art toward entertainment and away from the cerebral work of the previous generation. "I didn't want to make people *endure* performance, and I don't like to be bored, so I don't want my audiences to be bored either. I learned from Richard Foreman that it's possible to put onstage exactly what one wants to see there. One thing I like to see is the physicality of theater, so I do a lot of jumping around. For me performance art isn't just a live, visual medium. Anything at one's disposal can be brought in. But the fact that performance is constructed makes it different from theater. When I first did *The Ricky Paul Show,* the 'entertainment value' came from the character, a comedian I originally intended as a distant part of the whole picture. But, because the Ricky Paul character used words, everyone listened—and he really became entertaining. For me there is a difference between the passivity of watching entertainment and the involvement a work of art demands. And the more you see a work of art, the more there is to see. However, I'm not entirely happy with my colleagues' urge toward pure entertainment.

"My own approach is not purely comedic but analytic. I'm trying to show the tensions between characters, stereotypes, and comedians. I'm trying to *use* entertainment, to *use* laughter. I think that when people see *FunHouse* they laugh a lot but then find themselves feeling somewhat uncomfortable. I want to keep rattling people."

Bogosian identifies his approach more closely with such visual artists as Robert Longo, Jack Goldstein, Michael Zwack, and Cindy Sherman than with the theater. "The point is to create a sense of distance from totally familiar images. We're not making, for instance, a dreamworld, like the Surrealists of the 1920s. We're making a media world, in which there is a vibration between the self and the roles one plays. Then the question in the work is: where does the stereotype end and the real self begin? And the point is not how many roles you can play but the identity thing, the transformation.

"Also, there is a tension between the audience's attraction and repulsion to the images. When I presented all that sexist stuff in *Men Inside,* the men watching identified with it, but at the same time they said, 'What a shithead I am.'

"The format I use is more like TV or radio—or the theme album, a new development in rock and roll when I was growing up. You didn't just buy the album for one song; you listened to the whole thing. And from album to album you got the same musicians and the same ideas—just as in my performances people can say, 'Oh, it's Eric again.' So you get these short bursts of information. But then, when you listen to the radio and watch TV, you also get subliminal content: life is hopeless, you're a piece of shit, run scared, don't join unions, women are objects . . .

"I want to assemble another set of bits and pieces but with a different subtext. Maybe there's more than meets the eye; maybe things work against each other in subtle ways. You see, what I do isn't mere reportage. The media have no rational or consistent philosophy, and that leads to madness. There has to be a consistent way of looking at things with human values, not technological, capitalistic values, at the center."

Village Voice, July 19, 1983

Dario Fo's Theater of Blasphemy

Dario Fo, the prolific Italian playwright, director, and actor, has been popular all over Europe for more than 20 years. Yet in the United States his name has begun to crop up only recently. Most Americans who've heard it know about his three plays—slapstick comedies with hard cores of radical political provocation—that have been produced here since 1980: *We Won't Pay! We Won't Pay!* about housewives who "liberate" goods from their local supermarket in response to inflation; *Accidental Death of an Anarchist,* about the role of the Milan police in the real death of an anarchist in their headquarters; and *About Face,* in which the owner of Fiat is kidnaped by terrorists, rescued, and mistakenly given the face (and wife) of one of his workers. (In 1983, we're seeing more of Fo in New York, as the Public Theater produces *Adulto Orgasmo Escapes from the Zoo,* a one-woman show for Franca Rame, Fo's wife and colleague, coauthored by Fo and Rame and played here by Estelle Parsons.) Some remember that Fo and Rame were denied entry to the United States in 1980 because of their political activism—to the left of the Communist Party. But because Fo has never been here few know about Fo the great clown and Fo the cultural historian, two sides of the man that emerge in his one-man performance *Mistero Buffo.*

Although Fo has been performing *Mistero Buffo* since 1969, it is a piece that seems particularly well suited to the 1980s. If Fo manages to get into the United States later this year, as he hopes, and performs the piece here, the issues he raises will be familiar to every stratum of his audience, from the most general spectator to the performance art world. In *Mistero Buffo* Fo interlards renditions of medieval mystery plays with political and historical commentary, as well as with reflections on current affairs; he concocts for us that peculiar brand of subversive laughter that is edged with ironic insight, the laughter of the grotesque popular theater that jeers at officialdom in every form.

In the 1980s, when we once again feel the need for a political theater but regret the often mirthless rhetoric of much leftist theater, Fo provides a model for a polemics of exhilaration. In the 1980s, when means are scarce, he makes a portable, poor theater in which the body is the irreducible element and special props, scenery, costumes, and lighting are dispensed with. (It is the focus on the body, too, that gives Fo's work its earthy, burlesque humor.) In the 1980s questions of language preoccupy both artists and critics; Fo's *Mistero Buffo* is an excursion into the mechanics and politics of language. And, in the 1980s, when questions of reconstruction and authenticity pervade the performing arts, Fo gives us a reconstruction of ancient texts that are not simply historical curiosities but living lessons in understanding both the texts and the style of their performance. His brilliance as a reconstructor has been to vitalize the texts with language, timing, and gestures that are vigorous, direct, and instantly comprehensible.

I recently saw Fo perform *Mistero Buffo* and spoke with him and Rame in London. In keeping with their practice of performing in occupied factories, workers' cooperatives, and other alternative circuits, they were on hand to reopen Riverside Studios, the center for avant-garde and political theater and dance that had been closed since last November, when a funding crisis led the staff to occupy the building and take over the administration of the center from the local borough council. (Fo, Rame, and their theater company had themselves occupied a building in Milan in 1974 and converted it into a theater.) Fo's London performances vindicated the beleaguered Riverside: one critic wrote in the *London Times,* "No firework display, brass band parade, or grovelling apology from the Hammersmith Council Liberals could have given the reopening of the Riverside Studios a bigger send-off than this one-man show." Houses were sold out every night to such enthusiastic audiences that, when the run at Riverside ended, Fo went on performing at the local church.

Fo took the title *Mistero Buffo* from Mayakovsky's 1918 farce celebrating the Russian Revolution, a modern slapstick version of a medieval morality play, in which the earth is destroyed by floods, the bourgeois drown, the workers build an ark, and a radical Christ figure walks over the water to cheer the workers on. Mayakovsky wrote in his preface to *Mystery-Bouffe* that "in the future, all persons performing, presenting, reading, or publishing *Mystery-Bouffe* should change the content, making it contemporary, immediate, up-to-the-minute"; the only thing Fo's show shares with its predecessor is the title and the subversive, satiric use of the medieval religious drama to make political jabs.

Of course, the church in medieval times knew very well how dangerous and powerful theater was; the mystery plays, mixing vernacular languages with Latin and thrown outside the church into the marketplace, carried potent antiauthoritarian messages to wide audiences. Both Mayakovsky and Fo seized a moment of history when drama was rich, lively, and necessary because its uses were rapidly changing. If we think of theater in our day as something safe and defused, Fo shows us differently—not only in his own performance, not only in his history lessons about medieval theater embedded in *Mistero Buffo,* but even in the Carter administration's denial of his visa.

Fo's *Mistero Buffo* is a changing set of texts. Each particular performance is chosen from a repertory, which, done in its entirety, would run over six hours. In 1977 Fo performed a "definitive version" of the play on Italian television, in four 50-minute segments. The play is performed in the style of medieval *giullari,* strolling players who were an early version of alternative, underground theater, constantly on the run from censorship and persecution. A number of texts in *Mistero Buffo* deal with the origins and traditions of this form of solo storytelling, some of which crystallized in the more conventional commedia dell'arte.

In London Fo began each evening with a modern example of what a *guillare* might have done with topical material of his own day. He recounted the story of the Pope's assassination attempt—an affront, he explained, to Catholics and atheists alike because of its total lack of style. Like a nightclub comedian, Fo interrupted himself and digressed, his easy banter about the pope as a TV personality in Italy, even a force of nature, suddenly coming into hard focus on the description of the assassination and a graphic depiction of how the bullet went into the pope's sphincter ("What an outrage!" he stopped to comment, "the Pope doesn't have a sphincter; he has a sacred conduit"), came out his navel, ricocheted off the columns of the Vatican, and went up to heaven.

The program I saw in London continued with three texts: "The Resurrection of Lazarus," "The Wedding at Cana," and "Boniface VII," and with two "grammelots." Based on fifteenth-century nonsense language developed by the *guillari* to circumvent censorship, Fo's grammelot is malleable, manic gibberish that, depending on which sounds are stressed and what gestures supply a substratum of meaning, can sound like various languages or dialects. Before the enactment of each text or grammelot, Fo explained (through a translator) the action and the context, again in a half-serious, half-playful badinage. "Lazarus," for instance, was an ironic thrust aimed at people who sold indulgences in the church, an observation that led Fo into a meditation on the selling of fragments of saints and of false saints. Saint George, he warned his

British audience, was in fact sold to England by Genoan bankers, and the whole thing was just a swindle. So Christ's first important miracle is depicted in "Lazarus" as taking place in a cemetery that has become a marketplace, with people arriving early to get the best seat, yelling at each other to sit down, selling fried sardines, and picking pockets. When the translator leaves the stage, Fo performs the monologue with the help of a homemade subtitle contraption that allows his brilliant timing full play as he rapidly shifts characters—now a cynic, now a fan, now angry, now elated—until an entire crowd populates the stage.

In "The Wedding at Cana," Fo explains, we see an early notion of Christ—not the standoffish, fifteenth-century figure who doesn't participate, but a jovial, loving fellow who urges, once he has changed the water to wine, "Drink, people! Be happy here on earth. Don't wait until you're dead. Don't look at life as a waiting room." Loving, that is, except to the rich, and here Fo explains how venetian blinds, horses, and the expression "Oh Christ!" all were invented as a result of Christ's stern attitude toward the rich. The story of the miracle at Cana is told in the monologue by a drunkard who quaffed the wine Christ made—and in the text he stops his narration of the miracle to give a connoisseur's critique of the wine's flavor and texture—but not before the drunkard fights with an angel to see who will tell the tale. The angel, with his flowery language and pompous manners, stands for the scholastic, conservative elements of the church, while the drunkard, with his crude, robust talk, is an allegory for the logical, progressive side. Fo is remarkable both as a foppish angel and as the ecstatic, garrulous tippler, ending the monologue with a virtuoso oration on how God's great mistake was in not teaching Adam how to press grapes the moment he created him, "because if Adam had had a glass of wine in his hand when Eve offered him the apple, he'd have kicked the apple and crushed the snake's head—and we'd all be in Paradise! Cheers!"

The grammelot "Scapino's Teaching Lesson," in which Scapino, the commedia dell'arte character used by Molière in Le Bourgeois Gentil-homme, teaches a banker's son how to dress, walk, speak, and use techniques of hypocrisy and violence, provided Fo with an excuse for an introductory disquisition on bankers and their role in world history ("Capitalism starts when bankers organize wars, instead of princes and kings"), on the use of the law to maintain power through violence, and finally on the situation of prisoners in Italy. ("Our 5,000 political prisoners waiting for judgment have everything—including a rope to hang themselves with. Our prisons are so popular; they're booked up five years in advance.") As he launches into his onomatopoetic babble, Fo warns us not to try to understand what might sound like French. "People who know French will find themselves lost; people who don't will understand everything—this evening represents the triumph of ignorance." Suddenly, Fo's gestures, face, nose, eyes, forehead, and walk transform and tighten, as if his entire body had acquired a French accent. He kisses babies, twists the curls of his peruke, pokes at the lace trimming every part of his suit, is launched across the stage when the wind turns his mantle into a cloak, and fences. "Enough hatred and violence," a title reads. "Dialectic does exist—let us discuss things." But Scapino's discussion turns into a gory fight. "No to violence—direct, that is," the title concludes.

For the grammelot "The Technocrat," Fo's features once again utterly metamorphose, loosening and spreading until he has become a grinning, drawling Texan. This grammelot, in which an American scientist lectures on the history of aviation from the first flying machine to astronauts and computers, provides a pretext for talking about the "progress" computers are bringing to factories—progress in unemployment, that is—and the progress of death spurred on by the nuclear arms race. Fo's scientist is like an overgrown child playing with toys in his bathtub, sputtering, sighing, chugging, and whirring as he builds his rocket and blasts off.

Finally, Fo performs "Boniface VIII," in which the thirteenth-century pope—so hated by Dante he was put in the *Inferno* before he was dead, and remembered for his nailing up of monks, his persecution of the Flemish, and his Good Friday orgy with bishops, cardinals, and prostitutes—sings a Gregorian chant as he dresses for a procession. Bejeweled and berobed, walking along with the help of several monks who carry his train ("Steer more carefully! Am I a Pope or am I a wheelbarrow?"), he meets a counterprocession led by Christ, who ends up kicking Boniface on the backside.

To retell Fo's texts and comic one-liners is, of course, to give an impoverished account of his performance, in which the sense of the words is irradiated with wide, round, voluble gestures; a body that is large boned, loose, elegant, able to strike sudden, articulate poses; a generous face, topped by a white shock of hair, that is like a screen for a kaleidoscopic range of emotions; and an impeccable sense of comic timing. His are the skills of a Grimaldi, a Chaplin, or a Grock—an art of physically precise expression that, in the late twentieth century, seems particularly extraordinary because its use is so rare.

Born in 1926, Fo began his training as a child, learning the art of storytelling from the fishermen, glassmakers, and smugglers on the banks of Lake Maggiore (in Lombardy), called "bats," because of their nighttime jobs, who passed their time in all-night taverns spinning fantastic tales. The fishermen especially influenced him; for them storytelling was a kind of currency, with which they "hired" local kids to come and help with their work, and the openness of their gestures as they spoke and simultaneously knotted their nets is an important component of Fo's style. As an art student at the Brera Academy in Milan just after World War II, he got involved in the theater movement, centering around the Piccolo Theater, that involved artists from every field and forged connections with Parisians, including Picasso, the mime Jacques Lecoq, and Sartre, with whom Fo and Rame later became close friends.

"The important thing was that you took part in the whole movement. We were all together there—filmmakers, writers, sculptors, designers, journalists, actors, directors—and we all lived together and made a cultural life together. When I started performing (doing improvised comic monologues and then acting, with Franco Parenti, in a musical revue), we were just the group and there were no divisions— there were painters who did scenery but also painters who were actors, architects who were writers." In the early 1950s Fo wrote and performed comic monologues for Italian radio, collaborated with Parenti, Giustino Durano, and Lecoq on satirical revues, worked briefly on films, and married Rame, with whom he has collaborated ever since. The earliest revues were political (one included a sketch on racism) and were immediately criticized and censored. From the beginning Fo saw theater as a way of doing history in a Left-Marxist key outside of conventions and myths, breaking with both political and theatrical rhetoric.

In the late 1950s Fo and Rame formed their own company in Milan and began performing one-act plays and farces based on traditional comic forms, many taken from the repertory of the Rame family, a theatrical family dating back to the seventeenth-century. Throughout the 1960s the company put on comedies with overt political satire in the commercial theaters and on TV in Italy. But after 1962, when they quit their popular TV series in response to censorship, they did not appear on television again for 14 years.

In 1968 Fo and Rame decided to leave the commercial theater—
"We were jesters for the bourgeois, nothing more than a purge, a
sauna"—and to heighten their commitment, through *engagé* theater, to
Italian Left politics. They formed their own alternative theater circuit—
performing on the outskirts of the cities, where, in the nineteenth-
century, amateur theater was done—and played in churches, movie
theaters, factories, workers' clubs, marketplaces, and sports stadiums. At
first they toured under the auspices of the cultural wing of the Italian
Communist Party (from 1968 to 1970), but, after their satires on party
bureaucracy and policies brought them under attack, they broke with
the PCI and formed Il Collettivo Teatrale La Comune, the company with
which (in its various incarnations and reorganizations) they have
worked ever since, performing "interventionist" plays on themes from
abortion to terrorism, police brutality, fascism, workers' rights, prison
reform, women's rights, the drug trade, and nuclear war.

Fo and Rame are used to playing to audiences of thousands—an
audience that, as Fo points out, "will break down a whole sports stadium if they find out people have been speculating but who have a
different relation to us because they've organized our performance themselves, the profits go to a lawsuit or an occupied factory and not to us,
and, finally, because of our effect on the public. If we're performing in
the open air and it begins to rain, the audience demands that we continue." Performances are followed by debates, and at times the spectators reject the polemic of the show. But, Fo and Rame point out, in Italy
the audience comes knowing that their participation will be provoked in
one way or another. Not all of the spectators are sympathetic; when
About Face opened, hecklers threw stones, and the police often appear to
try to close down performances. "The police are our best followers,"
Rame quips.

Thus, for Fo even the question of language in his performance of
Mistero Buffo is a political one, not only the grammelot, an overt response to censorship, but also the mixture of Italian dialects that make
up the rest of the performance. Standard Italian is identified with the
elite class, while the language Fo uses—invented by clowns in the
thirteenth century—is not only proletarian but antinationalist, because
it can be understood by people from various districts. "All great poets—
some of whom were clowns themselves—have used this language.
Dante doesn't speak Tuscan; he speaks a mixture of dialects with a

Tuscan root. Shakespeare and Rabelais invented a language that was clearer and broader than everyday language, because they made use of all the dialects and all the languages at hand. This language of the great poets is very free and very rich."

The selection of texts, too, is a political question and also a question of theater aesthetics, for, although many of the texts have been published in various forms, Fo's task has been to clarify the original meaning of the oral performance, a meaning that becomes altered and softened in written transcription. "The text itself is meager. You have an oral text. But then you have the gestures, the rhythms, the timing—and the transcriber substitutes words for these elements that weren't in the original—as when you make a film and you write different scripts for the words and the action."

When Fo began to perform these texts he found that the audience understood various passages before he finished speaking, because the last section of the passage had been interpolated later, by another writer. "So I learned to read the texts, finding out where the text itself stops and could be substituted by gesture. All theater texts live on the basis of synthesis. For instance, when I sing the Gregorian chant in 'Boniface VIII,' then ask for my hat, the passage consists simply of 'The hat. The hat. No, you are crushing my head.' [Here Fo gestures imperiously, places the hat on his head, then screws up his face in an apoplexy of surprise, pain, and rage.] In the original it reads: 'Give me the hat. Hurry up. Hurry up, we are late. Come on now, hurry up, give me this hat. I have to put it on my head. My God, what did you do to me? This is an iron hat! With this hat, you are crushing my head!' It's much too long."

The changes in some of the texts are even more radical. Compare, for instance, these two versions of Christ's answer to a servant who complains to him in prayer (published in an article in *Theatre Quarterly* by Tony Mitchell). The official version:

You madman, have you forgotten
What was written in my law?
The human race will always be at war
If you fight evil with more evil.
If someone wrongs you, embrace him
And you'll live in paradise with me.
I could have destroyed heaven and earth
But the Jews nailed me up on this cross.

But in Fo's version Christ advocates fighting back, not turning the other cheek:

Are your arms broken or something?
Or are you nailed up like me?
If you want justice, do it yourself,
Don't rely on someone else to do it for you.

"Christ never spoke like the official version would have it. Christ said, 'I'm not here to bring peace, but war. What I'm saying can't be understood by everyone, because I'm a provocation.' But there's love in this talk too, which you can only see when you understand the cultural context of the time, the mixture of races. Christ was revolutionary because he broke up the nationalism and separatism of the Jews. He said all people were chosen. But then, in the Middle Ages, the Church became the mediator between the lords and the peasants. When capitalism was born in the Renaissance, people began to challenge the power of the aristocracy. Capitalism says, 'Every man on earth is able to become somebody through money. All people are equal—but they don't have the same value.' And the Church says, 'Yes, that's justice.' So we start all over again."

Fo's response, in theatrical terms, is also to start over, to reclaim the "illegitimate," popular tradition of the *giullari,* with its roots in Roman times, which blossoms in Greek, Arab, and Sicilian culture in the fifth century then in medieval Italy, only to disappear and reappear sporadically since then. The vitality of the "living newspaper" aspect of this tradition, the mixture of entertainment, information, and persuasion, is a powerful brew in Fo's hands. "Popular culture doesn't just mean taking things that are of the people *per se,*" Fo has said. "It means taking everything that the masters have taken from that culture and turned upside down, and revealing their origins and developments." Making things topsy-turvy, exploding the powers-that-be with ironic laughter, is the heart of Fo's method.

Village Voice, August 2, 1983

Mario Pirorano and Jutte Lollesgaard acted as interpreters during the interviews with Dario Fo.

Bucking Broncos in the Bronx
(Urban Western Rodeo)

A rodeo in the Bronx? It seemed such an oxymoron one *had* to go see it. For Carlos Foster, the organizer of the event, that contradiction in terms is the friction that he hopes will spark the imaginations of the neighborhood kids. Foster, a black Cuban cowboy who has lived in New York since the revolution, runs a self-financed program ("no grants, no subsidies") that uses horseback riding as a strategy for keeping kids in school and away from drugs. Foster rents horses that kids in the program learn to ride and care for, and in return the kids promise to behave. The horses are both a reward for the week's good conduct and a living lesson in Foster's four-point philosophy. Donald and Damon Reinhardt, two kids who are obviously reaping some of the benefits of Foster's program, listed the four points as we waited backstage for the rodeo to begin: challenge facing, decision making, discipline, and control.

I wondered, as I found a seat, whether these four points are both necessary and sufficient for kids to live a good life in the United States in 1983. I thought about the last rodeo I'd seen—in Texas, nearly 20 years ago—and a welter of macho images danced in my head. I thought about Foster's energy, grace, and assurances that for the neighborhood kids this rodeo went far beyond the gratification of the weekly riding sessions: a chance to see black and Hispanic as well as white professional cowboys in performance. For Foster it was a chance to produce a show *for* the neighborhood *in* the neighborhood. "This is probably the first rodeo in New York that isn't in Madison Square Garden," he reminded me. "I rode the streets on horseback for weeks selling tickets." And, as the rodeo itself began with a fanfare of riders, horses, and banners circling the indoor stadium at top speed, I thought about all the various forms of high art spectacle whose roots lie in the perfection of "typically" male skills of warfare and dominance: Western ballet, Kabuki, the Indian dance-drama form Kathakali. The dances and dramas derived from these martial displays have outlived their social, economic, and historical contexts, but the sheer virtuosity involved in refining those skills remains astonishing.

In most of the events everything happened so fast, you could barely see the contestant. In the first half of the program the events were competitions that raced against time—either how long a rider could stay on a bareback or saddled bucking bronco or how quickly one could wrestle a steer to the ground or rope a calf before it ran away. There was a complex excitement in these bouts, the sense of the animals chafing at the gate, the heightened suspense of knowing each contestant would succeed or fail within a matter of seconds, and then the hint of brutality involved in subduing the animals through timing, dexterity, and sheer strength. But if you blinked you could miss a round.

The velocity of the individual events was tempered by the announcer's commentary and also by the antics of a clown, who supplied a poetic retard by repeating the action of the cowboys in symbolic, absurd form. At one point the announcer asked for volunteers from the audience, and hundreds of kids flocked to the arena. The clown led out *his* version of a bucking bronco—an impetuous little mule—and the first 20 kids got a chance to identify with the cowboy's humiliation at being thrown as each and every one slid gently to the ground.

The second half of the program included not only bull riding and cowboys working in pairs to rope a calf but also two events for women: barrel racing and exhibition riding. The pace here was more relaxed; form, rather than speed, dominated. This was especially true in the exhibition section, more like a gymnastics competition than a Wild West flash of bravado. For the first time the personalities of the riders emerged as we saw the same performers—J. J. and Stacey Pryor, 15- and 13-year-old sisters—circle the ring repeatedly, dancing on horseback like two American sylphs, balancing on the saddle or flinging themselves sideways to ride perpendicular to the horse's flank.

At first the rodeo seemed to me nothing more than a contradiction, a superfluous display of skills that make sense in context but when transplanted to urban ground simply lose their meaning. And for me, a born-and-bred city dweller, to wrestle a helpless animal to the ground does seem somewhat savage. Yet the spectacle as a whole belied the stereotypical macho images I brought to it. After all, there was something very magical about seeing herds of cattle reposing under the elevated subway tracks. There was a satisfying blend of excitement and elegance in the sequence of events. None of the animals got hurt. There were all kinds of families enjoying themselves, the kids especially riveted to the action. And our inner-city kids could do a lot worse than to dream of becoming some kind of hero.

Village Voice, August 16, 1983

When Church Picnics Make Sense

(Bread and Puppet Theater)

There's a different spiritual temperament in Vermont. The landscape is vivid, green, and raw, as if the mountains had freshly churned up the earth. The ubiquitous cows spread themselves over the meadows like a tablecloth of tranquillity. Lightning flashes in three different colors and the Northern Lights coruscate in the cool night. On the road to Glover there's a rocky hillside garden that looks just like the Renaissance paintings of Gethsemane. "We never even see the sky in New York," my friend observed, "but here it's so enormous, you can begin to see why some people believe in God."

In this setting the tone of Bread and Puppet's annual weekend-long extravaganza—somewhere between medieval mystery play cycle, peace rally, and church picnic—makes sense. Every year we make our pilgrimage, a journey that is as much a remembrance of the halcyon days of the late 1960s as it is a movement through space. And every year the circus becomes more and more abstract, more and more sacred in mood. Political content is still scattered through some of the sideshows and of course in the leaflet rack (centrally located), the perennial Hiroshima House (a zen garden-like mausoleum of grey papier-maché corpses), some of the poetry readings, Paul Zaloom's civil defense primer, and this year's "Homily for Peace," put on by parents, teachers, and Physicians for Social Responsibility. But in the larger events—the daily circus, with its homespun wild animals, tongue-in-cheek antivirtuosity, straggly brass band, and gentle gusto; and the more mythically proportioned pageant, heralding each evening's flame-colored sunset with marching bands and puppets four times the size of humans—the political meaning has become diffuse and almost entirely metaphoric.

Last year's *Domestic Resurrection Circus* was united by the overarching theme of Saint Francis, but, if Bread and Puppet subscribes to any religion, theirs seems an early, primitive version of Christianity or an animistic faith. The banners in the circus parade celebrate Brother Sun, Sister Sky, but also such humble household gods as Sister Coffee and Brother Bread.

The poster for this year's show depicts a huge, kindly face in the sky blowing on a slumbering farm. In the sideshows, for instance in "Gardens Were before Gardeners," cosmic events like the changing of the seasons are reimagined as anthropomorphic doings, even miniaturized beyond human scale as tiny puppets hoe, water their plants, and pick their fruit.

There was no single theme this year, but the motif of "The Dangerous Kitchen," threaded through several sideshows and the pageant as well, combines a number of Bread and Puppet's concerns and approaches. The kitchen is the heart of the home, the symbol of domesticity. Each day the world begins again with breakfast; in the kitchen here the family gathers for communal meals, and guests are drawn into the family circle. If small, humble, and local are beautiful, the quotidian kitchen is the essence of beauty and the good. So the notion of "The Dangerous Kitchen" strikes an apocalyptic note.

In the sideshow "Kitchen News" two poor elderly puppet women, evicted from their housing project in Hoboken because it is about to be converted into condominiums, see the world outside their kitchen via television. The danger in this kitchen is two-sided: the women represent the suffering of the innocent at the hands of the powerful and are potential insurrectionaries as well because they recognize that their suffering is neither merely personal nor local. "I guess we don't have it so bad," the puppets murmur when they hear about homeless Guatemalan refugees. In "The Dangerous Kitchen of Marina Tsvetaeva" the political content is less explicit. A woman reminds us that Tsvetaeva hanged herself in her kitchen then recites some of the poet's verses as she walks through a wooden hut, rinses dishes in a pan, and ignores the ominous rope loop hanging at the threshold. Tsvetaeva's nocturnal broodings speak in universal terms, yet they are allegorical laments for the freedom strangled by Soviet power.

In the pageant a giant husband-man and husband-wife are rolled in on an immense bed. They give birth to a dozen or so white-clad humans, who are ritually transformed into vegetables, spices, kindling, and a match—ingredients for the wife's huge soup caldron. The couple sit at their kitchen table and sip coffee. But a demon dancer on stilts—representing the Superior Forces—brings drought, a heart attack, milk inspection, and tax collection to this placid kitchen, and a silver airplane perched atop a 20-foot scaffold sends a dose of "Bad" into the soup. While an awful army of airplanes produced by the caldron marches over the landscape, destroying cows, flowers, birds, chairs, and, finally, a city, the giant couple sits and weeps. But the inhabitants of the city rise and, forming a great ship with chanting, playing drums and cymbals, waving banners and huge blue hands marked with red hearts, they return to the kitchen. The wife takes fire from her hearth, ignites the enemy plane, and joins the ship. For one more year, at least, insurgent good has triumphed over the powers-that-be—both earthly and galactic.

Village Voice, August 30, 1983

Fat Sunday Fantasies

(Dimanche Gras Show)

Everyone knows about the spectacular parade that happens every Labor Day in Brooklyn when the "island" whose West Indian population is larger than that of any single Caribbean country swells with visitors for Carnival. Modeled after the Trinidad Carnival, after 16 years in New York the Brooklyn version has a life and reputation of its own. But, then, the West Indian Carnival is not a monolithic tradition; its complex history reflects waves of political change since European plantocrats and African slaves first began to mix their cultures in the New World. The elements of African performance that colonialists both encouraged and feared began to emerge after Emancipation (1834), when Carnival moved from elite to working-class hands; after independence from Britain in 1962, Carnival's importance as a symbol of national identity was consolidated. As Carlos Lezama, the president of the West Indian American Carnival Day Association, points out, "It is a myth to perceive Carnival as simply a theme for revelry and attitudes of gay abandon. Carnival is also a major force and contributor to the formation of a sociological framework."

In Trinidad, Carnival takes place just before Lent. In New York, Labor Day is a kind of compromise—a blend of festivities from various islands that celebrate Christmas, Lent, and Emancipation Day (August 1). And, although the Labor Day parade itself constitutes the core of Carnival, the festival really consists of five days of events—beginning the Thursday before Monday's parade. Dimanche Gras, on the eve of the parade, is modeled after the Trinidadian shows that began after World War II as revue entertainments around the crowning of the Carnival queen. Here, on the brightly lit open-air stage behind the Brooklyn Museum, all of the ingredients that flow in and out of one's field of vision in the parade can be viewed and heard—unraveled, in a sense— in the static frame the theater format provides. The element of playful competition comes into sharp focus—between Mas bands (groups of masqueraders in opulent costumes), Ole Mas bands (teams of bawdy satirists), beauty contestants, calypso singers, steelbands, limbo dancers, stilt dancers. At the Dimanche Gras show the community leaders are honored publicly. And a momentum is built communally as the driving music moves emcee, performers, and spectators alike, nearly all night long.

The climax of the evening is the display of selected costumes in the competition for the king and queen of the bands. The elaborate costumes—some practically parade floats themselves—are assembled and last-minute touches added in the museum's parking lot. It's almost 3 A.M. when the parade of giant, glittering, swaying structures arrives and each fantastic creation takes its turn onstage. By now one's consciousness has entered a dreamlike state. The small human encased in each costume dances it into being, until it seems magically to come alive, a beautiful monster several times human scale. The excessive appendages, gauzy fabrics, and iridescent spangles used in most of the costumes give them the look of exotic, jeweled insects.

This year one was a creature that seemed part spaceship, part crustacean, with curved translucent wings/claws and 14 golden, cone-shaped antennas surrounding its red and green bodice like a quivering halo. Another was an enormous brown furry spider. A red long-necked mythological bird whirled in circles, its dancer creating the illusion, with a pair of fake legs, that he was riding it bareback. Another dancer animated an entire cartoon landscape on which a lizard chased a fly. But most magnificent—and the winner for king this year—was the Midnight Demon made by the Beauty and the Beast band, a shimmery silver man's body topped by a white-as-death, rictus grin mask and framed by gauzy, sparkling black wings, ten feet tall, that seemed a cross between a Gothic arch and a bat's wings. As each contestant turns and steps and manipulates his or her extended body around the stage, all the members of the dancer's band crowd onto the stage, yelling directions, making gestures both of pathways and encouragement, and generally egging the dance on. They're like a contrasting background—humanity multiplied and collectivized—to the lone, superhuman figure they've worked so long and hard to create for a brief but glorious moment. And that willful wastefulness, that building up of luxury that will be savored for only an instant, seems to me an integral part of these costumes' splendor.

The dancing of the costumes is the climax of Dimanche Gras, but another, more humble event struck me as spectacular in its own way. This year's Ole Mas, for reasons not made entirely clear, was a competition that consisted of only one band. The group, largely made up of kids, made typically scatological and satiric jabs at all the authorities connected to the Carnival. It was mind-blowing to see such overtly shocking material presented along with beauty contests and spangled costumes.

Men were dressed as pregnant women, women as men with pants stuffed to represent giant genitalia; a trickster figure fondled both indiscriminately. Hand-painted signs proclaimed all sorts of insults: So-and-so is an old witch. So-and-so licks So-and-so's ass. So-and-so shovels shit. And the statements were graphically mimed, complete with funky, home-made costumes and props. If you didn't know the intricacies of Brooklyn and Carnival politics, maybe you didn't get the point of every thrust. But even the references obscure to outsiders added to the incredible, paradoxical cheek of this event. After all, most of the subjects of all this "aberrant" behavior were probably sitting in the audience or even at the judges' table, remaining dignified pillars of the community in the face of outrageous irreverence—enough to make even the most impudent Dadaists appear bourgeois.

Village Voice, September 20, 1983

Hard Knocks and Culture Shock
(Yoshiko Chuma and the School of Hard Knocks)

Yoshiko Chuma's work lies somewhere between dance and performance art. There's choreographed movement in it but often all sorts of other things, including film, objects, reflex movement, pure play, brash sounds, the language of songs and stories. At a certain point in the 1960s the definition of *dance* could embrace all these things. A thing was a dance because its maker presented it as a dance, and pure abstract "dancey" movement was one of the things people were least interested in using in their choreography. But now that the definition of *dance* is so elastic you can put anything in it, and now that technical virtuosity and the vocabulary of classic dance forms have rekindled the imagination of downtown choreographers, it seems useful to make some distinctions again.

Part of what makes *A Night at the Millionaire's Club* edge toward performance has to do with format rather than content. The installment I saw on September 19, the first in a series of four late-night episodes, partook of too many kinds of art and entertainment structures to be narrowly labeled dance. We saw 20 little vignettes, including poetry readings by "guest star" Anne Waldman. In between each act Eliot Sharp, acting as deejay, played a richly evocative assemblage of music, from Balinese ketjak music for gamelan to punk rock to 1940s nostalgia. The performers—Donald Fleming, Kaja Gam, Brian Moran, Gayle Tufts, Nelson Zayas, and Chuma—seemed more like a band of musicians than dancers as they took turns in the limelight or directing a sequence. In between the segments casual offstage behavior—changing costumes, looking for props, quick consultations—was made visible in a way more often seen in musical performance than dance. So, in many ways, the performance seemed like a live album, maybe a live video disc.

But also, Chuma used the device of film "takes" to structure the evening. Each segment was introduced with a clapboard, and the activity for each take ended—often in medias res—when Chuma called "cut!" In fact, Chuma has directed several films. Here her action as film director became one of the subjects of the performance, even though no cameras were rolling. Carol Mazurek's wonderful black, gray, and white sets added to the film sense.

And, then, there was the Pyramid's physical setup. Some events happened on the tiny stage up front, but the entire crowded back room was the performers' terrain. I heard that the group intended to adapt their behavior to the cabaret setting but that, when one performer struck up a conversation with a spectator, he was rebuked: "Don't talk to me, you're supposed to be performing!"

Chuma once said that she started making performances as a reflex to the culture shock she experienced on arriving here from Japan seven years ago. Yet, perhaps because she looks at American culture as a fascinated outsider, her view of its past and present, as it emerges across her wonderfully orchestrated group of performers and the 20 disparate takes, is point-blank. Yet its accuracy in recreating moods and images is also mixed with gleeful extremities of style, childlike intensity and playfulness, a heterodox use of loud, abrasive music, awkward and nervous movements. She tries on America's trappings like a kid trying on her mother's discarded high heels. Chuma's appetite for the harsh, the gritty, and the agitated, as well as for 1950s nostalgia, also gives her work a punk look.

Dressed in a flowered satin dress and high heels, Chuma mimics a nightclub singer, but she is lip-synching to the raucous rendition of "Keep on Smiling" that the group produces from the back of the hall as *they* mimic a wholesome college choir. Gayle Tufts (whose every intervention was brilliant) belts out a full-bodied version of "Dem Bones," while the others hurl their bodies around, landing on whichever bone is the song's current topic—and in mid-breath and mid-dance, Chuma calls, "Cut!" The whole group drops it and goes on to the next thing. Brian Moran does a dance on the floor that involves dragging part of a truck grill around, and later he and Nelson Zayas mime a silent comedy/ cartoon scene as they unwrap sandwiches, do some girl-watching, Zayas swats a fly on Moran's head, and then they wind up their arms for a fistfight. Donald Fleming tells a story about stealing a loaf of bread with expansive gestures; the rest of the group forms a file behind him and copies his every flourish. The group plays "One Potato, Two Potato" and, later, "Time Bomb"—in which they toss a ball hurriedly to any other player in sight, while a clock ticks away, and at the sound of an explosion Chuma lets out a piercing scream.

Waldman was a gracious guest, but her elegant persona and her stylized reading mannerisms—which I have so enjoyed on other occasions—made her seem out of place here, a refined adult among energetic kids.

Village Voice, October 4, 1983

Unruly Dolls and Ritz Rockers

(Harry Kipper / Karen Finley / Breaker Contest)

Harry Kipper is one of the Kipper Kids. I thought their brand of cheery, infantile / scatological slapstick was peculiarly male, maybe even especially British. Now Harry Kipper has teamed up with an American woman whose flair for primal excess matches his own. Karen Finley's nervous edge makes her a less captivating performer than Kipper, whose piss and vinegar shenanigans endlessly regale one. Still, that she is a decorous-looking woman (at least at first) who pulls equally ribald stunts increases the taboo factor in her performance.

Kipper and Finley's evening consisted of two solo performances. Kipper's *Actor Says Goodnight* was a short string of activities. Through the rips in a white sheet he created a kind of homemade puppet show, flying airplanes and practicing ventriloquism on a rabbit toy who thoroughly doused him with paint. He emerged in his underwear and, in the dark, shot arrows at two figures that, it turned out, were made of water balloons, keeping up a winning patter all the while. He showed us a collection of dolls—all into s/m. And he sang a song—a recent collaboration with William Blake. Like a bright child entertaining and shocking the grownups in a bedtime performance that incorporates any object at hand in a stream of libidinous narratives, Kipper finally had to call it quits when his time ran out.

The audience had been turned to face the kitchen counter that usually forms the back of the performance space at Franklin Furnace. All sorts of objects that Kipper hadn't used remained, including a table, glasses, bowls, a suitcase, and, lurking ominously under everything, a plastic covering on the floor. It wasn't just for the water balloons. Finley, with a patter more manic and fragmented than Kipper's, became an entire cast of characters and ran around using up these props and more in *I Like the Dwarf on the Table When I Give Him Head.* She pulled bottles of wine as well as a tape recorder from the refrigerator. She knocked over the table and broke the glasses. She pulled a can of tuna ("actually," she announced later, "it was a can of catfood") from her underpants. Slashing open her pink party dress, she showed us her breasts, atop a purple long-line corset. She made a winter panorama with a box of Ivory Snow and played digging her car out. She smeared chocolate frosting all over her face ("I hope that's chocolate frosting," someone behind me murmured). And, finally, she pulled her dress up and her pants down to take a sponge bath in a suitcase full of dish detergent and water.

At the end of her bubble bath Finley talked about the madness in the world; the last image in her performance was her repeated shriek: "Laugh, lady, laugh!" In a sense she weakens the power of the Kipper-Finley evening with her annotation. We already know that this messy, scabrous conduct exhilarates us exactly because it represents—no, more than that, it *is*—by its very transgression of every sort of social constraint, both a comment on society's structured inhibitions and a triumphant exercise of freedom. The Lords of Misrule don't have to explain why they turn the world as we know it upside down.

The Ritz has been sponsoring a series of challenges, by borough, among New York breaking crews. On September 27 the winning crews from the earlier contests competed for a $1,000 prize. The contenders were Rockers' Revenge (Manhattan), Rockwell, Inc. (Manhattan), Dynamic Rockers (Queens), Royal Rockers (Bronx), and Electric B-Boy (Brooklyn). I thought I'd seen all the possible breaking moves, but the playoffs proved that this is a form of dancing that keeps on expanding its vocabulary. All the routines incorporated various spectacular elements from other kinds of street dancing, many of which are of course recognizable from other Afro-American dances and rites—the snakelike undulations of electric boogie and the Yanvallou or the all-over body trembling that is reminiscent of women "moved by the spirit" in church. But the Dynamic Rockers won the top prize with choreography that also moved the spins and other floorwork of breaking into the air, as they worked in pairs, one dancer acting as support while a second spun on his head or shoulders. They teamed up in formations to step in perfect synchrony, red costumes glittering, or formed a pyramid for more dancers to vault in flying leaps, looking somehow like a combination of astronauts and circus acrobats. Two young women in the crew took their turns as well. The crowd went wild.

The crew that came in second was Electric B-Boy. There were only two dancers in this group, and one of them, a boy who couldn't have been older than 12, was utterly captivating. His partner was left miles behind as he boogied electrically, striking poses and touching his body with a narcissistic panache that must have been born of hours of practice in front of a mirror.

Village Voice, October 18, 1983

A Good Friend Is Hard to Find & the Way of What?

(Tony Conrad / George Coates Performance Works)

When Tony Conrad arrived in New York in 1962, you didn't have to choose any one particular art to specialize in. Conrad, trained in mathematics and computers as well as music, worked in both avant-garde music and film, performing with La Monte Young, Marian Zazeela, Terry Riley, John Cale, and others, composing soundtracks for films (including Jack Smith's *Flaming Creatures* and, since *The Flicker* (1966), a paradigmatic structural film, making films and videos. Starting in the early 1970s, Conrad began to mix his film and video formats with performance. In works like *Deep Fried 7360, Curried 7302,* and other works, he commented on theories of film "material" by cooking, hammering, or electrocuting film to the point where it could only be shown outside of the film projector; *7360 Sukiyaki* was a "tableside" act of cooking in which the whole dish was eventually literally projected (i.e., thrown) at the screen. More recently Conrad has been working on a trilogy of genre films—war, women's prison, and high school—that incorporate performance art techniques in both shooting and screening.

Conrad is well-known as a performance artist in Buffalo, where he teaches film and video, but his New York City appearances are rare. His one-night performance of *Your Friend* almost didn't happen, because the Artists Present Artists series was locked out of the theater it had rented on the day of Conrad's performance. He volunteered to do the performance anyway—in front of the theater's locked doors, followed by readings of petitions and press releases.

You can't really complain that the performance lost something by happening outside instead of inside the theater, since it certainly wasn't Conrad's choice to be outside. The problem was that the text of the performance itself isn't the whole performance; the social interaction between Conrad and his spectators is the subject for an ironic inquiry into a style that is more television evangelist / traveling salesman than either actor or street entertainer. *Your Friend* engages the audience but in ways that are both tongue-in-cheek and earnest. The spatial separation and concentration that a theater space provides are essential components of its impact and irony.

Conrad, in white jacket and bowtie, introduces his assistant (Melody Davis) and explains in a golden-tongued voice that his aim is to keep in touch with experience—and that he's going to show how this can be done even by amateurs, in the privacy of one's own home, all by oneself.

He demonstrates the various prongs of his program. Scientific: he shows how to start your own space program and builds a rocket out of matches, tinfoil, baking soda, and a paper clip. Creative arts: he plays a bass cardboard box (gigantic), a tenor, an alto, and finally a soprano (tiny), whacking each with a stick of appropriate size until it stops making sounds and falls to pieces, then passes out pieces of toilet paper to the spectators and urges us to invent our own musical uses for the material. Hygiene: he exhorts the members of the audience to reclaim their bodies for themselves and asks for volunteers who would like to learn to shit. He summarizes the workings of the digestive system, using plastic models of vomit and shit. He unreels a film, meditates on inside/outside splits, and teaches us to sing a simple song: "I'm a friend of Tony Conrad." The audience is chanting, Conrad is playing and conducting, and a voice comes on over a tape recorder: "Tony, what are you doing? Tony, what are you doing? Tony, what are you doing?" The terms of the entire evening shift as Conrad answers in a kid's whine, "I'm playing with my friends!"

Conrad's irony is a strange mixture of all-American geniality and innocence that could be for real and a satiric stance toward his own sincerity, a mixture of banality and transgression. In *Your Friend* you feel he is mocking something he actually believes in by presenting a deliberately simplistic, corny version of a very complicated ethos. The platitudes ring true, but the rub is that they can't convey all the contradictions of the experiences that produce them; their veracity is as flimsy as the success score cards Conrad and his assistant hand out to every spectator. On the one hand, life is just an absurd game, but, on the other hand, to play that complex game well, to plunge into mental vertigo and still come out standing, is the only way to live.

The Way of How is a concatenation of aural and visual images that never really hangs together. I suppose by calling the event a reverie George Coates figures the burden of making meaning is no longer on his shoulders, but even dreams and reveries have causal and symbolic links. One underlying theme in this performance is that of an alternative, fantastic biology, à la Alwin Nikolais or Pilobolus, but not as dancerly. Hospital imagery comes and goes too. And, as the two tenors (John Duykers and Rinde Eckert) wander on to sing arias and less recognizable things, you sometimes feel that there's a missing opera happening offstage. But none of this makes you want to work at making links in your own imagination. It's all just out there, and there doesn't seem to be any reason, logical or intuitive, for any of the stuff to happen, despite the fact that there are some lively or surprising sounds and visions at times. Duykers delivers a word salad monologue with pomp, and he wittily sings the names of various composers in each one's own musical style. People turn into mountains or a giant creature who births a little bug straight from a video game screen. The musical effects are both human and electronic; composer Paul Dresher weaves a thick tapestry of sound that at times incorporates earlier moments (the program notes are quick to inform us that "there are no pre-recorded sounds used in performance," lending the entire performance a dreary, didactic tone).

It's all rather thin fare, partly because of its internal contradictions. On the one hand Coates claims a heritage from John Cage, a desire to expand awareness of the ordinary, and this is expressed through the performance of ordinary tasks and sounds. On the other hand, these actions, demystifying theater, are countervailed by all the special effects that are used to fabricate illusion and magic—fancy side-lighting, scrims, shadows, sudden appearances. The result is an uncomfortable marriage of two diametrically opposed styles and functions of theater.

Village Voice, November 1, 1983

American Dreams

(Anne Bogart / Fred Holland)

"How then is the human race to deal with and how are the two sexes to share between them, this terrible power of life and freedom which both men and women desire and fear?" This is the epigraph for Anne Bogart's latest performance, *History, an American Dream,* a monumental piece with a cast of nearly 60 that tackles love, war, and politics.

Bogart's use of space aptly sets forth her epic vision. The audience is seated at the altar of St. Mark's Church, facing the main entrance; the entire nave of the church, including its balcony, is the arena for the sweeping, stylized action. Below, young couples (and one family: man, woman, and child) meet, dance, embrace, divide up according to gender to march as cheerleaders or athletes. Above, a pantheon of American public figures, from Tom Paine, Jane Addams, and Emma Goldman to Vince Lombardi, Douglas MacArthur, Anita Bryant, and Angela Davis, discourse on freedom, violence, sex, and human nature. When the main space is populated by only a few actors, we can see, in the rooms flanking the entrance, more actors sitting, standing, smoking, in assorted tableaux that are only partially visible. The effect seems to extend the performance into infinite space.

Not only physically but also thematically, the performance takes place on two levels. The American heroes and villains carry out a debate of opposing moral and political views, turning human drama into rhetoric—at times moving and passionate but nevertheless a set of abstractions. The spare architecture makes the church's balcony and railings seem at times like a New England pulpit, at times like a courtroom, at times like a lecture hall. The characters have names and distinctive appearances, yet they function as symbols. It is the mass of nameless yet highly individuated figures below that vividly plays out the crises and banal details that make life's pattern.

After the couples meet and mate (not all are heterosexual pairings), they change their clothes into war costumes, and, in shadows slashed by the beams of gyrating lights, they run, fall, slide, and collapse—their lives have been cracked open by war. Later, in a scene whose simplicity wrenches the heart, one by one each couple reunites.

I like *History* less than Bogart's *Women and Men, a big dance* of last year, perhaps because some of the power of her effects weakens on second viewing. The script here didn't live up to the force and poignancy of the action; at times the characters' speeches were reminiscent of a high school history pageant. This may have been intentional, since there was also an "instructor" on the main floor who announced the characters, but in any case it came off awkwardly. Still, the ambition and scope of the piece were impressive.

Fred Holland's *Jack Johnson (notes)* was a collage of slides, music, film, taped reminiscence, and staged action. As the title suggests, this was not a biography, but an elusive, atmospheric collection of fragments describing the life of the first black boxer to win the world heavyweight championship, which he held from 1908 to 1915. The piece was an affecting meditation on the contradictions of a black man, a winner, both lionized and victimized by white society. His success, his money, and his predilection for white women cut him off from black culture, but his race set him apart from the whites around him. This is a different side of American history than Bogart's American dream.

The scene is set in a gym, where Holland as Johnson has his head shaved then is carefully dressed and his hands taped by his trainer (played by Hank Smith). He works out for a long time, warming up, punching a bag or the air, jumping rope, rinsing his mouth with water. The real-time workout is punctuated by bells that mark out increasing lengths of activity. Meanwhile, a woman in a bathrobe (Ariella Vidach) enters and cuts up vegetables, cooks a chicken, reads and drinks. Johnson comes home to her, the two erotically embrace, he leaves, and we hear the shower go on. The smells, sounds, and unhurried actions, all for real, create a striking sense of physicality and immediacy; the tedium and loneliness pervading the scene are intermittently broken, more dramatically by the kiss, less so by the grace of Holland's/Johnson's movements.

Later the trainer goes out the window and is attacked; Holland dances a dance built of feinting, rocking, crouching, and jumping moves; he builds a toy train set and the train circles the track endlessly. A film, projected onto the window that marks the kitchen so that it bounces back on the kitchen wall but as if through memory's reflecting filter, shows actual footage of Johnson, knocked out finally as part of a compromising deal with the American government, intercut with a bullfight.

Village Voice, November 15, 1983

As the Egg Turns
(Rachel Rosenthal)

The education of Rachel Rosenthal reads like a who's who of the modern arts. As a child in pre–World War II Paris, she studied ballet with Olga Preobrajenska (the great Russian imperial ballerina who after the revolution trained a whole generation of European dancers, including Balanchine's "baby ballerinas"). When war broke out, Rosenthal's family fled to Brazil then New York, where she was drawn to the work of Pearl Primus and Katherine Dunham. She studied painting with Hans Hoffman, drama with Herbert Berghof and Erwin Piscator, and dancing with Merce Cunningham, whose company she performed with in 1950–51. Rosenthal cites her reading of Artaud's *Theater and Its Double* as a major force in her vision of performance.

Moving to California in 1956, Rosenthal set up her Instant Theater in Los Angeles. She describes it as an amalgam of collective ritual, abstract art, poetry, and dance that had roots in Zen Buddhism, chance, and Theater of Cruelty. In the 1970s Rosenthal was active in the feminist art movement in Los Angeles, and in 1975, like so many feminist artists on the West Coast, she turned to performance art as a possible means for transcending not only artistic but also personal and social boundaries. The early performances took the form of personal, autobiographical exorcisms.

Traps is a global exorcism. Can performance art change the world? In the cultures where it can (or seems to) performance isn't an esoteric form for art world audiences. Given the context of her performance, Rosenthal comes as close to restoring some kind of faith in the power of consciousness as anyone. There's something she understands about the charismatic, healing force of the performer who can inhabit and then shed personae like so many masks that is worlds away from the mystical mumbo-jumbo so often served up in the marriage of feminism and religion or in the fashionable readings of performer as latter-day shaman. If Rosenthal is any kind of priestess, she is the Zen sort, who whacks the neophyte across the ass and cracks the most irreverent jokes, all integral to subtly pointing out the way. No accounts I've read of

Rosenthal's "holistic" outlook and "ritualistic" performances prepared me for a presence so unpriggish, so ironic, so rough-hewn. On the other hand, her picture on the Franklin Furnace program—a woman with jutting jaw, shaved head, black gash of a mouth, pugnacious gestures, and camouflage pants—belied the moments of grace, coquetry, tenderness, or warmth.

The performance begins with the projection of a color slide of the ocean, out of focus. We hear the ocean's sounds as Rosenthal, in a white hooded cape and mask, scatters dried beans among the spectators. The ghostly figure stands still as Rosenthal's voice, on tape, recites the riddle of doctrine from Huang Po: "The fundamental doctrine of the Dharma is that there are no Dharmas, yet this doctrine of no-Dharma is in itself a Dharma." For Rosenthal the mind's own traps are fundamental, but there are also endless traps that are biological, social, political.

In a scene that seems straight from a Japanese Noh play she sits at a table, lights a candle, and repeatedly twists bits of paper into puppet moths that fly into the flame and explode. Disrobing to become the guerrilla soldier of the program photo, Rosenthal mimes shooting and tossing grenades, while she raves about insects in a virtuoso mad scene. Another change of character, and she is a simpering hostess. "I would like to tell you a little story in pictures." As she snaps her fingers to signal slide changes, she recreates the events that led up to her inadvertently causing the fall of her blind dog, Zatoichi, from her studio balcony. Now Rosenthal becomes professorial. The anecdote was an object lesson in how we lay traps—"acts committed by one part of you to entrap the other part." She illustrates her analysis of traps with poster-paper titles. But, after urging us to recall our own "recent and/or spectacular traps," she exhorts us to broaden our vision, to see how minuscule our own traps are from the perspective of the biosphere.

She tells a fairy tale about two countries poised on the brink of war. Then her honeyed voice mimics the narration of an educational film as slide images show, through the interaction of hard-boiled eggs (halved and whole) and small colorful toy animals, trees, and geometric forms, the story of viruses. The last slide shows the eggs destroyed by the invader toys. Rosenthal blows out the candle with a scream.

But there is a coda. "It can't end like this!" Rosenthal protests. She reminds us that we are not insects, programmed by our genes. She obsesses about scientific theories that point to hope for the future. Five times she picks up an egg from the white table. "Will it be all . . . ," she throws the egg on the floor. It splatters. "Or nothing?" The sixth time she throws the egg at the audience. "Chicken!" she reviles us as some duck. The egg is hard-boiled.

Finally, she urges us to look for the unexpected, untapped sources of affection in the world. Slides show her combing and caressing a pet rat, to the sound of Chopin. The final slide shows a whole egg. And somehow, that simple hope, utterly without sentimentality, makes you believe her.

Village Voice, November 29, 1983

Diaspora Dance: Sacred to Doo-Wop

(A Traveling Jewish Theater)

Hasidism, the mystical folk tradition of Judaism, has an odd relation to performance. On the one hand, its world is saturated with the sacred. To make or even see theater as we know it—that is, as a secular activity—would constitute a profane act. On the other hand, the daily lives of the Hasidim are framed and animated at every moment by strictly prescribed rituals that must be performed properly each time or the entire universe could perish.

The correspondence between ritual and theater is not simply metaphoric. The weekly Shabbes observance, for example, is a masterful piece of staging, down to the special costumes, lighting effects, timing, and strictly defined roles within the family and within the community. The traditional Purim *shpil*, a morality play given in the shul itself, is an actual dramatization incorporated, along the lines of the medieval church tropes, into the larger holy day ceremony.

In making an anthology of Jewish writing Jerome Rothenberg, the poet, understood the complexities of not only the relationship of a body-oriented mystical sect within a larger tradition that officially denies the body but also the (less obvious) connections between subversive Hasidism, its poetry and visions, and the writings and performance of a disparate collection of moderns, from Gertrude Stein, Tristan Tzara, and Louis Zukofsky to Lenny Bruce and Bob Dylan. In his *Big Jewish Book* Rothenberg juxtaposes events like the Living Theater's *Paradise Now* or various sound and gesture events à la contemporary performance art with texts like the eighteenth-century mystic Nachman of Bratzlav's "Vision Event":

> Imagine that you could constantly recall all that we know about
>   the future world.
> There is an angel with a thousand heads.
> Each head has a thousand tongues.
> Each tongue has a thousand voices.

Each voice has a thousand melodies.
Imagine the beauty of this angel's song.

The Hasidic cosmology is a complicated one that involves sexual imagery, oppositions of light and dark, male, female, and visual and conceptual metaphors for God and the soul that include the human body, a shower of sparks, and an esoteric system of numerology. It's a diffuse, elusive ethos with roots in the Kabbalah, or collection of mystical texts, and with thousands of branches, based on personal revelation, in Sephardic and Ashkenazic communities in Europe, America, and Israel.

A Dance of Exile treats a central theme of Hasidism—the primal exile not of the physical diaspora of the Jews but of the ineluctable separation of the human soul from God that prayer will ultimately heal—in a Rothenbergian spirit that embraces the elasticity and diversity of Kabbalah in the broadest sense (i.e., "tradition," paradoxically textual and personal). The performance is a kind of two-man vaudeville, a song-and-dance act that illustrates and comments on the condition of exile with nihilistic humor, the cryptic poetry of dreams, and a musical pastiche that ranges from Ladino songs to shouted incantations to nouveau doo-wop. The literary sources range from Rothenberg to Rilke to Gershom Sholem.

Although there's no linear narrative, the performance organizes itself around the encounters between a thirteenth-century Spanish Hasid who hasn't slept for 3,000 days (Albert Greenberg) and a Yiddish-style Bowery bum (Corey Fischer) who introduces himself as the Wandering Jew and punctuates his revelations with some angular softshoe. The two team up, spar, teach each other, and at times don masks to become more cosmic personae: a Lucifer and a Gabriel, if you want to think of it that way.

The evening begins and ends with the legend of King Saul's encounter with the Witch of Endor, the woman-shaman he seeks out, after he's banished all such seers, to help him save his kingdom; she refuses him, explaining that to call up spirits of the dead is now illegal. There's a connection between these women and the notion of the Shekhinah, the feminine aspect of God, that *A Dance of Exile* pushes. (The Shekhinah is said to have gone into exile, with the Jews, when the Temple was destroyed. She will be reunited with God, the sparks that are souls will be reunited with the holy flame, the essential source, and the universe, which we experience as fragmented, will become whole when all is redeemed.) But somehow even a broad reading of Kabbalah seems to me to go too far when it makes claims toward feminism. When Greenberg sings a Ladino translation of a song called "You Hold Up Half the Sky," I think even the plasticity of the Kabbalah is stretched beyond belief.

There are wonderful moments in *A Dance of Exile,* Fischer's dancing and gesticulations among them. But on the whole its own diffuseness serves not to reflect its subject but to make it even more baffling than it already is.

Village Voice, December 13, 1983

Murder to Go

I'm in Cape May for the weekend. The weather is glorious, and the architecture is stunning. All these restored Victorian manors in improbable colors with gingerbread trim, the serene ocean, the deserted boardwalk, the mild sun making everything sparkle—the ambience is one of an eerie, nostalgic beauty, of seeing this place somehow not only in the wrong season but also in the wrong century, as if a time machine had slightly misfired when it deposited me and my fellow tourists in this elegant resort whose heyday was 100 years ago. We round one more corner on our walking tour.

Suddenly the somewhat ghostly calm explodes, the present brutally forcing its way into pale meditations on history with a bloody splash. An ambulance is parked on the street, its lights flashing. On the roof of the Duke of Windsor hotel—where some of us spent the night—a corpse is being photographed. A police detective rounds up our shocked group and herds us into the hotel's sitting room for interrogation. Murder? Murder in sunny, sleepy Cape May? Each one of us looks around a circle of acquaintances innocently formed less than a day ago and shivers. Fifty minds begin to tick paranoiacally.

Well, maybe not all that paranoiacally. After all, we're not just 50 ordinary tourists, nor are we in town for the meeting of the Society for Architectural Preservation that's also pounding the pavements. This (staged) murder, along with a buried treasure and a second murder later in the day is exactly why we've gathered in Cape May this weekend, for some of our number are actors and most of us are spectator-participants in a performance called *Captain Morgan's Mysterious Manors,* organized by a company called Murder to Go that specializes in mounting "mystery vacations"—both private and public—designed for special locales, such as trains, ships, and Victorian seashore resorts. The thing is, no one is sure just how many or who of us are the actors. We've spent nearly every minute since we arrived in this town—every inch of which seems to have become incorporated into a gigantic theatrical set—witnessing and overhearing the clues that, with the discovery of John Dannenbaum's body, we are beginning to marshal into 50 different structures of coherence.

I'm a total murder mystery addict, but, as the weekend approaches, I'm getting nervous about going on this particular adventure. What if it's like a snuff film—I mean, what if the whole thing has actually been fabricated by one of my enemies as an elaborate cover-up for really bumping me off? That there were ads in the *New York Times* is no solace—I've read *The Red-Headed League!* I've never heard of David Landau, the director of Murder to Go, but the name has a familiar ring. Maybe I gave him a bad review once, and he has a fine sense of poetic justice. Maybe the subtitle of this play is: "The Death of a Performance Critic." I dismiss these fantasies as childish nonsense and try to drag them out of the corners of my mind by cheerily telling everyone I know about my plans. "Do you think it'll be like a snuff film and you'll really be murdered?" my friends respond unanimously.

Friday dawns clear and sunny. I take myself firmly in hand. This is not anything like a snuff film, I assure myself. This is just another attempt to break through the obdurate conventions of the murder mystery genre. Remember the mystery dossiers of Dennis Wheatley and J. G. Links in the 1930s, complete with letters, maps, press reports, photographs, and the fatal tablet of arsenic (rendered nontoxic, of course)—and the solution sealed inside the back cover of the "book"? Remember Chastain's *Who Killed the Robins Family?,* the mystery-as-lotto-book you responded to by sending your solution of the crime to the publisher who locked the answer in a safety deposit box? Besides, Murder to Go has already staged several versions of *The Mystery Express* on the train to Montreal.

I while away the bus ride from Manhattan with a good mystery. Four hours from Port Authority I stumble into the Victorian Rose, a little bed-and-breakfast guesthouse, where I've been assigned to room with Margo Adler from National Public Radio. Once we get to know each other, we figure there can't be any mystery two nosy, aggressive girl-reporters like us can't solve. I feel courage flowing through my veins again, especially after we sip the Captain Morgan's Spiced Rum that's been left on our doorstep. Captain Morgan, it seems, buried some treasure at Cape May in the seventeenth century, and the liquor company that makes the rum, a subdivision of Seagram's, is donating the pirate's papers to the Cape May historical archives in the town library. They're also footing the bill for the party Saturday night.

Our group, which is staying in three different houses, meets for dinner at nine o'clock at the Washington Inn. On the one hand, I'm trying to figure out who's an actor and who's a spectator, who's a potential murderer and who's a potential victim. On the other hand, I'm trying to find a ride back to New York on Sunday morning. And, besides, I'm curious who else would end up on a mystery vacation. If it doesn't turn out to be a snuff film, I think, I can only hope that it isn't a singles bar either.

There's an architect from Manhattan, Andrew York, but for suspiciously vague reasons he won't commit himself to drive us home. There are a lot of people from Philadelphia. There are several lawyers (none of them of the criminal persuasion, though), one clothing manufacturer, an envelope manufacturer who reviews classical music on the side, a bunch of people who work for Seagram's, two college freshmen with split majors in criminology and theater, a few Long Island matrons. There's even a descendant of Captain Morgan, Loretta Morgan, a glamorous historian who looks like she stepped straight from a James Bond film in her glittery dress. There's a brother and sister, Philip and Sarah Jackson, who grew up in Cape May—their father drowned ten years ago looking for the Morgan treasure and they've come back especially for this weekend, to make their stab at it. A few people are mystery buffs, but a surprising number are simply looking for an exciting vacation.

A representative from Seagram's presents the town librarian with Captain Morgan's 300-year-old map of Cape May. It shows Indian camps, a fort, a river, the shoreline, and not much else. Loretta Morgan reads a cryptic poem written by the pirate that, the legend says, gives secret instructions for finding the treasure. (We'd already found copies of the poem, with contemporary maps of the town, in our room.) The poem is studded with ciphers and compass points. It also mentions a certain A. Smythe. "Did you check the local phone book yet?" the woman on my right at the dinner table whispers.

As soon as coffee is served and people have started to mill around again, looking at the old map or visiting the bar, a man suddenly jumps up, snaps his fingers, swears, and runs out of the room. I grab Margo, and we're hot on his heels, with about five other people. We chase him around the block, and then a number of things happen, although I can't vouch for the proper sequence. Suddenly we're rushing back and forth, from one familiar landmark to another, and we're witnessing odd scenes—elliptical frictions—between the man we've been tailing, John Dannenbaum, and one couple in each hotel. It seems to have to do with the treasure. Dannenbaum quarrels with an old couple, the Thorns, in the sitting room of the Brass Bed. Next he has a run-in with the Jacksons on the porch of the Victorian Rose. He kisses Sarah, and she slaps him. Finally, in the Duke of Windsor he spats with York and Morgan.

We are vigilant. Dannenbaum disappears with Morgan into her upstairs bedroom then slips a note under the opposite door. "Meet me at the boardwalk at midnight," one of us shamelessly reads to the rest. We're forming teams, identifying the main characters, splitting up to chase this one this way, that one that way. By midnight, when Loretta Morgan stands windblown on the beach, the rest of us are there with her. York meets her. They embrace then head back to the Washington Inn. We definitely feel like voyeurs. Suddenly, shots ring out in the Duke of Windsor. We're rushing back and forth along the now familiar streets of Cape May, and, at 1:30 my feet wear out, and I sit on the porch to rest. Someone says something will happen at two o'clock, and it's just before two that Margo and I, having just gone to bed, are awakened by a woman's screams.

The next day at breakfast our host at the hotel tells of a double murder that happened exactly 100 years ago. Percy Morgan, a descendant of the pirate, was found murdered at a stable on the site of today's Washington Inn. A leading suspect was a man named Dannenbaum, whose family was connected with the Brass Bed and the architect Stephen Button. But Dannenbaum was killed later that day at the Mainstay Inn, a gentleman's gambling club formerly known as Jackson's Clubhouse. An architect named York was involved as well. Things are beginning to repeat themselves; history begins to form patterns. York was found murdered later the same day.

So we take our walking tour and discover the body. Detective Lyric, a model of the hard-boiled dick except that he works for the Cape May police (supposedly) instead of as a private eye, manages to grill us with the requisite plucky irony. It's damn hard to remember the order of things. Last night seems like a fog, but somehow we manage to reconstruct what happened. By now we're all working together. If someone overhears something, they run to tell the group. The grapevine guarantees that you don't always have to witness the evidence yourself.

Still, Margo and I secretly conduct our own excursion. A stroke of genius—we read Captain Morgan's poem as a contemporary description of the town. We pace off the 854 paces, find basketball courts—"Some boucaneers/Jumped the ring running footraces"—and then the reference to Pan must mean the bandstand near the mall. . . . we're in the middle of the woods and it's time to meet the group again. If anyone was tempted to come here this weekend to find swinging singles romance, they wouldn't have the time or energy to conduct it.

In the middle of our tour of the sumptuous Mainstay Inn—an extraordinary work of preservation—the second murder takes place. Philip Jackson. And here we had eaten lunch with him, exchanged the most banal remarks, tried, five or six of us, to transpose his copy of the seventeenth-century map of Cape May onto the contemporary one and to mark off the treasure spot, reading the poem as strictly, as nautically, as seventeenth-century, as possible. The tension escalates. We're rounded into another sitting room for another interrogation, until Morgan and York grab the sextant (evidence in the first murder), sight it against the setting sun, and we all rush to the boardwalk to dig up the treasure.

Things are relatively quiet for a couple of hours, until the party that night, when our Detective Lyric reviews the evidence, and each one of us casts a vote. Fourteen of us guess right. (I won't reveal the villain, since the performance will be repeated.) Even the murder victims come back for curtain calls.

The script wasn't great, but in a way it didn't matter. The situation supplied a lot. No script can account in advance for the material an active audience will bring to an open-ended context. So a lot depends on improvisation—Sarah and Philip Jackson, for instance, reminiscing about their father and their childhood over lunch. The feeling that everything that happened was part of the set of clues meant that the script could be skeletal and still the performance would be rich. And the grapevine accounted for a lot, too—if an event happened even with only a few witnesses, the entire group eventually learned about it. The sense of cooperation was key to the excitement and intensity, but so was the fact that an entire murder mystery unraveled in just over 24 hours. The social glue supplied by constant action together—by living together, actors and spectators, all constantly under one another's gaze—outweighed what, on deeper inspection, might emerge as flaws. For instance, the clash of styles between Lyric's hard-boiled brilliance, the Victorian setting that would seem to call for a British-style detective, and the buried treasure motif.

What was impressive was the way the performance was tailored to the locale, the way the town's history, right down to famous names, was incorporated into the fabricated plot (for, of course, stopping off at the local bookstore in a spare moment to find a better map, I thumbed through the local guidebook and discovered that, although there was a Dannenbaum, a York, a Jackson, and a Stephen Button, there were no murders on October 29, 1883, and Captain Morgan was nowhere to be found). And just as impressive was the handling of logistics, the timing that made us turn the corner and discover the first body or let us remain uncertain who was missing from the tour of the Mainstay just before the second murder or had us digging for treasure in the setting sun.

And, although there's something odd about the mixing of roles that had to happen on this weekend—the fact that we spectators all began, in each other's eyes, as suspects but all ended up as detectives—the nature of this performance, this do-it-yourself, not-quite-theater, felt satisfyingly apt for a mystery form. It's no accident that, although mysteries rarely work well on the stage, the theater and its relatives (magic shows, ballet, sports events, etc.) are favorite settings for the mystery novel. One is a metaphor for the other, for not only does the mystery setup presume that at least one person has been playing a role (that is, the murderer has constructed for him- or herself a new, innocent persona). The form also describes the interlocking tasks of the two major characters in a way that sets two kinds of performance into battle: the murderer, who is a kind of performance artist constructing an entire situation as a one-person show; and the detective, whose moment of triumph takes the form of master storytelling.

Village Voice, December 20, 1983

Man in Shadow

(Robert Whitman / Sylvia Palacios)

Robert Whitman's *Eclipse* is in many ways complementary to his *Rain-cover* of last year. Like so many of his performances, both works mix cosmic and earthly imagery—the meteorological and the visceral—and elements of nature and of work in poetic, dreamlike structures. Apparitions are engineered with elaborate stage machinery, not always seamlessly, thus with a crude magic projecting palpable visions rich in verbal associations, sets of cultural categories and oppositions. Things fall according to the laws of gravity but are answered by other things that improbably rise. Fire and water mix. People are moved by invisible forces. Films show static objects.

With its film of a city skyline, its set of laundry hanging out to dry, its burning room, and its endlessly emptying drum of water, *Raincover* evoked an urban reverie. *Eclipse* is bucolic in tone. Its first tableau is the opening of a wooden gate by a man dressed all in silver; inside the gate a back-projected film shows a cow to the accompaniment of recorded bird calls and other animal sounds.

Raincover contraposed fire and water in a bright, transparent key; its colors were the primary ones. *Eclipse,* not surprisingly, is cast in penumbra, and its elements are air and earth. The secondary colors play off the primaries like a minor melody alternating with a major chord. Much of the activity takes place behind a black scrim. Air is made visible by the movement of autumn leaves—in the opening film the leaves "fall" upward to reveal a group seated at a white-clothed dinner table, and later the performers and stagehands empty sacks of leaves that swirl around the filmed image of a hand gesturing repeatedly. But other things fall as well. A large rock slowly and soundlessly crashes through a wooden table. A man suspended nine feet above ground opens his coat, and first gravel then glitter cascades from his armpit.

Near the end of the performance the title image is played out in a film that shows the obliteration of a human head, rather than the sun. That primeval emblem is a chilling conclusion to the sequence representing the passing of autumn into winter, linking the extinguishing of light, of the sun, and of summer to the blotting out of human consciousness, of life. The sparks and floods in *Raincover,* the glowing object created at its end, are answered in *Eclipse,* despite its quiet humor, by a stark, dark dirge and a rising black sun.

After Whitman's piece the audience is led to another room in the building for Sylvia Palacios's *Irregulars.* Like Whitman, Palacios deals in unexpected images built of quotidian objects and actions. Her stage machinery is less elaborate, and her tableaux rely more on live human doings. In the past her performances have been evenings of short, unconnected works, primarily visual and nonverbal. *Irregulars* is a double departure in that it is a single stream of visual images that uses a verbal text (poems by Ron Padgett) in various forms—spoken live and recorded as well as written.

Still, the visual track predominates, and, since the imagery is rarely connected to the poems' content, the words disappear quickly, while many striking visions remain etched in the memory. Six electric blenders filled with a deep blue liquid line the front edge of the stage space, like footlights. The performance begins when all six start to whir simultaneously, whipping their contents into the ice-blue froth. Three actors are stationed on chairs attached to the back wall and raised well above the floor at odd angles. Two more stand on high side platforms and send words, painted on white signs, to one another by means of a clothesline and pulley. In the opening and closing scenes a woman lies sleeping in a slowly revolving bed made of newspapers. A woman general in Khaki drag struts or sits quietly with two other women, at a long table also made of newspapers.

Palacios's favored medium has always been the paper cutout, and here the most successful fusion of word and image is the short vignette to the poem "Cut Shadows," in which paper models of things—like staircases—are contrasted to inverse cutouts that can be seen as their shadows or their absences.

The performers in *Eclipse* are Rachel Liebling and Peter Melville; in *Irregulars,* Palacios and Charles Allcroft, T. W. Allen, Delia Doherty, Paul Martin Narkiewicz, Ilse Rumpler, Benjamin J. Slazer, and Denyse Schmidt. The production staff for both performances: Richard Kerry, Peter Melville, and Marcia Scanlon.

Although both performances are under an hour long, making a double bill seem a sensible presentation, both require that the spectator concentrate with full faculties. The result is that one's attention flags somewhere in the middle of *Irregulars.* I would prefer to see each event separately.

Village Voice, January 10, 1984

Canny Cantata / Peaked Paik
(I Giullari di Piazza / Nam June Paik)

Alessandra Belloni has adapted this seventeenth-century Neapolitan Christmas play into a kind of folk opera in which a double plot is punctuated by vaguely connected songs. The result is something like constantly switching TV channels on Sunday morning—if they'd had TV in Baroque Italy. There's good music, fine singing, a little dancing, a situation comedy, a religious drama, and, although nothing particularly falls into a linear narrative with anything else, the glue that lingers in the background is this Holy Child. I don't mean this as a criticism; this fragmentation adds to the invigorating sense of wonder that made me wish this two-and-a-half hour spectacle would never end.

La Cantata dei Pastori, which was written by Andrea Perrucci, takes place just before the birth of Jesus. Mary and Joseph are traveling to Bethlehem and looking for a place to stay. The Devil tries to intercept them and halt the Savior's birth by sending out his minions to harass them. Meanwhile, Razzullo, a commedia dell'arte character, who is always complaining that he's famished, is also traveling to Bethlehem. Every time it seems he is about to get a meal, the antics of the demons affect him too. There's a Sybil, come back to life from Egypt to announce the birth of Christ, a dragon that Mary kills with the help of the Angel Gabriel, a tempest, a hunter, a fisherman, shepherds, dances, a procession. In the music, directed by John La Barbera, there are all manner of love songs, religious songs (sometimes a union of the two), ritual chants (to make the sun rise, to exorcise the plague), lullabies, worksongs, and songs of social criticism, played on an ensemble of instruments including bagpipes, a mandolin, tambourines, and a baroque guitar.

Although the dialogue is spoken and sung in Italian, the plot is simple enough, the action clear enough, and the masked players' performance style expressive enough to successfully convey the meaning. But there is also a narrator (Carl Asch, who triples as Saint Joseph and a Demon), who dances, juggles, and summarizes the plot from time to time in English.

All of the actors, except Giuseppe De Falco, the hungry Razzullo, play at least two roles. Maybe this is for the sake of economy, but the doubling has its added, subtle, even ironic effects. There is a peculiarly modern, psychoanalytic twist in the fact, for example, that Belloni plays both Mary and Belzebu, the head demon. Elisa Mereghetti, who co-directed the play (with Belloni), plays a fisherman and the Sybil, and Saro Castorina plays a hunter and the Angel Gabriel—two instances of casting that stress the humble, peasant stratum of the Christmas story.

There's another modern twist that comes partly from the Italian conception of the centrality of the Virgin Mother but also, I'm sure, from Belloni's adaptation and especially from her powerful, robust performance as Mary. The mixture of pre-Christian elements in the songs and symbolism with this view of the Madonna—who makes the sun rise and slays dragons, among other things—hints at an interpretation of Christianity that embraces goddess worship. And, of course, the Italian version of class struggle is made clear through the interpolation of the Razzullo story—being a scribe, he must go hungry because he refuses the jobs offered him by the peasants—and through the traditional songs that protest the power of the rich and strong or that complain of the scarcity of food in the countryside.

The first event in *A Counterpoint to Good Morning Mr. Orwell* at the Kitchen was a public viewing on multiple receivers of the New Year's Day transmission of *Good Morning Mr. Orwell,* a transatlantic television satellite broadcast originating in both New York (Channel 13) and Paris (FR 3). Conceived by Nam June Paik, the show has a list of credits too long to name here, including director Emile Ardolino and writers Mitchell Kriegman and Leslie Fisher. George Plimpton hosted the New York edition of the broadcast.

The stated purpose of *Good Morning . . .* was to challenge the pejorative Orwellian view of technology by using it as a productive medium to unite disparate performers in disparate places into a single (though pluralistic) global village. (Although Plimpton mentioned that Orwell's other point in *1984* was the specter of totalitarianism, that topic was never broached in the show.) Another, implicit purpose for the program was to expose avant-garde performance to a broader (TV) audience than the venues for live performance, such as the Kitchen itself, can garner. Maybe television *is* the performance medium of the future, even the present. But one wonders what will become of the avant-garde if it simply copies popular forms. If it's only a bad version of the real thing, why not turn the channel and watch the real thing? *Good Morning . . .* had its marvelous moments—Laurie Anderson and Peter Gabriel's opening number, Allen Ginsberg's song on how to meditate, lots of footage of break dancing, Merce Cunningham's implacable movements, some of the psychedelic imagery of John Sanborn and Dean Winkler animation in *Act III*, a promo tape for music by Philip Glass. But both format and content often seemed like a weak mixture of the "Ed Sullivan Show," "Saturday Night Live," and MTV.

The current avant-garde in dance and performance emulates popular forms for all sorts of reasons, not only for accessibility but also for vitality and meaning. That it strongly rejects the previous generation's serious, analytic, intellectual attitude toward art was evident in *Good Morning . . . ,* which skipped from luminaries of the 1960s to the 1980s with not even a fleeting glance at the 1970s. (A 1960s touch was inadvertently included when satellite breakdowns forced the participants and crew to improvise constantly. I'm told that technical problems in New York also cut out a lot of the New York material.) In fact, when the Kitchen began broadcasting the football bowls on two monitors and reruns of *Good Morning . . .* immediately after the live transmission, the program was vastly improved.

Village Voice, January 24, 1984

Performers against Intervention

(Artists Call against U.S. Intervention in Central America / Deep inside Porn Stars)

Of the several evenings constituting the performance festival section of Artists Call, I saw only the last two: the first mostly performance art and the second mostly dance. What was striking to me about both evenings was the remarkable pluralism of the programming. The roster of participants ranged from groups and individuals who primarily identify themselves as cultural workers—that is, their political and artistic activities are inextricably intertwined—to avant-gardists who don't ordinarily perform in a political context. The work ranged from agitprop exhortations to dadaist gestures, from multimedia barrages to solo presence, from pieces made about specific people and events in Central America to those that spoke generally or even only vaguely to themes of revolution and imperialism. And, although a few pieces were wonderful, some boring, and more in between, all had admirable intentions.

There was something else unusual about these evenings—the mixture of political instruction and art; people who had recently visited Nicaragua as part of an artists' group told of their experiences, and the emcees reminded the audiences why these Artists Call events were taking place. I would have preferred more hard information and analysis about the present situation in Central America and less 1960s-style romantic rhapsodizing about revolution (after all, no one in the audience had to be convinced that what the Reagan administration is doing to aid repressive governments is wrong and that to build a true people's culture is good). But at least the attempt to raise consciousness was there, and Robbie McCauley's slide show, juxtaposing atrocities in Central America to police brutality (especially to blacks) in the United States spoke louder than words.

Of the performances I was particularly moved by Jana Haimsohn, whose sputter of vocalization and convulsive gestures metamorphosed from images of animal sounds to speaking in tongues to a state of possession by the soul of a baby shot, along with other children and women, by soldiers. Haimsohn's control in rendering utter loss of control was impressive. Herb Perr, Irving Wexler, and Marlene Lortev's affecting piece contrasted slides of the Caribbean and Central America as a vacation paradise and as a battlefield, while the three masked performers took turns satirizing various unconcerned points of view about U.S. intervention there and calling for political action, in classic agitprop style. Lortev ranted, as a coffee addict whose pleasure must be sated despite the human toll its commerce exacts.

As a whole, the dance evening was more satisfying with its strong, disparate dances. Grupo Bambule (Awilda Acosta, Linda Delerme, and Pat Rampolla, plus musicians), a Puerto Rican folk dance group, portrayed three women shackled by women's work then throwing off their chains. Hallie Wannamaker's solo, *General Hospital* (danced by Ann Lall), was a starkly, tensely expressive dance to the accompaniment of a recorded voice reading a newspaper clipping about a soap opera actress who saved the stray cats living in the ABC studios from threatened extinction. As the text was repeated several times, more and more phrases were replaced by references to Central America, until the actress was transformed into a political hero carrying out inspiring revolutionary deeds to save human lives. The text was both funny and heart-rending; the dancing seemed an almost negligible appendage. Johanna Boyce cast her thoughts about El Salvador into a powerful autobiographical form, reminiscing about her teenage romance with a Salvadorean student, his letters to her about the political oppression there, the blossoming of his political consciousness, and his eventual psychological defeat. This tale was interwoven with the story of Boyce's brother's death and of her own education and growth, all of which the choreographer told in a matter-of-fact tone, while her constant stream of intricate but matter-of-fact gestures made delicate images of working, dismantling, and constructing.

Ishmael Houston-Jones's dance on the first evening's program, however, touched me most deeply, because it expressed so frankly the ambivalence much political art refuses to tolerate. (Ron Littke's piece on the same program had a similar theme.) Houston-Jones galloped, flung himself, fell, and posed with his usual amalgam of violence and grace, while he told of his recent visit to Nicaragua and West Germany, his attempts to assimilate all that he had learned and thought about there, and his uncertainty about what kind of political action to take or whether he would even end up taking political action. "Maybe," he pondered, "it's easier to support a revolution that's far away, in a warm country it's nice to visit in winter. Maybe this is a case of political jerking off." Maybe, as he concluded, there *are* no easy answers.

The last performance in a series (with exhibition) on feminist pornography, organized by Carnival Knowledge, was *Deep Inside Porn Stars,* a purported fly-on-the-wall's view of a rap group (in the political, not the musical, sense) formed by seven actresses in X-rated films: Veronica Hart, Gloria Leonard, Annie Sprinkle, Veronica Vera, Sue Nero, Kelly Nichols, and Candida Royalle (their stage names). The framing device splintered quickly as each woman took her turn standing in a spotlight to address the audience directly, telling about her background or her philosophy of life and showing slides that projected not only her sexy superstar image but also her "real" self, and sometimes performing a dance or a song.

The conversation among the group that served as transitional glue between the soliloquies was a strange mixture of feminist polemics, union-organizing rhetoric, locker room and pajama party talk. The ethos that evolved in the course of the evening was a kind of glorious hedonism buttressed by First Amendment rights, the Protestant ethic (a girl has to make a living somehow), and a reductive version of feminist assertiveness (we should have the right to do anything men can do, no matter how exploitative or corrupt; the very fact that a woman does it makes it good). But, oddly enough, this theme was countered by a surprisingly puritan, conservative view that emerged only toward the end: the best sex, and the best life, is simple—monogamy, marriage, and motherhood.

Village Voice, February 7, 1984

Sportin' Solos and Makin' Whoopi

(John Malpede / Whoopi Goldberg)

Two tendencies are emerging clearly in performance art of the 1980s. One is the explicit borrowing of popular and folk entertainment forms as both structure and style: the comic routine, the TV variety show, storytelling, even circus. The second, perhaps a by-product of the first, is the wholesale use of character, especially the device of switching characters. Where avant-garde performers in the 1970s exulted in the self and explored issues of identity through revelatory personal display, now they are involved in the flip side of that quest, endlessly trying on personae. But it's not exactly a Stanislavskian enterprise; as in the work of Eric Bogosian, who may be the godfather of this genre, seamless narrative is ruptured each time the character changes.

John Malpede's recent solo performances are instances of the character-switching genre, and the characters he plays are stock ones from popular sources: the deejay, the TV interview host, the carnival con man. In *Out of the Public Eye* he spreads the format over a group (Malpede, Ann Magnuson, and Frank South). The characters remain more or less constant—a famous athlete and two magazine interviewers / TV sportscasters. But, aptly enough for a performance about sports, the roles are tossed from actor to actor like so many balls. The result is like a cross between Howard Cossell and Tom Stoppard.

Most of the script is devoted to two interviews, one of Bobby Kubey (Malpede), a born-again Christian quarterback. But embedded within these scenes are more plays on role playing, including watching and constructing one's roles through television. The interviewers are trying to capture the "real" Bobby. Both Bobbies enact the same solo nightclub routine in which a coach plays mindgames with a basketball player in a story about a baseball team. Both Bobbies constantly watch themselves on TV and even treat themselves to instant replays of their games and their ads. Bobby Kubey even shows his interviewers a tape of his epiphany—which, he explains, came upon him while he was at home alone watching TV—as he reenacts it for them, turning the event into a duet with himself. Finally, there is a taped, "on-the-spot" interview with a hunger artist who is fasting in a sports stadium, as a kind of athletic event. Malpede is brilliant as the aging Slavic émigré artist who balefully scoffs, in response to Magnuson's beaming journalistic platitudes, "Vot's to admire? I don't eat because there's nothing I'm interested in eating."

On one hand, the string of solo characters is a metaphor for personality splits or for the schizoid sense of contemporary reality. On the other, it is a structural alternative to combining characters in a linear narrative that is familiar from live, radio, and television variety acts. Whoopi Goldberg's *Spook Show* somehow happens on both hands, careening from bathos to pathos, from comic sketches that would be at home on TV to digs at the audience to genuinely tragic studies. Goldberg is black, and her very first confrontation with the audience is the title of her performance; her program note instructs those who might be ignorant that *spook* is a verb and a noun with two meanings: a ghost and, in derogatory slang, a Negro. (My dictionary lists yet another meaning, a shy or ugly girl, which also falls under Goldberg's purview, though she didn't list it.) Goldberg recoups every meaning of the word. Her characters—a junkie on a tour of Europe who meets up with a spirit of Anne Frank, a 13-year-old Valley Girl who aborts herself with a wire hanger, a crippled woman whose lover helps her discover a proud sense of physicality, a winsome child who fantasizes that she'll grow up white and rich—are the disinherited, the ghosts of the earth. And Goldberg's rendition of them haunts us, as she leads us in with laughter and then suddenly turns the tables, casting us into horror or awe or just quiet dignity.

Although at times the script could be tightened—the first monologue is too long—one thing that is flawless in Goldberg's performance is her incredibly accurate perception and portrayal of gesture and personal style of both blacks and whites. As she turns her back to the audience between monologues, she seems to transform her face and body entirely, as well as her voice. So often comedy depends on the cruelty of poking fun at people; Goldberg's humor is partly amazing because it is built on empathy.

Village Voice, February 21, 1984

The World According to Chong
(Ping Chong)

In Ping Chong's most recent performance piece, *A Race,* a group of android insects is graduating into the human world. As we witness their commencement exercises, we hear their headmaster tell them, "You will learn how to remember . . . and how to forget."

Memory is central to Chong's work, not only as a recurring theme but, more fundamentally, as a wellspring of imagery and even methods. At times his stage seems like the mind's screen, where enigmatically evocative impressions gleam in immaculate detail or flicker momentarily. But this screen is not only a visual one; Chong's multiple media mimic different ways of remembering, from the recording or retelling of history to the wordless redolence of familiar music, to the engrams of the muscular system. Chong's performances mix images of the distant past and the present just as our memories do. In *Lazarus* (1972) a biblical story is reenacted in New York. In *Nuit Blanche* (1981) we trace the history of a family. In *A Race* we seem to watch an incident from humankind's prehistory while we listen to reminiscences about the event we are watching.

You can see Chong's work as operating on a microscopic scale—hypnotically concentrating on the infinitely burgeoning moment—or as a global view of the village Earth. It all depends on where memory turns into history. Noël Carroll has written (in *The Drama Review*) that Chong offers us a view of human life as a behavioral surface, bereft of context but mysteriously *there.* The events he portrays, with their fragmented narratives and displaced time schemes, translate as both distant and slightly skewed. Like the Russian Formalists, he is able to comprehend the ordinary by making it strange. Chong referred to the early pieces by his Fiji company as "bricolages"—a French term Chong took from anthropologist Claude Lévi-Strauss that means "new worlds created out of any and all materials at hand." But, like an ethnographer, he is inevitably stuck outside the society he describes, and, since his subject is humankind, he is everywhere a perennial Outsider to whom the views, habits, and ceremonies he studies are exotic and inexplicable.

For Chong, who was born in 1946 in Toronto to parents who had emigrated from China and, with difficulty, finally settled in New York a year later, a childhood as a "ghetto kid," and, in particular, growing up in the intimate world of New York Chinese culture of the 1950s, has deeply informed his work. "The issue of memory in my work is directly related to my sense of exile from my own culture," he remarks, "or what vestiges of my own culture I had. When you leave your culture, you don't know you're giving something up. But if you don't live in that culture—if you're an alien in another one—you can't stay with it; it's dead."

Chong's parents owned the first dim sum shop on Bayard Street, but they were also performers in the Chinese Opera, and in his earliest childhood they performed (in the local moviehouse) on a daily basis. The Chinese Opera gave him a model for a theater that was non-psychological and full of pageantry.

After studying art at Pratt Institute, Chong found himself in the midst of various dilemmas. He felt the urge for a live, three-dimensional, time-oriented art that painting didn't satisfy. He also felt estranged from Western painting and found the cultural adjustment of leaving China-town disorienting. A devotee of films, beginning with the Chinese films of his childhood, after he saw *The Red Desert* and *Citizen Kane,* he found himself committed professionally to film. He trained as a filmmaker at School of Visual Arts for three years. And yet, when he finished, he still felt the need for alternatives. He took a course with Meredith Monk in 1970 and felt he had come home. He began to look at dance and to find an open format for his own artistry.

Since meeting Monk, he has not only performed in her work (including leading roles in *Vessel, Small Scroll,* and *Quarry*) and collaborated with her (on *Paris, Chacon,* and *Venice/Milan*) but also made his own body of performance works. "For me, the most important influence has been Meredith's unbridled imagination. It was completely liberating."

Although Chong doesn't use dance in the strictly technical sense, dancing is crucial to his work in two ways. It is through highly stylized movement sequences that the characters in his pieces become social-ized. Acculturation becomes palpably physical. In the fairy tale *Rainer and the Knife* (1981), in which a boy's lost knife is used to kill a dictator and then the innocent boy, recovering his knife, is punished for the murder, Rainer's education consists of his learning his mother's sema-phoric gestures. In *A Race* the acolytes wear black bands on each hand that individuate their fingers, and in one sequence a guardian shapes the pliable body of one acolyte into a more recognizably human piece of anatomy, rewarding him periodically with Pavlovian feedings. But also social dance, sparingly used, is a powerful symbol for social relations in Chong's work. In *A Race* one measure that the acolytes have not yet achieved humanity is that their group rendition of the two-step is all too rigidly symmetrical.

But language is equally charged. In *Fear and Loathing in Gotham* (1975), a tale of child-murder based on Fritz Lang's *M,* the killer, a Chinese immigrant, is shown in the full agony of his alienation when he tries to learn English from a record. In several of Chong's pieces the dialogue is multilingual, and for the spectator who understands only English even that language is often cast as baffling. Answers come before questions; facts float in a sea of nonsequiturs. "On the one hand, language is a personal defense strategy. I want the audience to understand the other side of the fence, what it feels like not to comprehend. But then, sometimes you see a situation better when you don't understand the language, because you pay attention to everything else. You can't be passive about language: language is culture. I sometimes feel that in each letter is the essence, the history of a civilization."

There is a tension in Chong's work between the dark themes of passion, melancholy, and death, and the jewel-like, lucid precision of the images, meticulously crafted. There is another tension between the idiosyncratic and the universal, a constant vertigo in which scales of meaning shift and humans oscillate between being of earthshaking importance on a personal level and being just one more insignificant species on this planet in this millennium. The moment expands intensely until it explodes into eternity, into a long-distance perspective. This has always been part of Chong's style, but the equivalence of all things in nature is especially striking in *A Race*. It comes, Chong says, from his recent readings in natural history. "I've learned that there are different realities in nature. For instance, there's a bamboo that only flowers once every 100 years. Just thinking about that kind of timing can entirely change your experience of time."

Although Chong's oeuvre is saturated with political references (*Humboldt's Current* and *Nuit Blanche* are both "about" imperialism, and many of the other works can be read as allegorical indictments of political oppression), that aspect of the work does not predominate. "If I were to be seen as making a political statement, I would say it is a very general one—holding the fort for the irrational. *Folktales,* the piece I'm preparing for LaMama for next year, which is based on stories from Italo Calvino, Lafcadio Hearn, the Brothers Grimm, and African folktales, will be an attempt to deal with primal material in a contemporary setting. I'm interested in the archaic, archetypal, sometimes savage elements in these tales, and in the relation of the organic to the highly technological.

"The self is animal, primal. And my work is a way of moving toward that, looking at it, and understanding it—even if it only begins by visualizing it."

Village Voice, February 28, 1984

In Love, in Murder

(Eric Bogosian and Michael Zwack/Black Light
Theater of Prague)

A sign on the door to the Kitchen explained that Glenn Branca's music for
I Saw the Seven Angels would not be performed live but on tape. After the
performance people grumbled that the music served only as prologue and
epilogue and what was the point of having it at all? And although Michael
Zwack's slides, monumentally projected on the screens stretching east to
west (in what is usually the length of the Kitchen space, but here served as
the width), provided a suggestive visual track, the text so dominated this
performance that it is hard to see why it was so insistently publicized as a
collaboration. Perhaps for history's sake: a note by Bogosian explains that
the origins of the piece lay in an unrealized performance by Zwack and
Bogosian for the Greek-looking ruins of the Seaman's Home on Staten
Island. "I would read passages from the Bible, hidden in the labyrinth of
corridors. Michael's paintings would be hung on the cracked and peeling
walls of the abandoned rooms. We never made the piece, but the idea of
combining a dense, obsessive text with evocative imagery has stayed with
us, leading to this production."

The text burgeoned into a collage of "classics"—from Blake, the
Bible, and Shakespeare to Flaubert, Henry Miller, Burroughs, Genet,
Norman Vincent Peale, and Hitler. The visual images were also all from
published sources, and they too ranged from the sublime to the
sordid—at times illustrating the text in a literal way (pornography for
Sorrentino's "Sexology"), at times waxing metaphorical (four Renaissance sculptures of David for *Death in Venice*). And, since the texts
roughly alternated between taped and live readings, the actors' solo
presences served as another visual element.

In a sense the performance itself was classic too: a series of soliloquies that moved in a perfect circle over the fundamental stuff of human
life—innocence, love, sex, religion, murder, and death. But in the juxtapositions and in the readings themselves, there was an irony that moved
the spectator uneasily between a sense of wonder and a sense of horror.
The acting style was exaggerated in places, making it clear, for example,

that Bogosian was satirizing Peale; in Bronwen Crothers's two live readings, though, the stylization became mannered. At times, however, the acting style was naturalistic and remarkably veracious, provoking fear and pity, for example, in the tale of child torture and murder in Vietnam (from *Nam* by Mark Baker) and in an account of the Ted Bundy rapes and murders in America (from *The Only Living Witnesses*). In Jordan Lund and John Woehrle, Bogosian has gifted actors.

Bogosian's world emerges in this piece as one in which the human experience is a jumble of spiritual rapture and carnal sensation given order by one's moral perspective; the points on the life circle are not as distinct as we would like to think. In this view any human act is the result of an admixture of desires, fears, obsessions, and ideas. There is violence in love as well as in murder. But there is also a distinction— one of proportion and context. Morality is not a case of either/or but of how much, where, and why.

In certain ways Jiri Srnec's Black Light Theater was amazing and in other ways disappointing. The basic device of this theater, which dates back to the Black Cabinet technique of ancient China, is the magical animation of objects through the manipulations of actors made invisible by black clothing, performing in front of a black curtain. A little Day-Glo paint and a black light adds to the illusion. Although *A Week of Dreams* suffered from a trivial plot (a taxi driver keeps having dreams based on objects passengers leave in his cab), dreadful music (an Eastern European idea of American jazz/movie music), cutesy pantomime, and impossible sightlines, some of the effects were marvelous. They brought to mind the methods and images Ericka Beckman uses in her films, especially the anthropomorphism of everyday things and the play of scale: laundry dances on a clothesline, a mermaid visits a flooded bedroom, gigantic spectacles become a bicycle. This is the stuff of spectacular fairy tales and surrealist visions. But, for some reason, here rich symbolism was avoided and possible visions remained merely shallow effects.

Village Voice, March 6, 1984

Jerkman's Progress

(Jill Kroesen)

When I was a kid, I thought regular grownups didn't have problems with their love lives.

I won't say how I know this, because it would implicate too many people and my friends would kill me, but now that I'm well over 30 I profoundly realize that not only does all that stuff never get resolved, but, in fact, it all gets more and more adolescent. And, ironically, if you're a feminist, this creeps up on you in the most acute and alarming way, leaving you no choice but to laugh at a situation that a few years ago you never would have admitted even to your best friend. Now you check in with your best friend daily to catch up on the gossip. But there's a self-mocking edge to indulging in this high school behavior that provides a salutary distance even while you luxuriate in your petty/earthshaking crises and in living out clichés. Or anyway, that's how you rationalize it.

Jill Kroesen knows this too. She is even more extreme, describing romance in essentially infantile terms. Like Kroesen's other performances, *The Lowell Jerkman Story* is an avant-garde musical that presents a sketchy narrative as an excuse for the songs, part new music, part rock, and part nursery rhyme; the resulting performance is a cross between a *True Romance* comic book and a child's living room skit. Since the locus of the hero's (villain's?) story is the downtown New York performance scene, an added attraction of *Lowell* is that it features a cast of "stars," live and on video.

In the prelude to the story proper Kroesen sings her "Penis Envy Blues," a plaint so accurate, concise, and fetching I wonder no one has written something like it before. "I was a girl who looked up to her dad/One day I noticed it was a cock he had," she croons. And later: "You can stick that dick in far/Drive trucks as well as cars/Lift pianos and things all day long/Oooh, I wish I was that strong." And later still: "You get taken seriously when you talk/You don't get raped at night when you walk." After she threatens to become a man by buying a dildo and calling herself Jay, God punishes Kroesen by turning her into a boy—Lowell Jerkman.

Lowell's father (played by Joe Hannan, who also plays keyboard throughout) hates him, and girls think he's a creep. Lowell decides to go to New York to become a rock star so he can have lots of girlfriends. When he arrives, a naive jerk, he has to learn how to survive in the cruel world of new music, including catching the attention of Rhys, the music curator at the Kitchen (played by Rhys Chatham, former curator of music at the Kitchen), and learning how to look mean without using drugs, which are too expensive.

To complete his education, Lowell realizes, he has to change his clothes from jerky to slick. And when his appearance changes, his being does too. Dressed all in black, with five women (Pooh Kaye, Nanette De Cillis, Jey Hiott, Lisa Love, and Sharla Perel, who also play drug dealers and a dancing chorus) clinging to him adoringly, he has become arrogant and successful as well as a misogynist. He expounds his philosophy of life as a heterosexual male artist in New York, to wit: women have mothering instincts and need babies or boyfriends to satisfy their biological urges. Men, on the other hand, need territory to satisfy theirs. This is why men have such a hard time in the city, except for gay men, who don't need as much space because they can get along with people. Women don't have any problem living in cities either, which is why there are so many of them in New York and why people like Lowell Jerkman can get so many girlfriends even though he's mean to them.

Lowell shows how mean he is in a series of typical phone calls to the girlfriend chorus. And he also shows (in a film) why, deep down, he's afraid of sex. Lowell's theory explains once and for all why we straight women have so many problems: there is a conspiracy among straight men to keep us out of the competition (intellectual and artistic) by making us fall in love with them so we stay up all night crying and never get any work done. Besides, every time a man makes a fool of a woman, he gains the equivalent of 160 acres.

There are, however, exceptions. Lowell introduces Ned (played by Ned Sublette). Ned belts out his theme song, "I'm the Bravest Man in the Whole Wide World 'Cause I Ain't Afraid of Girls," a kind of country and western ditty:

I ain't afraid when they're beautiful
I ain't afraid when they're real smart
I don't get nervous when they're fabulous
I ain't afraid they'll fall apart . . .

Finally, we are introduced to a dominatrix who runs a school for bad boys where Lowell is sent to be disciplined (along with most of our politicians). This leads to a screening of Kroesen's rock video in which she plays a secretary on Capitol Hill who spills all the pols' sex secrets.

I suppose Kroesen could be accused of a heavy hand, a lack of a clear feminist analysis, a totally disjointed narrative, and artworld in-jokes, and her cast of an amateurish acting style. Kroesen herself whines and giggles until she gets behind the microphone, when suddenly her voice becomes creamy and powerful. But what some might see as flaws I see as the stuff of a goofy, childlike, farcical, right-on-target style.

Last week I accused Eric Bogosian of failing to truly collaborate. I have since learned that Michael Zwack not only contributed the visuals to *I Saw the Seven Angels* but also participated in the selection of the texts.

Village Voice, March 20, 1984. Lyrics © Jill Kroesen.

Theory, Praxis—and Vodka

(Komar and Melamid)

Vitaly Komar and Aleksandr Melamid have an extraordinary sense of what's timely. And not only because of their general program—Soviet émigré painters and performance artists who work as a team, they comment on socialist realism and monumental art in a peculiarly American postmodern vein, like a Russian version of the Metro Pictures crowd but with a wry sense of humor. But, more incredibly, Komar and Melamid chose to make a painting-in-performance of John Hinckley's assassination attempt on Reagan on the very day that the Secret Service shot an armed man on the White House grounds, only hours after arresting someone who had scaled the fence. Now that's timing.

Actually, Komar and Melamid have an extraordinary sense of everything, from timing to art history to humor. Their paintings as well as their writings tweak the mind (see, for example, their ironic but perspicacious analysis of post-October Soviet art as icons of a new cult of the dead in "In Search of Religion," *Artforum,* May 1980). But *Art Belongs to the People* was particularly gratifying because they are remarkable performers, as affable as they are funny. And I should say right here that all of this was conveyed with wit and ease by the translator, Jamie Gambrell, who is an art critic as well as a gifted interpreter.

Like so many other Soviet émigrés, Komar and Melamid are suspended between two cultures; unlike others, they freely acknowledge the bitter contradiction of being simultaneously product and critic of both the Soviet Union and the United States. They celebrate as well as attack Soviet and American art, and, while they censure the USSR for its violations of human life and dignity, they certainly harbor no illusions about life in the United States.

Art Belongs to the People (School of the Arts) was an experiment in art education, as its subtitle suggests. Komar and Melamid invited four émigré Russians, nonartists, to serve as guinea pigs. Their task was to execute the monumental historical painting Komar and Melamid had planned. The program note promised that "using bullhorns, projected examples from art history, inspirational music, and vodka, Komar and

Melamid will employ a carrot-and-stick approach to teaching the participants how to paint. At the same time, they will provide brief lectures on history, ideology, and aesthetics, interpreting, as it were, the fundamental principles of contemporary self-expression." And so they did.

Now, because both audience and performers were drinking vodka throughout, the performance became progressively intense, hilarious, and chaotic, and, also, my notes became progressively illegible. But I remember a lot of good moments. First, we saw a lot of slides, not only commemorative medals, like Komar and Melamid's double self-portrait, amazingly similar to all those familiar profiles of Marx, Lenin, and Stalin, but also various historical genre paintings, which our learned professors subjected to a formalist (!) analysis, photographs from famous ballets, such as the one in which Baryshnikov plays young Stalin, and the fruits of Komar and Melamid's own archaeological digs. They explained to their "students" the importance of collective work as well as artistic freedom in their creation (but "first discipline, then freedom!"). They showed examples of their previous pedagogical successes. ("So if we can teach a dog how to draw a bone, we can certainly teach you how to draw Ronald Reagan.") They gave a little lesson in color theory. ("Color cures inferiority complexes, toothaches, alcoholism, pregnancy, and sweet tooth.") And then they let their students loose.

Lena, Misha, Olya, and Seriozha (for some odd reason the two women wore leotards and tights) each stationed themselves at one-quarter of the massive black canvas, on which gleamed the outlines of a slide projection recording the assassination attempt. Egged on by their masters, they outlined their portions in chalk ("Faster, faster! Seriozha, why can't you work as well as Olya?"), then took up paintbrushes and cans of bright paint. Now the plot thickened, along with the style. ("Misha, what are you doing, painting that eye in the middle of the canvas? Who do you think you are, Schnabel?") The action paused for another lesson, ostensibly in anatomy but with digressions into the artists' favored theme of genre painting—necrology—and then for a lesson in patriotism. Fortified with more theory and vodka ("Without it [the vodka], collective work—and patriotism—is unthinkable"), the neophytes finished their mural to the strains of "The Star-Spangled Banner."

Village Voice, April 3, 1984

Zaloom Society
(Paul Zaloom)

Paul Zaloom's solo performances are a cross between poor theater and mass media. He makes videotapes but out of paper (remember "crankies"?). He does TV newscasts, only he performs them live. He makes cartoons out of the dross of mass production, animating found objects like car parts, broken appliances, and scraps of foam rubber, plastic, and Styrofoam. The "poverty" of his style is both an aesthetic and political stance, for, despite the diversity of his media, his art is that of a miniaturist, and he speaks of and for the downtrodden.

Zaloom's latest performance follows his favored format: first an animation, then a hand-puppet show, and finally a lecture. In *Creature from the Blue Zaloom* he has nearly perfected this format, in terms of timing as well as range of content, which moves from environmental concerns to commentary on computers and TV to the politics of local real estate to nuclear arms.

In "The Future" Zaloom plays a cast of characters (he can switch accents trippingly) who introduce us to aspects of what world's fairs used to call "tomorrow's world." Books are arrested for championing freedom. A French chef tosses the Ocean of the Future as salad, adding oil, lead, human sewage, and all sorts of fish (including an octopus played by a distributor cap). Space of the Future, it seems, will be like a Darwinian highway with no rules, where all sorts of unidentified flying objects will battle it out for survival of the biggest. The Climate of the Future, once the earth's geography has been meddled with beyond repair, will move from greenhouse to desert. And, while TV looks like it will be the same anon as it is now ("Buy me!" squeals a palpitating box of corn flakes), computers will be a real throwback to primitive information science.

"Leonardo's Revenge," a puppet play, is a timely commentary on the housing crisis on the Lower East Side. An artist named Leonardo (you know, the one who does all those paintings of sloe-eyed children they sell in dime stores) gives us a tour of his place on East 9th Street. We meet his neighbor Judy, a purple-haired punk; his dog, who does some tricks; his mother, who washes his dishes with her steel-wool hair, reminds him he once was Lenny, and tells him she saw an ad for his apartment in the newspaper; his shrink, who, making an emergency housecall, looks around, likes the space, and decides to bump off his patient to get the apartment himself; and finally the landlord, who explains that since the artists have raised the property values, it's time to get rid of them and bring on the Yuppies. From time to time a leviathan head emerges from the depths of the puppet booth—Leonardo da Vinci himself (Zaloom with a Santa Claus beard, a white mop wig, and a wonderful Italian accent), discoursing on art, genius, and work. At last the modern-day Leonardo, despairing over his eviction, tries to commit suicide but realizes he can't—because he's only a puppet. When the landlord sends a bomb that blows up the building, Leonardo, Petrushka-like, survives . . . and in human form.

In "Basic Intelligence" Zaloom appears in suit and glasses and, explaining that he is one of thousands of Civilian Defense Department employees, delivers a slide show lecture on books you can buy from the government. Like Zaloom's "video" lecture illustrating what to do in case of nuclear attack, this show is based on real government documents—and all the information (as the program notes point out) is true. We learn, from selected excerpts from the *Dictionary of Military and Associated Terms,* put out by the Joint Chiefs of Staff, that certain terms are not to be used—*total nuclear war,* for instance—and how to understand concepts like "gross error" (an attack that doesn't reach target) and "disaffected person" (includes people who criticize the government). Through other publications, such as "New Thrusts in Technology" (a chapter in *1983 Weapon Systems*) and *Soviet Military Power,* we see phallic might stalking the world, all those tanks and howitzers with their nuclear heads, as well as ways for any citizen to sell all sorts of things to the military and then (in *How to Buy Surplus Personal Property from the Department of Defense*) buy them right back. There is even a little session on art criticism, as we see selected paintings celebrating the U.S. Air Force, all of which (in Zaloom's ironic analysis) base their touching effectiveness on the analogy between planes and birds—showing us, finally, how "natural" our military is.

Creature from the Blue Zaloom is as horrifying as it is hilarious. While you're laughing, part of you is also crying. Zaloom's agitprop theater is unusual partly because he's not simply exhorting us about things we already know or feel; he informs in a way that is direct—and electrifying.

Village Voice, April 17, 1984

One Flew over South Pacific

(Anne Bogart)

As her performances over the past year testify, Anne Bogart is gripped by a triple theme: the effects of war on Americans' daily lives, the ways men and women learn their social roles, and love—its pains and possibilities. These are monumental preoccupations, but Bogart manages to handle them with poignancy and without sentimentality. The heroism of the ordinary is the best way I can think of to characterize her style, in terms not only of theme but also of form—massive casts of characters, young actors who seem both vulnerable and shining with potential, and repetitive, nonnarrative scripts that show both the individuality and the commonality of her nameless protagonists.

Now Bogart has reworked a preexisting piece (a gesture that fits the current trend in postmodern theater) to reflect on her chosen subjects through an artifact of the historical moment that obsesses her. *South Pacific* was written in 1949. Most people remember it as a mawkish piece of World War II boosterism, set on a navy war base on a Polynesian island and having very little to do with politics, but in fact its concerns are very close to Bogart's. Her rereading actually changes nothing in the text but wrests meanings from it that were either merely latent or undercut in the original production. This is not a parody but a soberly ironic interpretation that looks at the original with historical consciousness. In the program notes Bogart points out that, although plays are open to multiple interpretations, most musicals are restaged as copies of the original Broadway version. Bogart's *South Pacific* "begins with a respect for the material" and looks for a more complex understanding of "what has always been assumed to be (incorrectly) a simpleminded approach."

The basic premise for this production is that the musical is being acted out by mental patients who are war victims themselves. Putting on this musical is part of a behavior modification program. Thus, the doctor, always onstage, oversees the production, hugging a patient after a taxing solo and nodding encouragement here and there. But, also, the lighting technicians, dressed as doctors, look like clinical observers as they watch from their booth above; the musicians and stagehands, also in medical whites, double as hospital staff. And every actor has multiple roles, beginning with his or her "real" identity (as patient) and continuing to the second level of role playing, on which the major characters are split and played now by one, now by four, actors (not always of the same sex). The very fluidity of role identification, and the further ambiguity of gender within a role, provides multiple, provocative readings, for whenever a conflict takes place it has various incarnations; love scenes often appear in both heterosexual and homosexual form.

Nearly every lyric resonates with new import. When Nellie Forbush, the nurse who has fallen in love with a French planter, announces that she's from Little Rock, we can no longer view her as a "typical" American. And the fact that her major struggle in the plot is to overcome her racist reaction to Emile's previous marriage and his half-Polynesian children suddenly takes on a new cast. But also, when Nellie wonders "Who is not running away from something?" and later, when she sings about her "normality" in "I'm in Love with a Wonderful Guy," we reflect on a congeries of issues—on people who run away to war or from unjust punishment as well as those who rebel and those who end up in mental institutions. That "most people long for another island" ("Bali Hai") surely had figurative meaning in the original version as well, but as sung here its metaphysical significance increases.

With Vietnam in mind, the relationships among the American military personnel, the French colonialists, and the native population are transformed. Bloody Mary, who sells souvenirs and lures the sailors to Bali Hai, is a small-scale entrepreneur who challenges the colonial attitude, encouraging love even if it crosses class lines (though it's true she wants her daughter Liat to marry a planter, in the end she lets her have her way—or would have let her, if Lieutenant Cable, Liat's lover, hadn't died in action), and paying native workers more than the colonialists. Billis, the guy who always wants to find women and exotic rituals, in this view becomes something beyond a troublemaker. He is an insurgent, even if a blundering one, who resists blind obedience to military authority. Emile, too, is a rebel who fights against bullies and for love and freedom.

I don't have room to write about the many other revelations in this production—for instance, the protofeminist anger in the songs "I'm Gonna Wash That Man Right Out of My Hair" (as well as its metaphoric refusal to give in to obsession) and "Honey Bun"; the various attitudes toward love that emerge, from fear to ambivalence to joy; the way the violence of war is made palpable throughout but especially in the Goya-esque battle scene; the opening scene, in which four psychotics as children demand, in "Dites Moi," why life is beautiful; the surprising song "Carefully Taught" (in 1949?), which bitterly explains that racism is not a natural human trait. Nor to write about the cast and other collaborators on this project, all of whom contributed to its brilliance.

Village Voice, May 1, 1984

India's Theater of Cruelty

(Kerala Kalamandalam)

Like other great forms of dance-theater spectacle in both East and West (e.g., Kabuki and European ballet), Kathakali's physical technique is built on a martial art tradition. Its bravura flares in its battle scenes, although its delicate moments are powerful in their own way; the rhythms of peace and violence, like the varying rhythms and silences of the musical accompaniment (two drummers and two singers, one playing cymbals and one a gong), make a satisfying texture. Brutality, gore, and feelings of revenge are not only balanced but even framed and made more beautiful, by righteousness and holy virtue. Bhima's act of ripping Dussassana open and devouring his entrails is physically answered by his cosmic trembling with he sits at Krishna's feet and receives his blessing. A rhythm is created, too, of the vision of human nature, from its most petty, frail, and nasty—cheating at a game of dice, sexual harassment—to its most profound and heroic.

Of course, all these things are present in the text of the play—in this case, the *Mahabharata,* or at least a few scenes from it: the dice game in which the oldest Pandava brother loses everything, including his brothers and their wife, Draupadi, to his enemy cousins, the Kauravas; Draupadi's audience with Lord Krishna; the negotiations between Krishna and the Kauravas; and the fateful battle between the Pandavas and the Kauravas. But through the Kathakali performance they are made physical, palpable, alive, in a way that seems just barely controlled by the stylized staging, as if the abstractions—the rhythms, the gesture language and exaggerated facial expressions, the elaborate costumes and codified colors of the makeup masks, the austerity of the set, and the blatant artifice of stage blood and rope guts—ordered and contained a chaos fleetingly let loose.

For all its majesty and stylized symbolism, for all its abstractness, the dance-drama—both in terms of the text and in terms of its performance style—is amazingly down-to-earth. It is both formal and crude, solemn and silly, ornate and simple. The first thing that happens is that the heroes come out and do a dance. What could be more straightforward? But then, when the narrative begins, the characters make their dramatic entrances from behind the Kathakali curtain, a bedsheet-sized cloth held up by two men that heightens theatrical mystery by concealing and revealing simultaneously. (The sense of mystery should be intensified by the shadowy illumination supplied by the single gas lamp downstage center; although the lamp was there, for the sake of tradition I suppose, this performance was lit by stagelights.)

The actors and musicians don't differentiate between "onstage" and "offstage" behavior of the sort we know in Western theater. They adjust their clothing, glance at themselves in the tiny mirrors at the ends of their tassels, walk to a props table upstage without any pomp to get an appropriate object, unembarrassedly try a second time if they fall from a footstool they've just grandly taken a stance upon. But, of course, most actions are just the opposite of casual, and the timing as well as the muscular configurations are utterly precise.

Given the fact that the text alternates between narration, dialogue, and commentary, all in a language I don't know, and that the mudras constitute yet another unfamiliar code, I was surprised at how much of the action was crystal clear. I don't mean to invoke the cliché that certain gestures are universal—because I don't believe they are—but there was no mistaking, for instance, what kinds of sexual abuse Dussassana was threatening Draupadi with just before he unwound her sari or how Krishna's anger at the Kauravas on the Pandava's behalf was fanned by their irreverence toward him in sight of all their court.

As I thrilled to Bhima's (literal) bloodthirst, watching him mime drinking Dussassana's blood, even though I'd seen him openly put on fangs and fumble for the stage blood, even though I'd seen the victim adjusting his guts and restuffing his belly with a rope that had fallen out, I suddenly thought of what we have in the way of an equivalent, in a culture where TV and movies have long since shaped our perception of violence and where for most people live performances not only are not a relevant or compelling form of drama but rarely include such physical extremes. I thought of Hollywood adventures, *Indiana Jones and the Temple of Doom,* for instance, whose locale is more or less the same as this story. Of course, there's no comparison in quality or range, but the difference between the uses of cruelty in the two seemed instructive: in the one a cheap, gratuitous, and overblown titillation; in the other, a meaningful and sometimes necessary part of life.

Village Voice, June 26, 1984

India's Theater of Cruelty / 251

What Becomes a Legend Most?

(Amateur Night at the Apollo)

I'm sitting in the audience at the final round of Amateur Night feeling like a stranger in a strange land. Is it because I am white in a mostly black audience, an audience that is raucously turning thumbs up or down at nuances of performance beyond my ken—forever beyond my ken, since no matter how much I value black culture, I can never have grown up inside it? Is it a matter of black and white, the gap between two aesthetics or repertoires, or is it the nature of live performance, that it speaks intimately to its own, circumscribed community—whether that means Harlem blacks, Yiddish-speaking Jews in the Catskills, or the downtown artworld—in a way that is neither possible nor desirable in the mass media? Is it that I don't frequent talent shows and don't know the rules of watching them? Not to mention that perennial sense of outsiderhood the critic suffers, like the detective, the ethnographer, or the voyeur?

Of course, it's all these things I'm feeling, exacerbated, I think, by the twin themes of nostalgia and promise that course through the evening. Nostalgia not only for the former brilliance of this theater, and for its importance, since the 1930s, to Harlem as a community but also for aspects of performance style that Hollywood, TV, the recording industry, and rock video have changed. And at the same time, the promise, with the blossoming of new styles in the 1980s, that change is perhaps not irrevocable; the promise, too, of a new Harlem Renaissance shaping itself. The reopening of the Apollo Theater last December, after all this time owned and run by blacks, is a symbol of that regeneration.

Nostalgia and promise are redoubled in the revived Amateur Nights. The Wednesday night talent shows, begun by Ralph Cooper with Frank Schiffman (later co-owner of the Apollo) at the Lafayette Theater in 1933 and moved to the Apollo (then owned by Sid Cohen) soon after, are themselves a glorious tradition, the meeting place of past and future where the children who will be tomorrow's stars are molded first in the images of the older generation. Here were bred the likes of Sarah Vaughan, Pearl Bailey, James Brown, Ronnie Spector, Dionne Warwick— and even the Jackson 5. Cooper still presides. The dancer Sandman Sims, long an Apollo regular, plays Porto Rico, the clown who shoots down the losers. And, as ever, the audience comments vociferously throughout and casts its vote with applause at evening's end. In the 1930s Cooper broadcast the show over the radio; now the plans are to do live TV broadcasts from the theater.

Not surprisingly, several Michael Jackson imitators are in the finals, including five-year-old Tyrell, who is dressed in a little black jacket, black pants, white shirt, bow tie, loafers, white socks, and all. To see the imitation is to illuminate what is special about the original. Tyrell does the requisite turns, pauses (it's those loaded stillnesses that drive the audience wild), footwork, glances over the shoulder, moonwalks, and distinctive Jackson hand gestures. He's undeniably adorable, but he doesn't sizzle, and what's more, the moves he shows us in the first half-minute of the song are the only ones he knows, so they get repeated ad infinitum. It's almost like the difference between a parrot and a human: one repeats its learned phrases incessantly, while the other can generate an infinite number of new, original utterance.

There are a couple of group dances to *Thriller,* with kids dressed as monsters and a few, inexplicably, in blackface. The audience does not go for any of *that.*

There is a magician the audience at first disdains but then warms up to; a family of acrobats that could be said to take breaking to its extremist implications by doing away with the dancing and simply performing circus acrobatics, which the audience cheers at the moment but loses interest in at the final voting; a comedian who performs a conversation in heaven between Malcolm X and Martin Luther King about current events, including Jesse Jackson's campaign ("He didn't say 'Hymie,' " King explains. "He said 'hire me!' "). There are surprisingly few breakdancers.

But most of the young performers are singers, many of them obviously practiced in gospel music, that prime locus of great black performance, even if what an inordinate number of them sing is "I'm Not Living without You," from *Dreamgirls.* The first-prize winner, Myleka Thompson, belts out the song with a full-bodied, sweet sadness that could break your heart and that set me wondering. How is it that a pubescent girl can understand so much about the pains of love or at least create the illusion of an initiate into the mysteries of the heart? And if it's only an illusion, a product of style, how is it that she knows how to pour forth her heart, or her illusory heart, to the audience, to the congregation? Or is it that what she knows are the mysteries of performance?

Village Voice, July 17, 1984

Moon over Loisaida

(Revenge of the Full Moon Show)

You couldn't see the full moon for the storm, and it was hot into the bargain. You'd think on such a miserable summer night people would stay home or drift into some air-conditioned movie theater, but P. S. 122 was crowded, standing room only—even though the space had been reversed so that its center was filled with café tables and chairs and the performance space ringed the edge of the room. You could tell from the preperformance hum that this was an audience of aficionados, regulars of the Lower East Side club scene, and therefore familiar with at least some of the seven acts of the evening, all of which have appeared at places like the Limbo Lounge, the Pyramid, Club 57, 8 BC, and P.S. 122's own Avant-Garde-Arama. Somehow, as we sipped our beer and turned in every direction of the compass to watch the acts revolve around us, I sensed that it was too early in the evening and too well lit for this crowd. But they took it in stride.

Tom Murrin, the Alien Comic, was the emcee as well as the opening act. The Alien Comic makes strange his own habitat, commenting on every aspect of downtown life from punk fashion to the real estate crunch and problems of art as he sheds bizarre mask over mask and changes homemade costumes, crafted of plastic, paper, and junk, that double as scenery, all to the rhythm of a manic, punning patter.

Annie Hickman works in a similar genre, shifting rapidly from one persona-as-costume-change-as-body-art-as-sculpture-as-comic-turn to another. Among other things, she dons a full-scale bathtub and takes a bubble bath in honor of the full moon; later, in full frog regalia she dances an exotic finale.

Mimi Goese's *Getaway Vacation* is a different kind of character switching. She uses objects as props, rather than as body-altering devices, but transforms herself by other means—vocal and facial expression as well as gestures—to become a succession of deliberately stereotypical happy natives, from Polynesian to Parisian, in this squib on tourism.

I'm as mystified by Steve and Mark (Steve Buscemi and Mark Boone Junior) as ever. They are compelling performers and well suited as partners: Steve with his bouncy nervous energy and rangy frame is like a human rubber band, while Mark is his foil, a solid immovable wall. But their material—in this case, a comic routine about a team of bomb defusers—is a predictable cross between a bad 1950s TV situation comedy and a high school skit. I'm sure the "dumbness" in this case is deliberate, but the irony is so subtle it just seems to evaporate. I'd love to see these two wield whackier material.

Jo Andres's *Liquid T.V.* is mysteriously beautiful and disturbing, a mass of paradoxes. Andres, Lucy Sexton, and Anne Iobst look like Amazons in their short haircuts, black sleeveless T-shirts, black jeans, and black combat boots. They seem to stand six feet tall. They rock their hips as they advance in a kind of chorus line then drop their dancerly demeanor to walk back and begin again, in what struck me as a very tribal manner. Later they dance in front of TVs that face them, not us, so the effect is of an eerie, other-worldly light bathing these other-worldly maiden-warriors. And, still later, one reason for their sinister costumes comes clear when the lights go out and slide projections of a human figure dance and multiply through layers of cloth borne and twisted by agents now made invisible in their black garb. They rip apart a glowing figurine and smear themselves with his light. The Afro-Caribbean music gives the whole thing the crazy, magical tenor of a voodoo ceremony as reimagined by white girls.

Regrouping to perform as Dancenoise, Sexton and Iobst look like bikers in short T-shirts crisscrossed with silver gaffer's tape. They balance on Bustelo coffee cans and swing chains. The ushers have handed out clippings of the recent Satan cult murders on Long Island, and the women act out the suburban horrors, sparring with strings of (fake) green and yellow guts, attacking Ishmael Houston-Jones and John Bernd and dousing them with (fake) blood. They all slither around on the floor for a while and enjoy the glorious mess, while David Linton provides high-tension percussion as he tortures a guitar and while the spectators, half-fascinated and half-grossed-out, brush bits of colored oatmeal and dyed milk off their clothes.

By the time the Fabulous Pop Tarts appeared perhaps the evening had gone on long enough. Perhaps a group can never live up to a name like that. Or perhaps their indeterminate style, part 1950s doo-wop parody and part just bad singing, turned the audience off. In any case the house unabashedly emptied itself. But the batting average for the evening wasn't bad at all.

Village Voice, August 7, 1984

Rent Out-of-Control

(Jeff Weiss)

You could see Jeff Weiss's work as high melodrama, as tragedy, as farce, as a Broadway musical gone askew, or, if you think of performance art as metatheater, as an event that comments on elements of theater, i.e., as performance. On one hand *The Confessions of Conrad Gehrhardt (And That's How the Rent Gets Paid—Part 4)* is a murder mystery, a campy rendition of a genre piece with the piquant twist that the hard-boiled detective, Persky, is a closet gay in love with his quarry—the enigmatic Connie Gehrhardt, who protests that the brutal sex murders plaguing the city have been committed by his double. On another hand, Connie's sister Annie's suicide monologue in the mental hospital is a separate, genuinely moving small drama. On the third hand, there is enough raunchy sexual comedy in the scenes between Connie and his singing partner, the lesbian hooker Izzy (and between Connie and his son Buddy; and between Buddy and his mother, Wilma; and between Persky and his wife), for a month of sitcoms. (But sex here serves alternately as comic material and as menacing terror.) And then the piece is larded with show tunes performed to the hilt by the fine cast (in addition to Weiss and his costar, Dorothy Cantwell, who plays Annie and Izzy, this installment's guests stars were Willem Dafoe, Nicky Paraiso, Nancy Reilly, Kate Valk, and Ron Vawter), numbers that would be flashy except for their homemade production values—and, of course, their outré lyrics.

But ultimately this crossbreeding of genres and the plot itself leads us to the real content of *Confessions*—for Connie is an actor. The mystery and the tragedy, as well as all the incongruous hilarity, are in the essential problem of shifting identities, which is the crux of the actor's art. We don't know whether the murderer is yet another one of Connie's impersonations. We're not really sure of the main characters' sexual preferences. We don't know which of the disjunct scenes Weiss ceremoniously frames (by calling out their titles, then signaling "One, two, three!" to start and calling "Blackout!" to end) are "real" scenes from Connie's life and which are "fictitious" moments from his plays. This is not only Inspector Persky's dilemma but ours as spectators as well. We don't even know if Persky himself isn't simply one of Connie's fantasies. Connie keeps a Pinocchio doll for a mascot. And how the actor's rent gets paid is by living out lies—but some of them are uncomfortably close to the truth.

In each installment, different guest stars appear and various scenes (of the over 200 Weiss has written) are played out. The randomness of the plot details rubs against the focused purposiveness of the theme with a pleasurable tension that thickens the sense of fatefulness and paranoia. The obsessive, fragmentary form is this play's content. It's as if it doesn't matter what slice of Conrad Gehrhardt's life we become privy to; all roads lead to Rome, and all dragnets to Connie. Yet, at the same time, you could look at the arbitrary nature of each scene's choice not as a metaphysical comment but as a method for finding pretexts for virtuosic display. At times the plot is riveting, even overwhelming. Then, mercurially, it is tossed aside for a bit of brilliant clowning—as when, in a shadow play, Connie and Izzy make a baby to get on welfare and, at the height of their consummation, rave not with passion but with mutual disgust, or when Paraiso and Dafoe play transvestite hustlers who threaten to kill Connie by French-kissing him and then eat his remains.

And the virtuosity is powerfully physical. The wrestling and the sexual encounters that are the meat of the plot are only part of the intensity of the actors' thereness, especially Weiss's. His presence is so vigorous and so focused it cuts like a laser beam. And one of his most striking abilities is to seem to totally change his bodily appearance from one scene to the next, so that both Connie's identity as an actor and Persky's suspicions of him seem wholly justified. He is the young, muscular gay swain with Paraiso-as-fellow-actor, but practically wizened visiting with Buddy, and, in one of the most touching scenes of the evening, a tender husband to Wilma (played by Valk), gently shaking her ragdoll body awake as he sings "Sleepytime Gal."

Like its hero, *Confessions* is strong and vulnerable, violent and sentimental, nasty and hilarious.

Village Voice, August 28, 1984

Disposing of a Cliché

(Mierle Laderman Ukeles)

In certain ways, what Mierle Ukeles is doing in her performances, and in the two concurrent exhibitions whose openings these events celebrated, is unprecedented. "You mean that woman who went around shaking the hands of all the garbagemen?" my friends replied when I told them how I was spending last Sunday afternoon. (If they had been at these performances, they wouldn't use the term *garbagemen* anymore.)

But in other ways Ukeles is a member of a tradition—or, rather, of several related traditions—and part of what these events were about was firmly establishing the performance-art-historical context for the work. That is, Ukeles creates symbolic civic pageantry of the kind that in the West goes back at least to Roman times and that flourished in the courts of Renaissance Europe. In this tradition the spectacle per se is accompanied by speeches explaining the symbols and extolling the virtues of the heads of state. As Ronald Feldman pointed out in his introduction to *Cleansing the Bad Names,* in which bad names for sanitation workers (beginning with garbageman and descending pretty quickly from there) were written graffiti-style on the windows of Feldman's gallery and then washed away by various leaders of political, art, and civil service institutions, Ukeles is like that portraitist commissioned to represent the royalty, but with a peculiarly American, democratic twist: the subjects of her "portraits" are the city's working men, and those particular working men whom everyone most disdains.

Mayor Koch even showed up at the Marine Transfer Station to say a few words before *Marrying the Barges.* He noted that in Mayor Lindsay's time the going thing was Happenings, an elitist art (according to Koch, I mean), but that now things were different and Ukeles was part of a new movement to make art for working people. Of course, most of the people in the audience were the press and gallery goers. But, anyway, the commemorative speeches took up a good deal of each event. They were an integral part of what each performance was. And, while reporting this makes the whole thing seem sanctimonious, Ukeles herself was so earnest and well intentioned that it didn't come off that way at all. You couldn't help but be touched.

Perhaps even more impressive was the realization that, although the original idea may have been Ukeles's, there is definitely something special going on in the Sanitation Department when it appoints an artist-in-residence. And in his speech department commissioner Normal Steisel compared *Cleansing the Bad Names* to Rauschenberg's act of erasing a de Kooning drawing. I think this man is up to something.

The other tradition Ukeles sees herself as heir to is the Constructivist aesthetic, which is in fact a subset of civic art, at least in its Soviet form. Ukeles is involved in a celebration not only of people but also of machines—a project that includes, as it did for some Russian performance makers in the 1920s, choreographing machine dances—strange as that notion may seem to us in 1984.

Marrying the Barges was a machine dance, but it was also reminiscent of another ballet, at least in its theme—*Les Noces,* Nijinska's grave picture of a Russian peasant wedding. Four "married" barges, filled with garbage and led by a tugboat stationed at their center, coursed down the Hudson on their way to dump their cargo in the Staten Island landfill, as they do every day. Two empty, single barges arrived—not married yet; you could think of them as living together, Ukeles commented. One was old, and one, bright blue with orange interior, was brand new. The main body of the ballet unfolded as a second tug led the barges into the Marine Transfer Station slip, putting them, so to speak, into their nuptial bed and consummating the marriage—the identical ending to Nijinska's ballet. (A lot of people, busy listening to the speeches, never saw the married barges make their 30-second appearance and wondered whether the cast had been falsely promoted in advance—kind of like guest stars who put in a cameo appearance you can miss entirely if you blink at the wrong place.)

Cleansing the Bad Names was a mix of public rhetoric and action, a modern political ritual in which Ukeles put a lot of officials to work. "Now learn from the men who do this all the time," she gently urged. "Don't put too much water on the sponges or it'll drip on the person working below you. You'd be surprised at how little it takes to clean up." She called up nine teams of cleansers, an impressive array of art world officials, New York City pols, and sanitation workers—from officers to regular workmen to the guy who won the department's Mr. Clean bodybuilding contest. And they all got their hands dirty together—though the paint, it turned out, was harder to scrub off than expected. One thing Ukeles never talked about, in all the day's verbiage, was why she chose to translate the bad names into wild-style graffiti. Is she suggesting that it's graffiti writers who call those sanmen those names? I think not, and to bring up the volatile and quite separate issue of graffiti in this context only muddies the water.

Village Voice, September 25, 1984

Joe Lowery Logs On

Joe Lowery, whose *Adventure in the Real World* marks the opening of Franklin Furnace's performance season, is something of a scientist. He believes in experimental theater in the literal sense—as a place where you try to find out something about theater. A chemistry major in college, he has become fascinated by computer technology, and, since he bought his own Atari 800 two years ago, his performances have been high-tech interactive.

But, like many scientists, Lowery is also something of a mystic. And he has a social conscience. While he doesn't mind falling in love with his computer, he wonders how technology affects and reflects society. And, of course, Lowery is, after all, a performance artist, so the way all these aspects fuse is in the act of performance itself.

Adventure in the Real World is, among other things, an anthology of Lowery's concerns and methods in past performances. His use of computers, for example, began with *In Discrete Packages* (1983), done six weeks after he bought his own microcomputer. "This was just after *Time* had named the computer Man of the Year," Lowery explains. "I was interested in the different metaphors society uses to view itself, and ended up intertwining computers, performance, and Kabbalah—all of which, in their own ways, are somewhat feared and somewhat mystified." He used the computer to generate designs for the ten *sephirot* of the Kabbalistic Tree of Life (which also forms the human microcosm). The final sephira, which contains all the previous ones, was a computer listing of the previous nine programs.

What first struck Lowery about using the Atari for graphics was the intensity and range of colors the computer provides. (He used 256 colors in *In Discrete Packages.*) And, appropriately for a Kabbalist who has also worked as a lighting designer in the theater, he became fascinated with the possibilities for using computer light. In *The Return of the Missing Heir,* a detective genre piece, Lowery used the computer voice to speak the hard-boiled PI's lines and the graphics to create film noir images and shadowy lighting effects.

A piece like *Return,* or his two rap-and-rhythm-box pieces—*Rhapsody* (pre-Blondie), on becoming illuminated, and the more recent *Reagan*

Rap, a partly improvised rap culled from Reagan sayings—are exemplars of Lowery's desire to "balance high tech with something people can grab onto. Fun is vital to performance, but entertainment comes in so many different forms."

And, while the technology satisfies many current preoccupations, for Lowery the real emphasis of his work is the performing. "What I attempt is to regard performing as an art form by itself and as integral as 'visual' is to 'visual art,' " he has stated. The act of performance involves both the state of the performer and the state of the audience as well as their relationship, all of which Lowery has explored in his work. In *Squirt* he got the audience to egg him on in expressing his alter ego's violent impulses and, when he ended by plunging a knife in the wall, noted its horror at its own mob behavior. In *1 2 3* he tried to invoke what he calls a state of "group mind" in the audience through the experience of laughing together. In *The Diane Arbus Performance Retrospective,* in which the spectators saw poses created from Arbus photographs in carnival-type booths that accommodated them one at a time, Lowery noted with satisfaction both the unique situation for the viewer and for the actors, who put on the "show" three times a day. "They started acting like carnival performers themselves, commenting on the customers and feeling a strong sense of camaraderie. It brought up the issue of what happens when you repeat a performance. Does it become rote? Or can you experience it each time anew? In many ways computer programming is a good metaphor for performance, because the questions are basically who's being programmed and how do you respond to that programming?"

Besides his solo performances, Lowery is part of the Smith Bros., an improvisational group (the other brothers are Bill Gordh and Frank South), and is also a member of Interaction Arts, a collective of performing artists that includes, besides the other Smiths, Jerri Allyn and Debra Wanner. Though he was first inspired to do performance work by his experiences working with Richard Schechner and the Performance Group in the mid-1970s, it is the "tight family of performing artists" of Interaction that Lowery counts as his greatest influence.

The new piece was inspired by meeting a 13-year-old kid on a bus trip through the South and finding the whole concept of a generation growing up on *Dungeons and Dragons* awesome. "They're learning to team up and work together in another world. These games are like living novels, depositing you on the doorstep of another world, and letting you

make the choices." The performance is "a journey toward a confrontation. Along the way I will fantasize many solutions to the confrontation.
These 'solutions' will be performed live." Lowery sees the piece as an
exploration of the use of fantasy role-playing to solve problems, a
method that has led to many of his own performances. "What I'm
looking for," he muses, "is just an understanding."

During his first computer performance, Lowery ran into a bug in his
program and couldn't get the machine to work properly. He was intrigued by two reactions in the audience that suggested future directions
for computers and performance: during the performance the computer
nuts in the audience fearlessly spoke up with suggestions, and afterward
several people told him they were happy that the system broke down,
that computers aren't perfect after all. When we think of how computers
work in the performing arts, we often imagine them operating behind
the scenes, in ways that threaten to drain the humanity from the act of
creation—as in computer-composed music. Lowery offers a vision of
performing computers that is not only interactive but even viewer
friendly.

Village Voice, October 9, 1984

East Side Confidential

The revitalization of the Lower East Side has taken shape in ways that are almost predictable, given the history of art movements, institutions, and communities, especially in postwar New York. The artists move in, looking for cheap living and working space: the galleries follow, and so do the restaurants and bars, since the artists need a place to hang out that isn't exclusively neighborhood, and the gallery goers need something more expensive. And artists, in their hanging out together, make performances in the bars they've claimed as their own. The issue of gentrification aside, the rise of performance art in alphabet city is striking in a number of ways: its style, its audiences, its sense of itself. The issue of gentrification can partly be put aside here because often these performances, unlike the galleries, attract only other artists and friends, rather than rich art buyers—for obvious reasons.

If performance art arose in this century as a way of galvanizing artists' ideas into action, if at its height in the 1970s it continued as a gesture that subverted the value of the permanent artwork as commodity, by now it has become something else—a self-consciously de rigueur component of any new art movement. It is, as RoseLee Goldberg has suggested, the advance guard of the avant-garde.

But, while performance art perennially emerges to herald each wave of the new, the way it appears is not necessarily the same. Its very role in the arts institutions that serve as its venues shapes the meaning of performance art and defines its place in the movement it's associated with. In the 1970s, for instance, it was the gallery that presented performance (and analytic postmodern dance) as kin to minimalist painting and sculpture. After the performance the artists went out to party. In the 1980s, partly because performance paradigms are drawn more from the music world than from the visual arts (and because avant-garde and popular music have fused in all sorts of complicated ways), the party has come to the performance. Neighborhood bars become the stages where performance events erupt in the flow of an evening's drinking, socializing, being on the scene. Even a "theatrical" space like P. S. 122 often takes on a cabaret atmosphere, and it is the performance program at P. S. 122—originally curated by Tim Miller and Charles Dennis, now by

Mark Russell—especially Avant-Gard-Arama, that has set the tone (and frequently provides the personnel) for many of the clubs.

That this scene is both product and symbol of a specific youth culture shows up in more aspects than its style of art. Just walking through the neighborhood on the way to the Pyramid Lounge calls up memories of high school dances spilling out into parking lots and side streets, as gangs of girls meet up with flocks of boys or pairs of friends arrive for rendezvous. They're dressed up 1950s style; feeling old one night on Avenue A, I realized that, though I'm not yet 35, I had already learned to jitterbug before most of these people were born. Even better than high school, you can stay out late; things start to heat up here only after midnight. (The chic new restaurants bordering Tompkins Park serve breakfast specials until sunset.) One's sense of the border between life and theater is blurred en route to an evening's art/entertainment not only because the streetcorners are so lively and so full of people whose very appearance is a spectacular gesture but also because of the leisurely timing in this village. You can stroll unhurriedly for reasons beyond social ease; performances here almost never begin before an hour after curtain time.

The suburban high school ambience heightens when you finally enter a club and find yourself in something very like a 1950s rec room. In fact, Darinka (118 E. First St., near First Ave.), in my view the most homey of the group, *is* in a basement, complete with a makeshift bar and mismatched chairs that spectators pull up to the tiny stage. 8BC (337 E. Eighth St., between B and C) and Limbo Lounge (647 E. Ninth St., between B and C) are more cavernous variations on the same theme, with fewer chairs and less secure sight lines for the many who stand, though, since the floor was raised at 8BC, the stage seems lower and the clientele feels less preadolescent.

But the further east you go, the more the high school ambience is tinged with the wartorn visage that has traditionally spelled the East Village (at least, until Operation Pressure Point reduced drug traffic and stationed cops on every corner). One is reminded of Europe between the wars, Weimar-period Berlin perhaps, an image that recurs in the neo-Expressionist style of painting and performance here, in the aggressive music performances, with their overtones of Weill, and in the cabaret locale itself. One is reminded, too, of more recent global chaos. A new bar is named Downtown Beirut. P.S. 122 (First Ave. and Ninth St.) looks positively pristine by comparison.

The limitations and possibilities of the club venue demarcate Lower East Side performance style. The space is small and intimate, the timing is brief, and the stay is temporary. Not surprisingly, what happens here looks very much like cabaret entertainment: striptease, comedy, magic shows, cocktail music. Though Europe has a tradition of avant-garde cabaret art, here the mode is popular entertainment, but with an (ostensibly) ironic twist. Parody is the key to both the identity of this style and its problems.

The parodic twist comes from the context, from everything besides the immediate setting—the postmodernist impulse to quote from and recycle the past, especially mass culture (for example, John Jesurun's *Chang in a Void Moon,* a live movie spy serial); the younger generation of artists' thirst for narrative, melodrama, and just plain fun in the light of the cerebral performances and theatricalized masochism of the 1970s; a new primitivism that celebrates, among other values, intentional crudeness in production, the spontaneity of ad hoc events, and the transgressive gesture of reveling in bad taste; a deliberate stance of the kind of adolescent narcissism that makes kids think their private, hilarious satires on, say, Latin class would make a good TV show. This is, after all, a generation that grew up seeing something very much like that—refined to perfection—on "Saturday Night Live" and in the *Harvard Lampoon.*

The twist also comes from the way the performances are done, from what is quintessential to performance art as a genre. In performance art it is the *act* of carrying out some task that is stressed, not the task itself; when its subject is another form of the performing arts, like drama or singing, performance emphasizes all the details of its nature as performance, rather than its literary, scenic, or musical qualities. So Howie Solo, the emcee of a recent cabaret evening at Darinka, stylizes his hand and facial gestures to an extreme as he acts the role of a Catskills crooner but sings off-key. This is, after all, a generation that grew up watching rock and roll turn into theatrics.

Or the twist comes from mixing genres. The woman who emcees at Limbo, for instance, dresses in a gold lamé outfit but talks like a Holiness preacher. Tom Murrin, the Alien Comic, is a stand-up comedian who dresses in surreal disguises like a series of game show spectators dying to be picked out from the live audience. The rapid-fire pacing of TV meets up with autobiography in Beth Lapides's monologues. In fact, TV timing predominates; where in the 1970s performance art stretched one's sense of time and sometimes lasted for hours, in the 1980s performance time is telescoped.

But there are two problems with this parodic stance. For one thing, its irony isn't always evident. Quotation does not automatically create parody; a framework, context, or new perspective is required. In the 1970s Yvonne Rainer explored "deliberately bad performance" as one of several modes of removing material from its original context, but her way of using it was to make a new context by rubbing all the possible modes against each other. The other problem is that popular entertainment isn't popular for nothing. Its slickness and sophistication are what make it compelling—more than that, extremely pleasurable—despite its often vapid or objectionable content. Stripped of its attractions for the sake of parody, and bereft of critical commentary, this stuff makes a thin diet.

Village Voice, November 13, 1984

300 Puppets Set Skipitares Free
(Theodora Skipitares)

One of the ironies of the avant-garde performance world is that in its restless quest for the new it often turns to traditional forms of theater and to historical themes. At its best performance manages to find new uses for these old vessels—often because performance makers stumble into old-fashioned formats without being schooled in the conventions that may have proved limiting for "real" practitioners. Naïveté provides a fresh approach, revitalizing or even revising the past. In Theodora Skipitares's recent work two particular fascinations of current downtown performance art—puppet theater and American history—meet.

Skipitares's *Age of Invention* is an epic that stretches over the panorama of American history, with a cast of more than 300 puppets and only 7 humans. The puppets range from tiny masks, no bigger than the palm of your hand—red, brown, and white, with eyes that light up and detachable jaws that chatter, they dot a map that shows the population distribution of Native Americans, blacks, and whites during the Civil War—to life-size figures, the three inventors that are the "stars" of the pageant. Thomas Edison, for instance, has a hand manufactured by a prosthetic limb company that, operated with bicycle brake mechanisms, can pull a handkerchief from his shirt pocket or smooth his unruly white hair, and his mouth is sophisticated enough to spit tobacco.

The human performers, like the teams that manipulate each character in Bunraku, Skipitares prefers to think of as caretakers, not as puppeteers. "You watch six pairs of eyes following the puppet's moves as the puppeteers make it move, and you get a sense that they are looking out for its destiny," she muses. "I wasn't a kid who played with puppets. I came to work with them as a logical outgrowth of my work in figurative sculpture and in autobiographical performance, inspired along the way by Winston Tong and by Mabou Mines's *Shaggy Dog Animation*." She admits, though, that as a newcomer to the world of mechanical performers she uses some standard conventions of the art but often shocks old-timers by breaking time-honored rules.

Each of the three parts of *The Age of Invention* represents a century of

U.S. history and centers around "a high point of Yankee ingenuity," as Skipitares puts it. Benjamin Franklin is the exemplary figure for the eighteenth century; Edison for the nineteenth; and a fictional character, Michael Connor, based on the real case of a salesman who taught himself surgery and performed over 900 heart operations, for the twentieth. The complicated scenography includes a tableau of Washington crossing the Delaware, replete with an old-fashioned ocean machine that simulates rolling waves; a model of the Wall Street of 1882 that becomes fully illuminated in electrical Edisonian splendor; and a team of doctors performing open heart surgery. The music is an electronic score by Scott Johnson and Virgil Moorefield.

Skipitares trained in theater and art at Berkeley and did graduate work in theater design at New York University, working at places such as Brooklyn Academy of Music and the Performing Garage before beginning to make her own performances in the mid-1970s. At first they were solo autobiographical works combining personal images and objects with diaristic texts, but gradually she felt the need to broaden her perspective, and, searching for some medium that would give her other characters without other actors, she began to use puppets as "surrogate actors."

"In my autobiographical work, I was always veiled and masked," she explains. "The puppets freed me. They can bleed onstage. They can vomit. They can provide intensity that still remains at a distance." With the help of Eli Langner and other designers and engineers, Skipitares developed her puppets into complex mechanisms.

Visually she has tried to capture the artistic spirit of the centuries represented—American folk painting in the eighteenth century, a fascination with industrialization that alternates between the elegant and the rugged in the nineteenth, and a feeling of disintegration in the twentieth—and dramatically she has deliberately created the sweetly awkward sense of a high school diorama and pageant. But this is no naive celebration, no stale leftover of the bicentennial spirit. Inspired by her delvings into diaries, biographies, newspaper and museum archives, and architectural drawings, the author/artist/engineer has embarked on a rereading of history that gives body to details our textbooks swept under the carpet.

For instance, in this performance Skipitares wants to teach us the things about Edison that Con Ed is proud of but also about his anti-Semitism and his involvement in the invention of the electric chair. She includes Benjamin Franklin's long resistance to American independence and his explicit racism.

Each act begins with what Skipitares thinks of as "curtain raisers"— songs sung by women puppets—women buffaloes, pregnant pioneer women, and World War II riveters, who stand for the ordinary women whose lives form a backdrop to the extraordinary men who constitute the grand "myth of heroic invention, a male myth" that has come to symbolize American energy and ingenuity. "I guess I just wanted to rebalance things," she says.

Village Voice, January 8, 1985

Pencilvania or Bussed

(Beth Lapides / Kaylynn Sullivan)

The publicity for Beth Lapides's performance gave the true title of her work: in print that allows for more complicated graphics than newsprint does, it read "The Great American Novel," only "The Great" was crossed out and "A Good" scribbled in. In pencil. Something I liked about this performance was the quantity of personalized pencils I got in the mail in the preceding weeks as well as at the performance itself. I've been reminded of Beth Lapides every time I write for some time.

Something I didn't like right away when I walked in was the ballot we were all expected to fill out with said pencils—voting for one's three favorite Great American Novels. I don't like to think about novels that way. And I suspect Lapides doesn't either, given the Miss America pageant treatment the winners got toward the end of her monologue. But most of the audience took it seriously, and the polling results were predictable: *Moby-Dick, Huckleberry Finn,* and *Catcher in the Rye.*

But the ironic, lackadaisical tone of this performance—nouveau nightclub act, some singing, some comedy, with Lapides dressed in a white man-tailored suit—made you wonder what Lapides's point of view was, exactly, since she seemed inclined neither to repudiate nor to embrace any number of things: the notion of a novel or an antinovel, high art or mass culture, populism or cliquishness. More cogent than the evening's meanderings were some of the thoughts in Lapides's recent "Interview with Myself," included with the press release: "The Great American Novel is lots of smaller things making up a bigger thing. Like America. . . . I would say that the Great American Novel is made up of lots of good American novels. These novels in fact, inform our fantasy of the great American novel and so I would say really are part of it. All the great books have this idea of compilation in them. Look at the Bible."

Thus, for Lapides, not only is her performance part of the Great American Novel, but "so is the Macy's catalog. And blueprints for a split-level home in Ohio. And the operator's manuals for a Chevy and an Apple and a food processor. And there's a TV Guide from the week of the '84 Olympics . . . a Superman comic book . . . Lenny Bruce's monologues and the transcript of the trial of the Chicago Seven."

A Good American Novel included all manner of pedestrian things—word games with the audience, occasional songs, gossip in re: Lapides's domestic adventures with her boyfriend, a little plaint about holding out for a heroine, and a set of ten rules governing human behavior (the best was "Everyone thinks they're shy") that served us as a kind of funky homiletics, a presumably less pretentious version of the ten you-know-whats.

If performance is supposed, in Lapides's scheme of things, to restore a sense of humanity the idea of the novel deprives us of, that argument is supported neither by the conventional novels cited during the evening nor by most of the material. Though Lapides has a lively presence, she needs a better (ahem!) writer. The jokes often fell flat (she needs to work on her timing too), and the songs were largely undistinguished. That is, those Lapides sang. Lunatune, an all-woman group of a capella singers, appeared on the program as special guest stars and their own songs—including a feminist anthologizing of doo-wop lyrics on love and a satire on punk culture—were a pleasure.

Like *A Good American Novel,* Kaylynn Sullivan's *Nighttrippers* seemed like a good idea that unfortunately got trivialized in the translation—in the installment I attended, anyway. The handle for the performance was its unconventional format, which took on various meanings at different points in the evening.

Brought to the secret locale of the event (a different place each of the three Saturday nights) in a school bus with windows papered over, at first the spectators treated the situation like a kid's treasure hunt. But then we were ushered into a building that seemed to have a warehouse or garage for a foyer. Our hosts offered us champagne. As we perplexedly gathered in the vast space, we perceived that the architecture of a partially gutted, once elegant theater formed the stage for this performance, that the space had been reversed: we stood where the real stage had been and watched the action unfold on the stairs and risers (now stripped of seats) in the house.

In one balcony Henry Threadgill and his orchestra played a wonderful song that sounded like postmodern swing—a bit Deco, a bit Caribbean, a sweet stream of scat singing, but with some weird dissonances. In the orchestra, mezzanine, and balconies, there was a slow parade of silent men and women in exaggerated evening dress, including outsized geometric headdresses for the women and neon-color body paint for the men (design consultant: Alyson Pou). These ghostly figures drew near one another, drew apart, gestured, and cast glances. They eventually traced a steady course through all the levels of space and exited on the main floor. Whereupon the song ended, and we were handed a flyer and shown the way out, through the theater's front lobby.

The sense of the event shifted from a kid's adventure to a cross between an archaeological expedition and a séance. But, also, I had other fleeting senses of the event as well. Roped off from the performers, standing in a huddle, the spectators seemed like visitors to an aquarium or wax museum. The cast was racially mixed; the spectators were almost entirely white. Had the whole cast been black, I would be even more tempted than I am now to compare that uncomfortable voyeurism—especially given the evocative style of the music and costumes—to the practice, between the wars, of whites traveling uptown to black and Hispanic ballrooms and theaters. Were these the kind of nighttrippers we were being revealed as? Was the audience paying admission to be made fools of for elegant slumming? Or, questions of ethnicity aside, was this just the opposite of slumming—you too can be posh for an evening and even call it art?

As the rest of the spectators lingered inside, politely expressing their desire for more than the half-hour's doings, we headed back to the bus, where we read the history of the place—the Manhattan Opera House on 34th Street, long since partly dismantled and used for, among other things, union organizing in the 1930s, big band dances, music recordings, and ethnic gatherings—while the driver filled us in on the first two installments. In the first, he reported, the audience rode to a church in Harlem where some men were cooking dinner, playing cards, and cursing the audience if they came too close. The refreshment served was hot Champale. In the second, the group landed at the public baths on the Lower East Side, where women in white slips recited poetry. And now here we were, at the opera. The driver, for one, didn't know what to make of it. And I wondered why, with such an interesting progression, the three evenings had been marketed separately.

Nighttrippers could have been subtitled "The Great American Urban Place." But I wish that, beyond her sense of place, Sullivan had made what happened there, at the opera house in any case, more dense. In many ways it was reminiscent of, but less rich than, the work of Meredith Monk, with whom Sullivan has worked, especially *Vessel* (the bus trip, the use of architectural detail, the mysterious nontalking characters, the importance of the music). But Sullivan is trying to say something different than Monk. At least—I think she is.

Village Voice, January 29, 1985

Felines at the Finish Line
(The Cat Show)

It's been hard enough, these past ten years, to explain to family, friends, and colleagues what it means, exactly, to be a performance critic. But to explain covering the cat show. . . . Oy! Even to justify it to myself, at first, since I wasn't quite sure what it was, turned out to be quite a task—a debate between intuition, which told me to check it out, and reason, which speculated whether cats would be jumping through hoops of fire, chanting poetry, or posing in bathing suits. I argued with myself: "Why should I always only write about human performances? Don't animals have rights too?"

I learned a lot at the cat show. For one thing, when I got there I realized, of course, that (like the rodeo and the circus), the cat show is not an oxymoronic instance of "animal culture" but an event in human culture that sheds light on people's relationships—with animals and with each other. And I learned something about animal rights.

Madison Square Garden is filled with hundreds (though it seems like thousands) of cages, and in each cage is a cat—except for those otherwise occupied in the judging rings. Camped outside each cage is the cat's owner, eating, listening to the radio, talking to friends, or explaining things to strangers. Some of the cages are like small zoo cages. But others are regular boudoirs, replete with such amenities as purple chaise longues and a kitty litter box disguised as a bidet, or beds covered in blue gingham. One Maine Coon with tiger marks has set up bivouac in a jungle hammock inside a cage covered with camouflage. As calls come over the loudspeaker—"All Russian Blues, to ring 8, please! All longhair kittens, to ring 3! Norwegian Forest cats, to ring 2! This is the final call for Cat 83 in ring 12!"—the owners whisk their cats to the center of the stadium, where in 12 separate rings, divided discreetly by curtains, 12 judges from the United States, Canada, and Japan are conducting their *performances*.

Some of the judges, like Sue and Jim Becknell from El Paso, are gracious hosts, explaining as they handle each cat (and each successive round of cats) the protocol of what, to the untrained eye, looks both formless and mysteriously significant. In some rings judges are simply grading cats with numbers and letters; in others, ranking them competitively with ribbons. It turns out, as the Becknells explain, that first cats are graded on an absolute scale in terms of how they look and feel for a cat of their breed (Persian, Abyssinian, etc.) then, within that breed, of their division (solid, shaded, particolor, etc.) then, within that division, of their color (blue, calico, black and white, etc.). After the cats gain points for those three categories, the judge ranks the top ten cats in each division—his or her best cats. Finally, after each judge has seen all the cats, the final competition on Sunday afternoon is the Best of the Best—judged by Georgia Morgan, president of The International Cat Association (TICA). Most of the cats are pedigreed, but, as Sue Becknell explains, household pets can compete and are accorded the same dignity as the championship types.

But other judges have different acts. Larry Paul, from Atlanta, rolls up his sleeves and gestures like a magician, building the suspense as he announces his ten best one by one, planting a box of grits and a confederate flag on the top winners' cages. Yukimasa Hattori, from Nagoya, Japan, is swift and deft, almost perfunctory. Maureen Nottingham, in red curls and green eye shadow, a visual feast when she handles a red cat, draws the biggest crowds—cat lovers of every description from fat ladies collecting shopping bagsful of free cat treat samples to punks.

Around the periphery of the Garden are booths selling natural catfood, grooming equipment, toys, and every conceivable item—from sweaters to coffee cups—decorated with feline emblems. One of the booths, though, was distributing literature on animal rights.

Eve Ottenberg, who happens to be not only my youngest cat's godmother but also, at times, my political conscience, prodded me over to the table. And that information, especially in light of Peter Singer's article "Ten Years of Animal Liberation" (*New York Review of Books*, January 17) gave me pause. After all, I'd been pitying these poor cats, shut up in cages for the weekend and handled by a bunch of strangers. "Just remember that these cats," Eve pointed out, "are living in the lap of luxury compared to the millions of cats and rabbits and other animals who are being tortured in cosmetics and detergent factories and all sorts of other research labs. These cats, whether they win or lose here, and our cats, are the lucky ones."

Village Voice, February 12, 1985

Bloodsucker

(Ping Chong)

"The plague is here! Stay in your houses!" reads one of the 25 black-and-white title cards, taken from the 1922 silent film by Murnau, that flash on a screen early in Ping Chong's version, giving us a crash course in the iconography of the Dracula legend. Nosferatu, we know, is the source of the plague in the film, which served as the inspiration for Chong's newest performance work. But in our times that exhortation has a special, grisly resonance as well as a special humor. Is the plague the bomb? An epidemic of AIDS? Or perhaps the VCRs that keep us chained to our TV sets?

Unlike Werner Herzog's recent reinterpretation of the Murnau film, this *Nosferatu* is only loosely based on the film (which was, in turn, based on the Bram Stoker novel). There are the intertitles and the occasional flashes of certain key images, like Nina Harker's angelic face or the rat-visaged Nosferatu rising from the dead. But Chong is not interested in making new twists on an old story. He is interested not in the narrative but in the new images that infinitely fertile myth evokes. And he is interested in what those images might say for the present, not for a recreated past, not even for the recent past.

Nosferatu in certain ways represents a departure for Chong; its resemblance to a well-made play is uncanny, and it is impressive that Chong can pull that off. The actors deserve plenty of credit too. The set is, primarily, a room (sans fourth wall) in a fashionable apartment gleaming with high-tech appurtenances; the main characters are yuppies, and often their dialogue seems culled directly from some uptown cocktail party.

But these recognizable elements are skewed in structural ways and juxtaposed to unconventional elements so that the performance is unsettling, not only because of its powerful content but also because it keeps acting like something familiar only to change into something bizarrely unfamiliar. Much as Nosferatu, the vampire, is both dead and alive, human and inhuman beast.

For instance, the set is both a predictably bourgeois living room and something that has been constructed before our very eyes during the performance. Further, its glass table is lit at times from various angles so that it projects a shadow play on the side or back wall, lending a sinister resonance to the banalities of the ongoing bickering, gossip, and flirtation. A prelude to what takes place on this set happens in a timeless, characterless place—a platform in front of a dark curtain on which two angels wrestle (in heaven? before the world was created?). The curtains somehow recall a movie theater more than a proscenium stage, and, when they open, they reveal the projection screen on which we see the quotes from Murnau's film. And finally, toward the end of the performance, a panel below the screen in the rear wall of what has seemed a perfectly normal living room opens to reveal an entire new realm, where the classical figure of Nosferatu rises from the dead and enters—or, rather, *invades*—the living room to claim his bride.

Similarly in the action, characters' worlds overlap and intrude. The Harkers and their friends comfortably ignore the medieval/futuristic carnival of skeletons—from cheerleaders to punks copulating on the couch to a bride dressed in blood-red—that dance their gruesome, motley dance around the living room, mocking the yuppie complacency by coexisting in their space as reverse images of the "living dead." And, in the same way, the repetitions and reruns of both action and dialogue create a sense of unease—disease—and foreboding.

What, then, is the plague? Is it yuppiedom? Is this a piece about the emptiness of these people's lives? I think not. Unlike realistic plays, Chong's theater of images partly depends not on the unfolding of complex characters but on the brilliant arrangements of coded cultural types. I think Chong has chosen our newest social stereotype as simply a more extreme example of what he grimly sees in all our lives: a hollowness, a darkness, a mystery—the thing that seemed to have its origins even before the beginning of the world, when the two angels, clad in gray, with gray plastic masks and white shocks of hair (a cross between Pre-Raphaelite gravestones and Kabuki warriors), frolicked, caressed, and wrestled with one another until one tore from the other's breast not his heart but a dry black thing that is like a heart of darkness. The mystery is that the vision is grim but told with such striking, unearthly beauty.

Village Voice, February 26, 1985

Junk Alchemy

(Jack Smith)

Jack Smith's appearance on Millennium's recent slide art series, which also included new works by Lawrence Kucharz, Stuart Sherman, and Perry Hoberman, was remarkable for a number of reasons. One—for me and evidently for so many of the people in the crowded house, all too young to have been around in his heyday in the 1960s—was the experience of seeing a live Jack Smith performance. As the publicity for his event accurately noted, the work of this "almost mythical" filmmaker and performer has indeed influenced a whole generation. Yet *Death of a Penguin* was an important event not just for personal/historical "research" reasons but also for the sake of illuminating the present, because the ways in which Smith has influenced performance art for the past 20 years or so are complex and at times circuitous.

So much of what is central to current performance art—allusions to Hollywood, TV, and other aspects of mass culture; fusions of the homemade and the esoteric; funky, deliberately amateurish acting styles— stems from a set of fascinations and obsessions that can be traced back to Smith's sensibility. That sensibility is related to camp imagery but precedes it, not chronologically, I mean, but logically. This is the stuff of camp, the subject of it, without the arch ironic consciousness involved in striking the camp posture. This is the madness of inspiration, of a pure and personal vision.

And that, I think, is how the art of Jack Smith differs from even the performance art today that revels in certain similar themes, images, and techniques. Smith's performance used the iconography of Disney cartoons, movie stars, exotic dancers, of musty junkpiles whose particulars were hard to discern in the gloomy auditorium. But, unlike his contemporaries, the Pop artists, who took a cool, ironic stance in relation to this kind of imagery, unlike the Lower East Side cabaret acts of the 1980s, whose imitations of popular entertainers use distancing to either comment on or simply assimilate mainstream commercial art, Smith is a kind of alchemist. He's not interested in letting the real world into his art to focus on the concrete here-and-now. He uses the theater as an embodiment of the imagination, a place and a way to make magical, ephemeral things out of an eccentric assortment of dross, from old shawls, wine bottles, incense burners, and coffins to scratchy opera records to the actors themselves, in their unpolished intensity. In several senses his vision of the theater as the mind's marvelous garret resembles—and probably influenced—that of Richard Foreman.

Not a lot happened at *Death of a Penguin*. In the Jack Smith tradition the performance started late and then slowly. Informed by adepts in this tradition, I arrived just after nine for an eight o'clock curtain and found a woman dressed up like a harem dancer sort of setting things up, talking, and playing records. The slides had begun, their images sometimes partly obscured by the long scarves draped from the ceiling. Some time much later, Smith appeared, looking like some kind of mummy from the Bowery, in an overcoat and hat, his head wrapped in a bandage. He and Marisa read from a script written out on yellow legal pads. They didn't read all of it. And, as they read it, Smith also gave stage directions. "Say that again into the microphone." "Now go turn up the music." "Why didn't you light the incense?" This time he got an answer: "But you said to take a long time setting up and then you came out so soon!"

The stage directions were muffled, but then so was the actual dialogue. It seems there was a woman, or a female penguin, or a society lady, Yolanda La Pinguima, who escaped from the zoo and then died or was killed. She had a lover, or perhaps it was her murderer, named Sinbad Rodriguez. She always wore lipstick of a particular color— Desert Salmon. I guess the incense was to have been lit for the funeral rites and that we were seeing her coffin in the pile of indistinguishable stuff around which the actors moved. And maybe it was said somewhere that her body was beginning to rot and to smell. She was a mysterious creature, sitting on park benches, keeping her secrets.

The slides, meanwhile, showed landscapes that were hard to assimilate in cognitive terms. They looked like photographs but of no place that could be imagined on this earth. There were several different unimaginable places, actually—one a kind of grotto ("Boiled Lobster Color Slide Show of Crab Lagoon"?), one a kind of amusement park that seemed a cross between Disneyland and the Arabian Nights but in Germany.

And there was Smith, shlumping through it all, forgetting things, rearranging things, waiting, muttering, drinking wine, smoking, deciding on the spur of the moment to have an intermission, sending his costar out to do a sinuous dance after intermission, and, ten minutes later, coming out to take a bow, seemingly as unsure as the audience about whether, in fact, the performance had actually ended. And for all that awkwardness and messiness, potent, magnetic, almost frighteningly *there*.

Some time after the performance I read Jonas Mekas's *Village Voice* column from 15 years ago on the occasion of seeing a Jack Smith performance, *Jack Smith, or the End of Civilization*. The column was as extraordinary as the event it recounts, an event not all that different from the one I saw just weeks ago: there was Jonas, meditating on the personal meanings of this event, which (unlike the one at Millennium), had an audience of ten, most of whom were friends of Smith, and some of whom, including Jonas, were dragooned into becoming actors for the evening. The performance started late and moved slowly, not all that much happened, and what did wasn't clear, there was a coffin and a burial, and "I had a feeling . . . that only here, in this downtown loft, somewhere at the very end of all the empty and dead and gray downtown streets, was this huge junk set and these end-of-civilization activities. . . . It resembled more and more the final burial ceremonies, the final burial rites of the capitalist civilization, competitive civilization, these were the magic burial grounds and the burial rites of all the corruption, comfort and money and good living, and free gifts of the world that was now asleep, at 2 A.M., only Jack Smith was still alive, a madman, the high priest of the ironical burial grounds, administering last services here alone and by himself, because really the seven or eight people who were now his audience (the other three were on the set) were really no audience at all, Jack didn't need any audience, he would do it anyway, and I had a feeling that he did it anyway, many nights like this, many Saturdays, by himself, audience or no audience, actors or no actors, he reenacted this ceremony, the last man who was still around and above it all and not part of it but at the same time conscious of it all, very painfully conscious of it all, the sadness himself, the essence of sadness itself."

Thank you, Jonas. One can't write like that about performances now. And in fact, performances now that are like that aren't like that now.

Village Voice, March 19, 1985

Up the Kitchen!

Next week I go on leave for six months. It seems both ironic and fitting that my last *Voice* performance column for the near future should be about the Kitchen. I've been writing for the *Voice* about dance and performance art for 9 years, but I can't even remember the first time I ever went to the Kitchen; it must have been about 13 years ago.

But I wanted to answer William Harris's attack on Mary MacArthur, the director of the Kitchen from 1978 to 1984, in "Slouching toward Broome Street" (*Voice,* March 5), not out of nostalgia, not because of any personal or professional ties (I went on a three-week lecture tour of Italy in 1983 as part of a Kitchen package), but to clear the journalistic record. Harris celebrates what he sees as the golden years of the Kitchen, during the tenure of Robert Stearns (MacArthur's predecessor), and describes MacArthur's term as a time of troubles, both fiscally and artistically, basing his judgments, it seems to me, on inaccuracies and misinterpretations. Harris mentions MacArthur's successes—the great number of artists served, the development of new audiences through touring and broadcast media, and the phenomenal level of activity in every imaginable field of avant-garde art—as almost insignificant asides in light of the Kitchen's financial problems, as if its business were to make money, not to present art. But, at the same time, MacArthur's prowess as a fundraiser and grant getter is seen as despicable.

I spoke to most of the people quoted in the article since it appeared, as well as many who were not. The general response was that the remarks con Mary MacArthur were quoted, those pro simply ignored, and that the article was built not from evidence but on innuendo. Some, such as Eric Barsness, formerly the staff person for development, and Stearns, protested that they had been misquoted or quoted out of context; Stearns termed the piece "unnecessary, uncalled for, and untrue."

He may have his disagreements with MacArthur, but Eric Bogosian, like so many other curators or former curators I interviewed, is quick to point out that "her ethics are impeccable. The issue of my name being used on several grant applications is an oversimplification of a complex situation, which has to do more with the necessarily scattershot approach of applying to different programs, because of the kind of institution the Kitchen is, with the changing guidelines and require-ments of the National Endowment for the Arts (NEA) programs, and with recession, than with Mary MacArthur."

The article does not acknowledge that it was under MacArthur's aegis that Bogosian began his innovative dance programming—just as Bogosian's own career as a performance artist ("and, let's face it, that of my entire generation," he says) blossomed at the Kitchen during those years.

Harris criticizes the curatorial system as an instance of over-administration, implying that he prefers the single-vision approach of an artistic director, as at presenting institutions such as Dance Theater Workshop. But this seems to me to deny the possibility of different ways of programming and, especially, to deny the nature of a multiprogram organization like the Kitchen, a pluralism that largely accounts for its vitality and importance in the downtown arts scene.

People like David White at DTW, Mark Russell at P.S. 122, and staff members of alternative and intermedia spaces in other cities were all quick to point out the contradictions in the criticism leveled at Mac-Arthur. "The funding agencies encourage you to expand your staff," several of them pointed out, adding that the article might have been more helpful if it had examined the deteriorating situation of funding and institutions for the avant-garde rather than trying to find a scape-goat. White states (as do various others) that the comparisons between DTW, P.S. 122, and the Kitchen's budgets and other practices are "specious." Unlike other venues, the Kitchen does not rent space to artists but fully produces every artist that appears in its season—artists who range from performance makers to dancers to video artists. Harris often seems to overlook the primary commitment of the Kitchen; it began as a video center. Because its mandate is to present such diversi-fied programming, it has all sorts of behind-the-scenes costs, especially for equipment, that the other organizations don't have. This also means more administrative complexities and more areas that are difficult to fund. Neither the budgets nor the grant writing and funding practices of the organizations are comparable.

"In institutions like these, you constantly take risks. And if the money comes in, you look great. If it doesn't, you simply don't," says White. He (and many others, including sources at funding agencies) credits MacArthur for looking beyond narrow bases of support with the establishment of the Kitchen touring program and other strategies for disseminating avant-garde art. "She was responsible for the New Music Festival in 1979," says White, "which eventually became New Music America, the only freefloating festival around. She was responsible for the Media Alliance. She helped redefine the opera–musical theater program at the NEA. I've learned an enormous amount from her in terms of touring; she certainly paved the way for much of what goes on at BAM."

Harris reported that New York State Council on the Arts (NYSCA) and NEA have "tightened their purse strings," but grant figures for fiscal year 1984–85 reflect just the opposite. He notes that income from the NEA for FY 82–83 was $414,329 but doesn't mention that that figure includes part of a one-time challenge grant of $100,000 as well as deferred income; it's obvious, then, that NEA funding will never be that high again.

Bobbi Tsumagari, Interarts program specialist at the NEA, further clarifies the NEA's position. "The Endowment does not act unilaterally for or against an organization," she states. "The panel system prevents that." At least in Interarts, she adds, the panels understand that institutions project their plans so far in the future that specific details (for example, artist A rather than artist B) are not considered binding.

I can't agree with Harris's complaint that the curators are lackluster. In the dance program alone, following in Bogosian's footsteps, Jamie Avins has produced an astonishing roster of artists, all the more impressive because it mixes the known and the unknown (at the time), the past and the future of the avant-garde, from Simone Forti and Steve Paxton to Jim Self, Johanna Boyce, Ishmael Houston-Jones and Fred Holland, and Eric Barsness; from Bauhaus reconstructions to the first of the recent wave of dance-film collaborations. She also, in her first season, presented a concert of break-dancing and one of Toni Basil with Lockers and Poppers.

The performance programming, at first under RoseLee Goldberg then Howard Halle, has been equally far-ranging, from Nam June Paik, Bogosian, Longo, and Laurie Anderson to John Malpede, ABC No Rio, Thulani Davis, Komar and Melamid, and Expressionist and Constructivist reconstructions. And the same could be said for the music, video, film, and gallery programming.

Harris charges that under MacArthur curators were no longer artists. This is a curious comparison, since at least Tom Bowes, Anne deMarinis, George Lewis, and Amy Taubin all had more advanced careers at the time they were hired as curators (Taubin, in fact, had performed at the Kitchen in Stearns's day as well as having had her film work screened there) than did Bogosian, Longo, and Chatham, the earlier group. Halle is a visual artist, and Avins is a choreographer.

Harris charges MacArthur with sponsoring programs that simply recycled old hits. But the Kitchen has always been a place where one sees both older and younger avant-gardists. And let's get our history straight. Stearns didn't present only unknown artists; Paik had already been a "star" for a decade by the early 1970s, Philip Glass was well-known, Laurie Anderson already had been performing in other venues. It was under MacArthur that Fripp and Eno appeared at the Kitchen. And it was under MacArthur that the mix of the present and future avant-garde not only continued but expanded to include blacks, Hispanics, and Native Americans as well as whites, urban folk culture as well as "high art," mass media as well as the more arcane uses of all sorts of technology, presentations in the street, on television, on the radio, and in other theaters and venues, heralding the striking mix of popular and avant-garde culture that characterizes the vibrancy of the downtown art world in the 1980s and that has spread from Soho to the Lower East Side.

Is it MacArthur's fault that institutions change with age, that the avant-garde will never support itself on earned income or corporate funding, that neighborhoods such as the West Village, Soho, and now the Lower East Side become gentrified after the artists have settled them, that arts budgets are shrinking, that the avant-garde itself is in a state of flux? I hardly think so.

Village Voice, April 2, 1985

Index

Note: Articles (or significant portions of articles) on individual artists, works, or events are indicated by boldface page numbers.

physical skills, 190–91
"Resurrection of Lazarus, The,"
188–89
"Scapino's Teaching Lesson," 189–90
"Technocrat, The," 190
text selection and interpretation,
193–94
"Wedding at Cana, The," 189
Foley, Tere, 69
"Folk Dances from the Migraine"
(Bloolips), 108–9
Folktales (Chong), 236–37
food, 180–82
Footsie (Oleszko), 79
Foreman, Richard, 6, 14, **49–50**, 133
Forti, Simone, 158, 159
47 Beds (Gray), 152
Foster, Carlos, 195
Franklin, Benjamin, 270
Franklin Furnace (performance
space), 4
freaks, 55, 151–52
Friedman, Ed, 58
Frisch, Norman, **105–6**
Frohmader, Jerry, 101–2
Full Financial Disclosure (Burden),
117–18
Full Moon Show, 7, **254–55**
FunHouse (Bogosian), 183, 184
"Future, The" (Zaloom), **245**
Futurism, 1
Italian, 5, 9
Russian, 14, 98–100

Gabriel, Peter, 228
Gallo, Vincent, 122
Gam, Kaja, 203
Gambrell, Jamie, 243
garbagemen, 258–59
Garçon! (Burden), 117
"Gardens Were before Gardeners"
(Bread and Puppet Theater), 198
Garver, Fred Garbo, **121**
Gaulke, Cheri, 63, 168, **169–70**
gay art, 109. *See also* "Men Together"
gay artists, 113
Gehrhardt, Conrad ("Connie"), 256–57
General Hospital (Wannamaker), 230
genius, 25

Getaway Vacation (Goese), 254
Getting Ahead (McGee and Hughes), 92
Gibson, Jon, 83
Gilbert, W. S., 55, 56
Gill, Rena, 49
Ginsberg, Allen, 228
Giorno, John, 158, 159
giullari (strolling players), 188
Giullari di Piazza, I (group), **226–27**
Glass, Philip, 24
Gleason, Abbott, 95
Goese, Mimi, 254
Go-Go World (Fisher), **179**
Goldberg, RoseLee, 283
description of 1970s, 1
on performance art, 3, 6, 8, 9, 264
*Performance Art: From Futurism to the
Present*, 9
views of modernism, 8
Goldberg, Whoopi, 15, **233**
Goldenhagen, Carl, 76
Goldstein, Malcolm, 158
Good American Novel, A (Lapides),
271–72
Good Morning Mr. Orwell (Paik),
227–28
Good Writing about Good Food
(Schmidt), **180–82**
Goodman, Andrea, 67, 68, 76
Gordh, Bill, 7, 90, 262
Gordon, Peter, 38, 71
grammelots, 188, 189–90
Gray, Spalding, 6, 7, 10, 15, 148, **151–
53**, 160
Grayisms, 153
Green, Vanalyne, 92, **167**
Greenberg, Albert, **216–17**
Grommets, 7, **27–28**
Grupo Bambule, 230
Guerrero, Jenny, 87

Haimsohn, Jana, 28, 163, 229–30
Halle, Howard, 283, 284
hand puppets, 129–30
Handke, Peter, 134
Hanfield, Judith, 66
Hanna-Barberic Cavalcade (Scharf), 125
Hannan, Joe, 114, 241
Hannon-Bookwalter, Suzanh, 100

No Theater Company, **54–57**
Noise Bodies (Schneemann), 158
nonaction, 74
non-matrixed performing, 5, 9
nonspecialization, 4–5
Norton, Margot, 45
Nosferatu (Chong), **276–77**
Nottingham, Maureen, 275
Nuit Blanche (Chong), 234, 236

Obedience School (Nightfire Theater),
    173–74
Obrecht, Bill, 161
Oh, Dracula (Burden), 118
Oklahoma! (Rodgers and Hammer-
    stein), **64–66**
Ole Mas bands, 200, 201–2
Oleszko, Pat, **78–79**
Oliveros, Pauline, 6, 81
On Edge (Carr), 14
1 2 3 (Lowery), 262
Ontani, Luigi, **168–69**
order, 112
Orgel, Sandra, 62–63
Original Lou and Walter Story, The
    (Kroesen), **64–66**
Orlando Furioso (Ariosto), 132
ostraniene, 12–13, 17n. 35. *See also*
    enstrangement
other modernism, 8
Ottenberg, Eve, 275
Out of the Public Eye (Malpede),
    232–33
outsiders, 234–35, 236

Padgett, Ron, 225
Paik, Nam June, 14, 81, 82, **227–28**
PAINT YRSELF RED/ME &
    MAYAKOVSKY (Miller), 111
Palacios, Sylvia, 7, **225.** *See also* Whit-
    man, Sylvia
Palestine, Charlemagne, 28, **34–35**
Pandava family, 250, 251
pantomimes, 56
parades, 200. *See also* religious proces-
    sions
Paraiso, Nicky, 256
paratheater, 13
"Park, The" (Ashley), 38–39

parody, 266–67
Parsons, Estelle, 186
Part Three-Friction (Houston-Jones),
    107
Paul, Larry, 275
Paul, Ricky, 114
"Penis Envy Blues" (Kroesen), 240
Perel, Sharla, 241
performance art
    antecedents, 1–2
    Auslander on, 8–11
    Bogosian's views of, 183–85
    Carlson on, 8
    Carroll on, 7
    component of new art movements, 8,
        264
    content, 144
    descriptions of, 3–4
    difficulties of defining, 2–3, 6–7
    Goldberg on, 1, 3, 6, 8, 9, 264
    historical narratives of, 7–11
    locations for, 4, 264–65
    Lower East Side performance style,
        266, 278
    Lowery's views of, 263
    as metatheater, 256
    nature of, 5, 6, 266, 278
    in 1980s, 9, 120–21
    reflection of its time, 120
    Sayre on, 8
    tendencies in 1980s, 232
Performance Art: From Futurism to the
    Present (Goldberg), 9
Performance Art Magazine, 4, 6. *See also*
    Alive (magazine); *Live* (magazine)
Performing Arts Journal, 6
Perr, Herb, 230
Perron, Wendy, 12
Perrucci, Andrea, 226
Persky, 256–57
personal narratives, 11, 36
physical deformities, 55–56
Piccolo, Steve, 71
Piper, Adrian, 7
plagues, 276, 277
Plimpton, George, 227
polyvalent artists, 5
Pop Art, 161
pop culturization, 11

Wilding, Faith, 62
Wilson, Ann, **42–44**
Wilson, Robert, 4, 14, **24–25**, 42
Winkler, Dean, 228
Wither, Robert, 83
Woehrle, John, 239
Women Against Violence Against
 Women (WAVAW), 63
Women and Men, a big dance (Bogart),
 146–47
women body builders, 175–77
women in Victorian society, 55

women's performance art, 62–63
Women's West Coast Performance,
 89–92
Working Artist (Burden), 117

Young, La Monte, 159
Your Friend (Conrad), **207–8**

Zaloom, Paul, **154–56**, **245–46**
zaum (poetry), 102
Zayas, Nelson, 163, 203, 204
Zwack, Michael, 238, 242